Japan's Greatest Victory, Britain's Worst Defeat

JAPAN'S GREATEST VICTORY,

BRITAIN'S WORST DEFEAT

by

Colonel Masanobu Tsuji
Chief of Operations and Planning Staff,
25th Japanese Army, Malaya

Edited by
H. V. Howe
Military Secretary to the Australian Minister
for the Army, 1940–46

Translated by
Margaret E. Lake, B.A., Dip.Ed

SPELLMOUNT

British Library Cataloguing in Publication Data:
A catalogue record for this book is available
from the British Library

This edition copyright © Spellmount Ltd. 1997, 2007
This edition maps copyright © Spellmount Ltd. 1997, 2007
First published in slightly different form in
Japan as *Shonan: The Hinge of Fate* (1952)

ISBN 1-86227-129-1
ISBN 978-1-86227-129-6

This edition published in Great Britain in 2007 by
SPELLMOUNT (PUBLISHERS) LTD.
The Mill, Brimscombe Port, Stroud
Gloucestershire GL5 2QG

Tel: 0044 (0) 1453 883300
Fax: 0044 (0) 1453 883233
E-mail: enquiries@spellmount.com
Website: www.spellmount.com

1 3 5 7 9 8 6 4 2

Printed in Great Britain by
Oaklands Book Services
Stonehouse, Gloucestershire GL10 3RQ

Publisher's Note

THE EDITOR OF THIS VOLUME, H.V. Howe, first came across this book through a review of its original Japanese version in a Malayan newspaper. Realizing that the book disclosed aspects of the Singapore campaign that were not apparent to British or Australian historians, he contacted the author in 1953, stating: "It is, I think, of the utmost importance that history should be fully and accurately recorded, and this cannot be done unless Allied historians are able to read the Japanese account of the campaign in Malaya written by the officer principally responsible for its planning and execution. In order that the operations of the Japanese Army may be correctly presented to the English-speaking peoples of the world, I strongly urge upon you the desirability of publishing an English translation of your book."

After extensive correspondence, Colonel Tsuji finally replied: "It is my hope, emanating from the bottom of my heart, that it should be read by all the peoples who long for peace beyond past vengeance. I offer sincerely my profound respect to the officers and men who most gallantly fought in the battlefields of Malaya. . ."

Readers familiar with World War II in the Pacific will indeed find much to learn from this little-known work of a master planner and bold soldier. In Tsuji's account, the "disaster" of the largest surrender of troops in British history becomes—as it was—a spectacular victory, due to a combination of swift, pragmatic preparation, resolute execution and the impressive valor of the Japanese Army.

There is also much in this volume that will be of interest to professional military planners as well as historians. A few themes emerge that are as timeless as war itself: the difficulties of coordinating different branches of the armed forces, endless logistical problems, harsh terrain and unpredictable weather, squabbling between units for precedence and the "fog of war" that renders first reports from the battlefield unreliable. There is also the significant failure of the British to destroy the supplies they abandoned in their retreat, including fuel, ammunition, food and vehicles. Contrary to many examples of an attacking force becoming weaker as it extends itself farther into enemy territory, in Malaya the Japanese actually became better supplied as their offensive progressed.

It is rare for a military planner to place himself in the vanguard of an assault, but that is where Tsuji chose to be. As the eyes and ears of his commander, and as a roving courier, he had three of his cars destroyed by shellfire, and came under enemy gunfire on many occasions during the hundred days of the attack. He records countless acts of bravery, including Japanese officers cutting demolition wires with their swords as British engineers were preparing to detonate them, and innumerable cases of sacrifice by young Japanese soldiers.

Some of the personalities prominent in this book, including the author, have not seen their reputations survive the postwar era unscathed. Colonel Masanobu Tsuji, who was the planning genius behind the most impressive victory in Japan's modern history, went on to serve in a similar role with the Japanese Army at Guadalcanal and in the defense of the Philippines, where the results did not equal his earlier success. Allied historians have since also attributed to him unsavory characteristics, having to do with brutality and fanaticism on the battlefield as well as mistreatment of civilians. In this volume, the reader will fail to encounter a hint of the Japanese attitude toward prisoners that has since been revealed to have caused widespread suffering among noncombatants.

After the war's end, Colonel Tsuji was ordered by the Imperial High Command to "disappear," and spent the next few years wandering in disguise throughout Southeast Asia. Returning to Japan after reconstruction, he was elected to the Japanese Diet, subsequently serving in the House of Councillors. In the early 1960s he returned to Indochina, where he finally did disappear and has not been heard from since.

General Gordon Bennett has also been the subject of criticism since the war's end—not just for his handling of troops during the Singapore campaign, but also, unreasonably, for not allowing himself to be taken prisoner by the Japanese at the end of the battle.

General Yamashita, the "Tiger of Malaya," to whom this book is dedicated, was hanged by an Allied military tribunal for war crimes, shortly after the end of hostilities.

It has often been remarked that "history is written by the victors," a premise in keeping with Colonel Tsuji's account since, in 1942, at Singapore, the victors were the Japanese. As an insider's view of the spirit, skill and tenacity of modern-day samurai at the pinnacle of their power and success, his book provides us with a rare and valuable perspective on one of history's greatest campaigns.

Contents

PUBLISHER'S NOTE   V

INTRODUCTION   XIII

AUTHOR'S PREFACE   XV

PART ONE

War Without Preparation   1

The Doro Nawa Unit   2

Southward Advance? Northward Thrust?   10

Hasty Operations Orders   17

Whirlwind to the South   19

Army Commander Yamashita   25

A Secret Reconnaissance   31

Orthodox or Unorthodox Tactics?   39

The Army and Navy Operations Agreement   42

A Dream Plan   47

Towards Embarkation   49

PART TWO

The Threshold of Fate   55

Singora's Waves Are High   59

The Collapse of a Dream   62

The Assault on Kota Bharu   69

The Last of the British Far Eastern Squadron   73

A Death in Bangkok   78

PART THREE

Breakthrough on the Jitra Line   81

Extraordinary Tactics   84

A Chance Exploit   90

The Churchill Supplies   97

Advancing with the Calendar   98

The Capture of Penang   102

The Perak River Obstacle   103

Crossing the Perak River   107

PART FOUR

Dying Wishes to a Beloved Wife   111

Small-Boat Operations Dumbfound the Enemy   114

New Year's Eve on the Battlefield   117

"That Which One Sows . . ."   120

A Thrust Through the Jungle 123

Divergent Opinions 125

Two Young Warriors 127

The Fall of the Federal Capital 131

Are the Osaka Soldiers Weak? 134

The Bicyclists 136

PART FIVE

Ammunition Supplies 139

The Pursuit Sustained 142

Breaking Through Gemas 144

Command of the Skies 147

Is Jealousy the Monopoly of Women? 148

Mopping Up Bakri 151

The Arrival of the Assault Groups 153

Deep Emotion in Johore Bahru 156

PART SIX

Singapore—the Pivot 163

The Plan of Capture 166

The Battle Plan for the Assault 168

To the Heights of the Imperial Palace 171

Distressing Preparations 173

A Demonstration to Mislead the Enemy   176

The Blue Signal Flares   178

The Only Mistake   182

Slaughter on Bukit Timah   184

Welcoming the Kigen Festival   189

The True Spirit   194

Hoisting the White Flag   199

PART SEVEN

Rushing the Camera   205

Warning Against Celebration   207

Sharing the Joy   208

CITATIONS   213

APPENDIX 1: Read This Alone—And the War Can Be Won   223

APPENDIX 2: The East Asia Federation Movement   261

APPENDIX 3: The British Garrison in Malaya   263

Introduction

EVERY SOLDIER WORTHY OF THE NAME pays ungrudging tribute to the military capacity of his outstanding opponents. I have no hesitation in recognizing Colonel Masanobu Tsuji as one of the ablest of mine.

In his book he unreservedly attributes Japan's victory in Malaya to the patriotic fervor and self-sacrifice of the frontline officers and men of her 25th Army, which, in advancing six hundred miles and capturing Singapore in seventy days, achieved one of the decisive victories of World War II and accomplished a feat unparalleled in military history.

The trained observer must, however, conclude that the success of the campaign was primarily due to its extraordinarily thorough and quite original planning. The most unusual feature of this book is the author's account of the research into the techniques of tropical warfare. For three hundred days he and his small team—experienced only in the subarctic regions of Manchuria—lived and worked under primitive tropical conditions, and, divesting themselves of all the conservatism which usually afflicts army staffs, evolved the tactics, armament, and equipment best suited to jungle warfare.

For the first time in history an army carried out a blitzkrieg on bicycles, astounding the world by the sureness and rapidity of its advance, and exploding the myth of the impregnability of Singapore—which, as Colonel Tsuji emphasizes, had no rear defenses, a fact he states was unknown to Winston Churchill at the time.

No soldier smiles on defeat, and Colonel Tsuji is naturally distressed by the defeat of his country, which he ascribes to absence of inspired national leadership. Expressing the opinion that Sir Winston's character "savors of Zen mysticism," he pays him generous tribute as the type of leader necessary to carry a nation to victory through desperate circumstances.

Japan's collapse was not due to lack of spirit of her servicemen or her people, but to the weakness of her national economy, which, as the author points out, was clearly recognized by her Imperial General Staff, and by them was taken into account in weighing the probability of quick and complete victory against the inevitability of defeat in a prolonged conflict.

Colonel Tsuji's career proves him a master planner and an outstanding field officer. He now appears as an excellent writer and is to be congratulated upon his book, and also upon the motives which led to his escape from the Allied forces after the national surrender, of which he tells in another book, *Underground Escape*.

Like many soldiers in all countries he seems subject to strong religious influences, and, pondering the consequences of defeat in the light of his Buddhist faith, he determined that a paramount obligation was imposed upon him to work for the regeneration of his country. With the approval of higher Army authority he thereupon evaded arrest by Allied forces, disappeared, and for three years wandered through Asia, until, cleared of all charges against him, he was able to return to Japan, which he now serves as a Member of the House of Councillors in the National Diet.

H. GORDON BENNET
Lieutenant-General
Commander, Australian Imperial Force in Malaya, 1941–42
Turramurra, New South Wales, 1959

Author's Preface

THE CAPTURE OF SINGAPORE WAS indeed the "hinge of fate" for Britain and the peoples of Asia. Domination based on force must be overthrown by force. Only by sincere adherence to sound moral principles can a just and lasting peace be made.

As Chief of the Operations and Planning Staff throughout the Malayan campaign, I have dedicated this book to the memory of General Yamashita. In reply to Mr. Winston Churchill,* I would like to transmit to future generations the true facts of the campaign, which will demonstrate to all the sterling worth of the Japanese Army.

In military strategy Japan conquered spectacularly, in the war she was easily defeated. But, incomprehensibly, as a result India, Pakistan, Ceylon, Burma, Indonesia and the Philippines achieved independence soon after the end of hostilities. Indochina and Malaya had already become free almost overnight of domination by Europeans. These Asian peoples who were emancipated by the fall of Singapore will eternally pronounce benedictions on their benefactors.

Malaya's history is the history of the strong preying upon the weak. The Polynesian peoples who were the original owners of the country lived in the jungle, but were ousted by invaders from the Palembang Kingdom in Sumatra, who in turn were later overthrown by the Kingdom of Java. Thus, ownership of the country was changed for the third time.

Portugal, by great achievements on the seas of Europe and Asia, became very powerful and gained control of the Malacca Straits, and so Malaya received its fourth ruler. Before long, Holland took the place of

---

* *The Hinge of Fate*, volume ix of Winston Churchill's history of the Second World War, was published in 1951. The first edition of Colonel Tsuji's book appeared in Japan the following year.

Portugal, and when later Great Britain appeared on the scene to outrival Holland, Malaya received her sixth master—Stamford Raffles.

From the time Raffles founded Singapore, Britain's Far Eastern aggression and rule over the island lasted over one hundred and twenty years, and then in seventy days it was given a fatal blow by the lightning operations of the Japanese forces.

The halo of victory must shine on the Union Jack, but today there remains little vestige of its glory of former times. As Mr. Churchill proclaimed, the surrender of Singapore was Great Britain's "hinge of fate." In this single issue England was weighed in the balance and found wanting, and she forfeited the dignity of one hundred and twenty years. Although victorious in the war, she lost India and released her hold on Burma; and now, alas, she sees Malaya buffeted on the waves of her people's revolution.

War in these modern times has a new character, for it brings hardship to the victor as well as suffering to the vanquished. Is this not a revelation of Providence showing the limitations of government based on force? Today, however, the position of the world remains the same, for the guiding spirits of America and the Soviets are not awake to the change in historical philosophy, and continue to believe in domination by force. In the event of a third world war, whoever may be victorious there will be no crowning laurels of victory, but only skeletons exposed to the sun on the ruins of the battlefields.

When the dread threat of atomic war was looming over the world, Mr. Churchill was once again elected Prime Minister of Great Britain. Confronted by the rise and fall of their nation, this was the man in whom the people of Britain put their faith, and to whom they entrusted the destiny of their motherland. Immediately after his re-election he gave warning of the possibility of a third world war and made clear his intention to avert the danger by interviewing Stalin, or, if necessary, by cautiously investigating the establishment of American atom-bomb bases in England. While the Japanese Prime Minister, a younger man, was resting at Oiso or Hakone, Mr. Churchill, though well into his seventies, signified his willingness to travel to Moscow or to Washington. By his readiness to negotiate he hoped perhaps to influence even Stalin.

Mr. Churchill is a man I hold in the highest esteem. Glancing over his personal history, it appears that when young he cast away his military profession, but later, while on reconnaissance during the South African War, he passed too deeply into the enemy's lines, became separated from his compatriots and was taken prisoner. He seized the first opportunity to escape, and in constant danger succeeded in making his way through the enemy lines and eventually returned to his own people.

Subsequently he entered the political arena, and in the First World War, while holding the important Cabinet position of First Lord of the Admiralty, he visited the battle line in Belgium. While there inspecting the British Naval Brigade [at Antwerp], he found himself caught in the midst of a heavy German attack. He is reported to have telegraphed directly to the Prime Minister his wish to resign from the Cabinet and to be appointed to command of the Naval Brigade. There is nothing particularly surprising about his bravery as a young man; but now, when over forty years of age and a Cabinet Minister, he desired to cast aside his high position and fight with the officers and men in the front line; his ardor and fighting spirit gushed forth unrestrainedly from a deep affection for his country and his people.

Frequently during the Second World War, when critical situations arose, it was the strength of one man—Mr. Churchill—which brought the British people through. Then, after victory and the change of Cabinet, the shining laurels of victory were passed on to Mr. Attlee without regret or dissatisfaction, and Mr. Churchill, wielding his powerful pen, wrote his imperishable precepts for the nations.

There is a savor of Zen mysticism in this attitude of turning aside from fame and honor arising from distinguished service. Even before he had completed the manuscript of his memoirs of the Second World War, Mr. Churchill had to face the prospects of a third world war, which, if it should come about, would result in the annihilation of the human race. Not only the British people, but the whole world, was watching and hoping that he would prevent it.

When Mr. Churchill's Second World War memoirs were introduced to Japan by the *Mainichi Shimbun*, I was absorbed in reading them and craved for more. In point of historical fact, excellence of treatise, and lucid penetration of historical data, they must be the supreme war document of the present generation. Of greatest interest to all Japanese was of course the fourth volume, called *The Hinge of Fate*, which, published serially in Japan, presented Mr. Churchill's version of the campaign in Malaya. Even now, so long after the event, that book stirs up the feelings of the Japanese people not a little.

Prior to the outbreak of war in the Pacific, I was a staff officer of Imperial General Headquarters, and at the end of 1940 was assigned to prepare plans for operations in Malaya. Just before the actual commencement of hostilities there, we carried out maneuvers in tropical warfare in southern Indochina. From the beginning to the end of the

Malayan campaign I served as Director of the Planning and Operations Staff under General Yamashita, Commander of the 25th Japanese Army.

If one's memories are carried deep into the past, there are some hard lessons to be learned from experience. When I differ from Mr. Churchill's opinions it is because in reading his memoirs I discovered some regrettable mistakes; but they are small flaws in a gem the full merit of which none will deny.

In regard to the campaign in Malaya the only men fully qualified to reply to Mr. Churchill were General Yamashita, who has fallen on the execution ground at Manila, and his Chief of Staff, Suzuki, who too has vanished with the morning dew on Leyte Island. Today, however, reflecting upon the battles of years gone by, as General Yamashita is no more, I venture to substitute for the spirit of the departed hero; and wishing to reply to Mr. Churchill's memoirs, boldly and without regard for myself, I publish this review of the Malayan campaign from the Japanese standpoint.

Written ten years after the outbreak of war, it presents the views of one who was in close contact with General Yamashita throughout the campaign. With self-confidence and introspection it is submitted to aid the formation of a new historical philosophy by the youth of Japan who fought so hard and bravely on the battlefields of Malaya and who later suffered and gave themselves up to despair at the defeat of the Fatherland. In every epoch it is the disinterested and patriotic youth of every nation who are the pioneers and the backbone of their countries and who determine their destinies.

Notwithstanding the inspiring leadership of Mr. Churchill, the British Army surrendered an impregnable fortress almost without resistance in barely seventy days, even though its military strength was greatly superior to that of its Japanese opponents. The youth of the Army lived up to Mr. Churchill's expectations, but because of inefficiency in the British Army in Malaya, Japan conquered spectacularly.

In the war, however, Japan was defeated, notwithstanding the superiority of her youth. Was it perhaps because she had no such great leader as Mr. Churchill?

It is true that the history of Malaya is the history of the weak falling prey to the strong. To say the least, to the extent that we control a living world, so naturally we are prepared to defend it with our utmost effort. We cannot tolerate continued dependence of our Fatherland's destiny on international guarantees and the good faith of a foreign power. You, the Japanese younger generation, are facing a crisis. As one reflects upon the might of the nation which your seniors demonstrated on the battlefields of Malaya, where they displayed a dauntless spirit second to none, one sees the same devotion to our country in your reconstruction of the defeated Fatherland. This nation must not again be subjected to the tragic atom bomb. If possible, it must have peace without fighting, not only for the sake of Japan, but for the sake of all Asia. If this can be achieved, then the whole world must rejoice.

Already I have published a number of books, and from some of my readers and friends I have received rather scathing criticism as well as friendly advice as, for example, "He writes as if he conquered the world by himself alone," and, "He is not meditating on the punishment of defeat, he is inciting jingoistic thoughts." I do not think I will discuss these criticisms now, and in any case I positively have not the power to wield my pen in any other way.

All my life perhaps, the spilling of blood and the groping of my way along the road will be engraved deeply in my brain. I have set down only my own impressions, and as regards details of time, dates, military strength, names of people, and so on, it is difficult to guarantee the impossibility of errors of memory. Respecting the fundamental principles, however, I have a clear conscience, which is based on confidence in the records.

Meditating on the reasons for conquest in battle and defeat in war, I earnestly hope that a road may be discovered to lead away from domination by force to alliances based on moral principles and sincerity.

Today, ten years since the landing on Singora beach, this record is dedicated to the spirits of the now departed heroes General Yamashita and Army Chief of Staff Suzuki and the more than 3,500 soldiers who fell on Malayan battlefields.

Masanobu Tsuji
8 December 1951

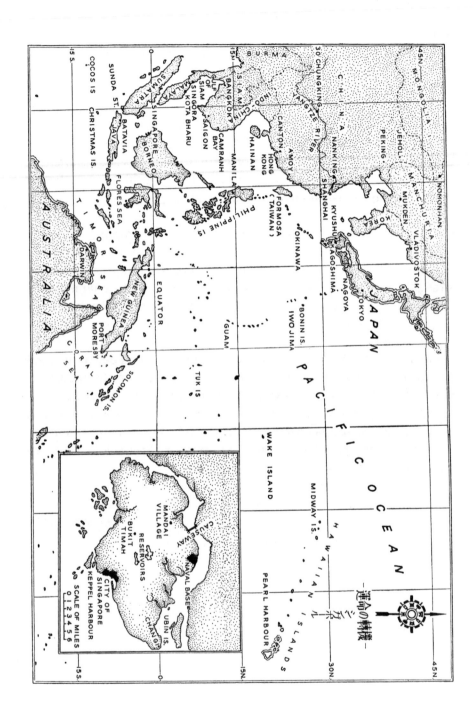

Part One

War Without Preparation

IN THE SECOND PARAGRAPH OF *The Hinge of Fate* Mr. Churchill states that "the onslaught of Japan. . . [which] had been long prepared. . . fell upon the British and American fronts—if such they could be called—with cruel severity." Was that really the case?

The fact is that after the Washington Conference of 1921–22,* the Japanese Navy had exhausted its energies in training in the arts of war and working over secret plans. In so doing it regarded both the British and American navies as potential enemies, and endeavored to make up for numerical inferiority by the superior quality of its ships and seamen. However, so far as I know, there had been no preparation of military plans against Britain and America by the Military Headquarters General Staff. Following the Russo-Japanese War, the basic policy had been one of preparation for another war against Russia; but after the collapse of Imperial Russia, for a period of several years there was no menace from the Soviet Union; and consequently little military planning of importance in Japan. After the Manchurian Incident [the Japanese occupation of Manchuria in 1931], we became fully conscious of the Soviet menace to the Far East and our military preparations were expedited. The concern of the Army was directed towards the north.

---

* The Washington Conference, signed by Great Britain, the United States, Japan, France, and Italy, limited the number of capital ships in the navies of the contracting powers. Old capital ships were to be scrapped, and building programs for new ones abandoned. Great Britain and the United States were each allowed 525,000 tons of capital ships, and Japan 315,000 tons. Aircraft carriers were limited in the same ratio of 5:5:3, Great Britain and the United States having 135,000 tons each, and Japan 81,000 tons. The agreement expired in 1936.

The capture of Singapore, Hong Kong, and the Philippines was discussed, but nothing more than a vague scheme was formulated for naval operations in combination with a few Army divisions.

The feeling that it was necessary to prepare seriously for war against the United States and Britain developed only after economic pressure was exerted against Japan by the United States following upon the movement of Japanese forces into Indochina; this resulted in the freezing of all Japanese funds in the United States, the annulment of the Commercial Treaty with Japan, and the prohibition of exports of petroleum and scrap iron to Japan. Correctly speaking, preparations for war against the United States and Britain date back to 6 September 1940 (14th year of Showa*) when the following decision was made in the Imperial Presence: "To complete the necessary preparations for war by about late October, resolving, as a matter of national preservation, not to avoid war with the United States."

In the following pages I shall describe how the preparations against the United States and Britain were arranged by Headquarters and on the fighting fronts as well.

The Doro Nawa Unit

EVEN IN OUR SUMMER DRESS we felt the heat at Taihoku [now Taipei, capital of Taiwan] on New Year's Day in 1941. At a crossroad in the military barracks a brand-new, spick-and-span signboard was hanging that read: "Taiwan Army No. 82 Unit," another name for which was the "Taiwan Army Research Section."

The barracks—a small, cramped house, formerly a brigade head quarters—were being extended. The fragrance of new wood was still in the air, and from early morning until late at night the sound of hammers and planes could be heard. Only thirty people lived there, and among them, raked together from every quarter of Japan, were officers, noncommissioned officers, servants, and typists.

Under the direction of General Itagaki, Chief of Staff to the Commander-in-Chief of Japanese forces in China, I (who had been driven out of Nanking General Headquarters, and although watched by the authorities from Tokyo, had worked for the East Asia Federation Movement** the central provinces of China) was appointed officer in charge of the Research Department of the Taiwan Army. When in the New Year I passed through the gate of the small unit of which I was now

---

* Showa ["enlightened peace"]—the era of the reign of the Emperor Hirohito.
** See Appendix 2.

a member, it was the first time in all my eighteen years as a commissioned officer that I had served in such a small force. It was also the last time.

With the sudden change in the bewildering international situation it seemed that the Central Administration in Tokyo had begun to think seriously that preparations should be made for a thrust southward.

Japanese soldiers were familiar only with the intensely cold regions of Manchukuo—now again known as Manchuria. None of them had any understanding of the meaning of the words "squall" or "jungle," much less any experience of these things. Consequently it was essential to begin to collect fundamental data for military operations in tropical areas.

The Doro Nawa* unit was organized with extraordinary urgency and given the name of the Taiwan Army Research Department. This small organization was supplementary to Taiwan Army Headquarters under Uemura, the Army Chief of Staff; in reality, however, Colonel Yoshihide Hayashi shouldered responsibility for the unit.

To this unpretentious and promiscuously chosen household was allotted the task of collecting, in approximately six months, all conceivable data connected with tropical warfare: the organization of Army corps, equipment, campaign direction, management and treatment of weapons, sanitation, supply, administration of occupied territory, and military strategy, tactics, and geography.

It was the duty of the unit to report on all these matters to General Headquarters in Tokyo. Furthermore, the scope of research extended over the whole of the Pacific war regions as well as Malaya, the Philippine Islands, Indonesia, and Burma. Funds apportioned to the unit for research totaled barely 20,000 yen.

Even among the commissioned officers chosen for the staff, there was not one who had had any real experience of the tropics. What's more, in the eyes of those at General Headquarters nearly all the members of the staff were persons to be ignored, held in contempt, or kept at a respectful distance. The founders of the Taiwan headquarters were like the new bride who is teased by the mother-in-law—the more she works the more the mother-in-law is burnt up with jealousy. There were many others also whose attitude suggested the well-fed faces of those in the Yoshizaki Temple.**

---

*Doro Nawa—a phrase impossible of literal translation. "Doro" means robber, "Nawa" means rope. You catch a robber and begin to make the rope afterwards. It means to make preparations too late. An English equivalent might be the "Barn Door Brigade"— after the expression of closing the barn door after the horse has gone.
** A reference well known to Japanese, denoting the attitude so often adopted by those in comfortable circumstances to others not so fortunately placed.

For these reasons we could not afford to slacken in our efforts to carry out the duties allotted us. On New Year's Day we were far from being in the mood for celebratory *toso* [spiced wine], as we had at once to abandon the idea of a one-year plan and arrange for the completion of our work in six months.

The ten research officials to whom were allotted the various items for investigation put heart and soul into their work; but they soon grew impatient, for they had not the faintest idea of where it would be best to turn their attention, and to make matters worse they were completely destitute of data.

There were many questions that had to be determined. For instance, what alterations had to be made in the organization of troops and the type of weapons and equipment used on the Siberian and Manchurian battlefields at twenty degrees below zero to meet requirements for fighting in the dense jungles of the tropics? How should tactics and strategy recently used against the Soviet Union be revised for action against British and American armies, and what comparisons could be made between the tactics, equipment, and organization of Soviet, British, and American troops? What should be done to cope with supplies and sanitation in tropical areas—and particularly with malaria? What measures should be taken in occupied areas to comply with the traditions and special characteristics of the inhabitants? What could be found out of the military geography of Malaya, the Philippines, Burma, and Indonesia? And so on.

It was first decided to map out the most important objectives on which to work, and then to assign specific tasks of investigation to the ten members of the research staff according to the ability and past experience of each man. My appointed concern was Malaya. I was to study questions of military geography, equipment, tactics, and supplies—the whole organization of a campaign.

Having such a meager household for carrying out our work, we cast our eyes on the headquarters of the Governor-General of Taiwan, like an old pioneer family trying to make a suitable alliance with a man of wealth. We secured the support of the headquarters, and with humble language and extravagant gratitude we sought assistance from all available men of talent, and knowledge from all possible sources. Apart from this help we were undermanned. The Director of the Southward Association, who had for ten years been engaged in research into trade with tropical countries under the jurisdiction of the Governor-General, was a Mr. En Imagawa, a senior official who benefited from a fairly liberal budget. He was of great help, as was also Lieutenant-

General Kikuchi, a former instructor on military geography at the War College.

With the assistance of the Southward Association it was possible to obtain information from everyone in Taiwan and Japan who had knowledge and experience of the tropics. From an old sea captain who had voyaged for many years to the south we received instructions in forecasting atmospheric phenomena, in disembarkation methods, and on coastal conditions. From officials of the Ishihara Mining Company we learned useful military facts about Malaya's geography. Professors of Taiwan University advised us on tropical hygiene and about counter measures against malaria. The Director of the Taiwan Bank gave us details on banking in the various countries we were studying. In addition, we learned much from commercial firms and private individuals, and in particular from the Reverend Mr. Kozui Otani immediately after his southern tour. All shared grudgingly their specialized knowledge with the new household in the barracks building.

This information alone was not genuine strategic material, but it was all useful knowledge about tropical countries from which it was the duty of those of us who wore military uniform to select, adjust, and adapt the points applicable to our purposes. From the total research fund of 20,000 yen given to us by Army Headquarters, a monthly budget of about 2,000 yen was set aside and the whole of this money was applied to the employment of our informants from outside.

For a period of two months, almost every day we pestered specialists from every quarter. We even used our siesta time for lectures, which were always eagerly attended. Soon all the research officers felt they had become no mean specialists of the Southward Road. This unimpressive group was certainly at that time the supreme authority in the Army on tropical warfare.

Taiwan's intelligentsia did not begrudge assistance for the Research Department, which was forging ahead; but, by contrast, as time went on, the jealousy of the Army Operations Section became intense. Even the 20,000-yen research fund allotted by the Central Department in accordance with regulations was grudgingly given, and in one month was cut by nearly 2,000 yen. This is to say that leadership of the Southward Association was kept under the jurisdiction of the Army Operations Section.

An officer from Military Staff Headquarters who was entrusted with an official inspection of the southern areas reported the valuable knowledge he gained, which enhanced the reputation of our unit. Important suggestions also arose from talks with Colonel Tanigawa and Major

Kunitake. The most important information gained can be summarized as follows:

1. Singapore Fortress was solid and strong on its sea front, but the rear, facing Johore Province, was practically defenseless.
2. The British Army was training aerial defense fighter planes in Malaya, but reports in the newspapers of the number of machines were intentional propaganda, exaggerating the real strength.
3. Coastal defense in the neighborhood of Mersing was strong and administration of the area exceedingly rigid and searching, travellers' arrivals and departures being rigorously restricted.
4. Land and air forces in Kedah Province appeared to have recently been strongly reinforced.
5. The British Army in Malaya numbered from five to six divisions with a total strength of approximately 80,000. The proportion of European troops was probably less than 50 percent.
And so on and so on.

Styling Singapore the "Gibraltar of the Orient" and boasting of its impregnability might possibly indicate a show of strength—or bluff. But the absence of rear defenses of the fortress constituted a very grave defect. The strength of its position was purposely and extravagantly propagandized without regard for the complacency which would be promoted among the public and even among those responsible for its defense. I was only one of many who were thinking seriously about the capture of the island.

Some men of excellent talent secretly helped the work of the Research Department. Major Asaeda was one of them. He had passed through the Army Staff College with a set of swords, and as a staff officer in Shansi he was famed for courage. He had then been selected for the War Office Army Officers' Bureau; but office duties did not suit his temperament. Casting aside an especially important post, he came alone to Taiwan, discarded his officer's uniform, and dressed himself as a coolie. He wished to work as a spy and expressed a strong desire to offer his life for research in southern areas. It was my first meeting with him, and I received the impression that he was a disinterested, death-defying hero. Alas, to our great sorrow, this very fine "coolie" was later cast into the jaws of death.

Revealing the state of Asaeda's affairs to Lieutenant-General Kikuchi, I employed him as a research officer of the Southward Association. He labored until exhausted, literally forgetting food and sleep. However, he had left his military post without permission, and was accordingly punished for the offense by three months' suspension from duty. At the expiration of this period he worked side by side with members of the Taiwan Army Research Department. He then wished to move on, so, disguising himself, he infiltrated into the southern part of Thailand, crossed the Malay frontier, and eventually brought back a valuable report on conditions there relating to the seacoast and contours of the land in various sectors. I shall refer to this again later in my narrative.

In the middle of February 1941, the Central Department in Tokyo ordered maneuvers to be carried out extending over a fortnight under the command of General Suzuki, Director of War Exercises, Headquarters General Staff. There was a nationwide selection of technical staff officers, as well as of staff officers detailed for special instruction in the embarkation and disembarkation of troops. I was added to the group.

Taiwan was headquarters for the maneuvers and Kyushu was regarded as the hostile country. Landings were made on the Kagoshima coast and the capture of Kurume was planned. As a result of these exercises, fundamental principles of operations were determined, but apart from wearing the dress and equipment to be used in tropical areas, the project was not characterized by either originality or peculiarity.

The maneuvers, however, brought together talented officers from all quarters, including naval staff men. During the two weeks' period they came to know one another by sight and became friendly. Later, these acquaintanceships were to prove of tremendous value on the battlefield. The maneuvers were probably of most value in assisting the allotment of duties in the Pacific war to those best suited to perform them.

Next, to examine from actual experience the information obtained by research and set down on paper, maneuvers were conducted in great secrecy in South China during ten days of June 1941.

These were carried out under the administration of the Taiwan Army, with direct command of the operations under the Army Commander, 23rd Army, who, for a fortnight, transferred his headquarters from the Pescadores Islands to Fuchow in order to be closer to the maneuvers. The Uzina Transport Department was temporarily moved to Canton to facilitate close cooperation with the Taiwan Army Research Unit, which actually directed the maneuvers in the field.

With Colonel Hayashi, I visited the commanding general of the 23rd Army at his command post at Fuchow. Wearing a bathrobe and narrow belt, he reluctantly received us in our full field outfits and paid little attention to our report on the maneuvers. Meeting him, I recalled a quite contrary experience in the Kwantung Army* when I served under General Ueda, who, even though he was crippled, invariably put on his uniform to receive subordinates on special duty, no matter if they arrived after midnight or in the small hours of the morning. Could there be a greater contrast than between him and this 23rd Army commander?

Restraining my indignation, I had to conduct myself submissively for the sake of our important maneuvers. Remembering that "Good advice is harsh to the ear and flatterers usually become uppish," I compared this general, still on the active list, with the noteworthy Lieutenant-General Kanji Ishihara,** Divisional Commander at Kyoto, for whom I had the greatest respect, and who had recently been placed on the retired list.

Investigation into the transport by sea of men and horses was the primary objective of these maneuvers. In temperatures of 120 degrees, men and horses would have to be packed like sardines into the ships, travel through heavy seas, and disembark on open beaches. How could this be done without heavy loss?

To ascertain the limit of endurance of the men, they were embarked "three to a mat" (an area of about 6 feet by 3 feet), and for about a week given a ration of water which had to be economized to the utmost. The transport of military horses on a sea voyage to the tropics had been thought to be impossible, but ways and means were worked out by which it might be done.

The most difficult problem of all was to determine methods of disembarking men and equipment on open beaches with due regard for dangerous coral or hidden and sunken rocks, but eventually, after considerable trouble, satisfactory routines were evolved. Our study of these matters was carried out with the utmost seriousness; it was as a sword smeared with blood.

These exercises ended our research, and the lessons learned were then put into practice as nearly as possible under active-service conditions. A landing was effected on Hainan Island by a battalion of infantry, a battery of artillery, and a company of engineers using bicycles and motor cars. The operation covered an area within a circumference of roughly a thousand kilometers. Bridges were blown up and repaired, and rapid assaults carried out as the troops moved through the tropical terrain. A great deal of further information was gathered during this practical experience concerning the organization of equipment, methods of fighting, the rationing of troops, and so on.

---

* Kwantung (or Kanto) Army—the Japanese field army in Manchuria.
** See Appendix 2, "The East Asia Federation Movement."

The results of all the research and experiments undertaken were classified under such headings as war technique, organization, military geography, rear-service duties, etc., and five months later they were submitted to Headquarters General Staff, Tokyo. General Tojo, the Army Minister, and General Sugiyama, the Chief of Staff, as though for the first time satisfied, with smiling faces said, "Many thanks for your trouble. You have done well."

And thus the labor of our unit was rewarded.

Among the things which stood out conspicuously was the pamphlet entitled "Read This Alone—And The War Can Be Won."* It was compiled in simple, informal language from a summary of the mountain of diverse research material, and was so prepared that anyone could read it lying on his back, on a hot, crowded, and uncomfortable ship. It had been approved by the Headquarters General Staff, and about forty thousand copies were printed for distribution to officers and men immediately after embarkation.

Meantime, the captain of a merchant ship who had made many voyages to the south gave us a secret chart of Indonesia, and from a Japanese resident of Malaya we received aerial photos of Singapore. These things had been extremely difficult to obtain.

Our task had been, as it were, to warm ourselves at another's fire and to produce something from nothing—a gleam of hope from bewilderment—and to accomplish in a short period a large undertaking by original methods. With the secret cooperation of two men, Lieutenant-General Kikuchi and Mr. En Imagawa, our task was well done, and its success was based on the serious and utmost effort of all the members of the research staff. Behind these and also worthy of special mention were our ten typists, who, until late at night, eaten by mosquitoes, silently and uncomplainingly typed away.

The "Doro Nawa" model of research, with less than thirty people in its household, in a period not exceeding six months, planned the military operations of the whole army which was to move south, and also the administration of the territories to be occupied, and I declare with humility that it provided the greatest, and in fact the only, instruction book on tropical warfare available to the Japanese armies. I think it was scandalous that the Army should have been so unprepared. But these are the candid facts: During the latter half of 1941 the armies which were to become engaged in southern areas abandoned their horses and were reorganized into mixed formations using bicycles and motor transport.

---

* See Appendix 1 for a translation of this pamphlet.

While reorganization was in progress there was little spare time for training, and most of the troops obtained their first ideas of tropical warfare
from reading the pamphlet issued to them on embarkation. Preparations
for war against Russia had been continued for ten years in accordance
with a full-scale military plan, and there is all the difference in the
world between those long drawn-out preparations and the ones undertaken prior to the Malayan campaign and operations elsewhere in the
Pacific. Tojo, the former Minister for War, and Muto, former Director of
Military Services, were responsible for the creation of the Taiwan Army
Research Department, and they gave the orders concerning the "Doro
Nawa" model for research work. At the Court of Justice at Ichigaya the
International Tribunal on War Crimes did not mention a word about the
short time devoted by Japan to preparation for the Pacific war. Could it
have been because the memory of such a meager, insignificant thing as
the "Doro Nawa Research Unit" did not remain long in mind? It must be
concluded, however, that lack of thorough preparation was one reason
for our defeat in the war.

Southward Advance? Northward Thrust?

ONE EVENING, HALFWAY THROUGH THE test maneuvers on
Hainan Island, we were just beginning supper in a coconut plantation.
We had cut open coconuts to drink their juice instead of sake, taken our
meals of cooked rice, salted fish, and pickled plums from the cellophane
bags in which they were wrapped, and were talking of the next day's
exercises when our excited wireless operator announced special news.
War had begun between Germany and Russia.

After the partition of Poland in the east, and having routed the British
Army at Dunkirk and Calais and destroyed the French Army in the
west, Hitler had suddenly, and without any notice whatever, pointed
the sword at Stalin's head and attacked Russia. During the summer of
1939, while the Kwantung Army had been engaged in a desperate battle against five times its number of Soviet troops at Nomonhan,* Hitler
had completely disregarded the Anti-Comintern Pact with Japan** and

* At Nomonhan, near the border of Outer Mongolia and Manchuria, Soviet
forces severely defeated a Japanese army in August 1939. The Red Army almost
annihilated one division.
**The Anti-Comintern Pact of 1936, signed between Germany, Italy, and Japan,
was designed to prevent the spread of Communism. The contracting powers
undertook not to enter into treaties with the Soviet Union except by mutual
agreement.

concluded a non-aggression treaty with the Soviets. This had brought about the collapse of the Hiranuma Cabinet at the end of August 1939. This treaty was again twice violated by Germany without warning.

I, at that time, felt intuitively that a dark shadow had come over the future of Germany, which had consistently disregarded inter national good faith. War must have a morality and a reason which is under-standable at home and abroad. From a propaganda standpoint, Hitler's attack placed the Soviet Union in a 100 percent more advantageous position.

Putting aside all questions of international morality, however, and looking at the position from a purely strategic aspect, the question arose whether the German nation had any real prospect of victory when con-fronted simultaneously by the Anglo-Saxon and Slavic races.

It appeared to me that Hitler had begun his attack on Russia too late to have any substantial prospects of success. If he could seize Moscow and Stalingrad and attack the Urals before the winter, he might win. But at the end of October snow would begin to fall over the Russian battle area, and I did not think he would be able to settle matters by that time. I knew from my experience of the life-and-death struggle at Nomonhan that victory over the Soviets would not be an easy matter.

Two days after the outbreak of the Russo-German war, I received a telegram announcing my appointment as an assistant member of the Headquarters General Staff But the maneuvers we had begun could not be stopped when we were only halfway through. They were designed to work out a technique for an attack and a long-range penetration of approximately one thousand kilometers into enemy territory—the distance from southern Thailand to Singapore—and were to take into account the probability of strong resistance along the whole route of the attack and the fact that all bridges would be destroyed and roads dam-aged by the enemy.

As I have already stated, the investigation unit for these exercises was a mixed organization of infantry, artillery, and engineers equipped with motor transport and bicycles, and the operation was carried out as nearly as possible under war conditions.

At the end of the Hainan maneuvers, I returned to Taihoku by plane to finalize my work with the Research Unit. Having done so, with regret I said farewell forever to the typists, servants, and office staff who had shared our anxieties since the establishment of the unit. I finally arrived in Tokyo on 14 July. Colonel Hattori welcomed me sin-cerely, saying, "For some time I have been patiently waiting for you to come along."

I did not know why I, who had previously been reproved by General Tojo, had been recalled to Tokyo. Presumably I would be required to participate in preparations for fighting either in the north or the south—I had no idea which.

My several years' experience with the Kwantung Army, and particularly of the fighting at Nomonhan, would be useful in the event of war against Russia. On the other hand, the research into tropical warfare in which I had been wholeheartedly engrossed during the last six months would be equally useful if the Japanese Army moved south.

The decision whether to thrust to the north or attack southward had not yet been reached.

When I arrived at Tokyo Headquarters I found an intimate friend, Lieutenant-Colonel Kumon, who was sitting at his desk looking perfectly happy. He told me there had been practically no discussion as to whether we should strike north or south, but that among the General Staff there were many who believed Hitler would force a decision in Russia in the late autumn, and that we should miss the bus if we did not hurry to get into the war, and that consequently our share of the spoils of victory would be decreased.

This view of Germany's prospects was finally accepted by the General Staff. The Kwantung Army had been increased in strength from 400,000 to 700,000 and renamed Kantokuan (Kwantung Army Special Maneuvers), and a war expenditure of a thousand million yen had been provisionally appropriated.

At dinner the day after my arrival there were heated arguments in my section on the prospects of war with Russia. I had been greatly surprised at what I had heard of the opinions of the General Staff, and stated my opinions as follows:

"Do we know the strength of the Russian armies in the Far East, which inflicted such heavy casualties upon us at Nomonhan? Soviet forces in Europe are positively not yet defeated, and even if Hitler carries on the war efficiently I believe his conquest of Russia will probably take him four or five years. When we were fighting at Nomonhan in 1939, he betrayed Japan and concluded a Russo-German non-aggression pact, thus without warning destroying the Anti-Comintern alliance. In Hitler there is not a vestige of international good faith. Japan will be staking her national destiny if she goes to war, so why should she consider aiding Hitler in his fight with Russia? If Germany wins and seizes Russia and Siberia east of Lake Baikal, what gain will there be for Japan or for Asia?

"For the past century or more, Britain has ruled ten times as many of the peoples of Asia as has Russia. Singapore is the key to Southeast

Asia. Its seizure will emancipate the oppressed peoples of Asia and will also exert a powerful influence to bring about settlement of the China Incident."*

Vehemently opposing war against Russia, I strongly advocated an attack to the south. Lieutenant-Colonel Kumon, with an uneasy expression, called me into another room. "The Central Department has been concentrating on ways to defeat the Soviets," he said. "As you have only been here a day or so, you do not know the position. You should keep quiet, otherwise you will again be dismissed by the Departmental Chief." He went on, "The other day when Staff Officer Obi came to Tokyo, and from his experience in Manchuria opposed war against Russia, he was stormed at by the First Department Chief, General Tanaka, and the Chief of the Personnel Bureau, General Tominaga."

Although I felt grateful to Lieutenant-Colonel Kumon for his kindly warning, I thought to myself, "Thank you very much for your advice, but I don't even mind being dismissed. I did not wish to come to Headquarters General Staff."

It was not very long since Matsuoka, the Minister for Foreign Affairs, had returned home after concluding a non-aggression pact with Russia, but already weaker-minded members of the staff were eager to follow the lead of those who advocated war against Russia—which they had opposed only a short time ago.

Since Nomonhan, Japanese resentment against Russia had been engraved even in the marrow of my bones. There was no reason to trust the Soviets, but the question was, "Should we side with Germany just because of Hitler's and Ribbentrop's bluster?"

To me it seemed that in determining our policy we should retain an Asian field of vision and maintain international good faith. Russia appeared to have accepted restriction of her Far Eastern territories to their existing boundaries, and as she was fighting desperately on her western front there was little or no immediate danger of her attacking to the east.

Since the beginning of the Manchurian and China incidents, however, Japan's relations with America had become strained. Although there was little danger of attack from the Soviets, it appeared quite clear that we would soon be challenged by America and Britain.

---

*A provocation by Japanese troops against a Chinese Army patrol on 7 July 1937 led to a full-scale Japanese invasion of China. This theater of war eventually accounted for millions of casualties and remained active until the Japanese surrender in WWII.

Owing to America's revocation of the Commercial Treaty, petroleum was no longer available to Japan from the East Indies, and the freezing of Japanese credits and of the property of Japanese residents in the United States intensified the economic war. I felt at the time that we could not escape war with America unless we evacuated Manchuria.

At the end of 1939 and during 1940 the Japanese Government, while doing everything possible to avoid war with America under any circumstances, ordered an inquiry into the extent of our national resources to be carried out by the War Department and General Staff Headquarters. The results, according to our mobilization plans, may be summarized as follows:

1. Raw materials such as iron ore and aluminum could be obtained from the southern regions to the extent of the transport available, and would be diminished in proportion to our shipping losses. In the third year of war, however, we would experience extreme shortages of non-ferrous metals. The same would apply to liquid fuel. Moreover, serious shipping losses would also result in corresponding reductions in imports of coal, which would cause a general decline in industry.
2. Even if we avoided war, and America and Britain terminated their anti-Japanese economic measures, lack of liquid fuel would be fatal to Japan. In 1941 the Army and Navy had in storage roughly 1,170,000 kiloliters of aviation petrol [about 240 million gallons] and about 4,400,000 kiloliters of ordinary petrol [about 970 million gallons].

Accepting these findings as a basis, General Staff Headquarters demanded of the War Office another estimate of national resources, the report on which was as follows:

1. Allowing for maintenance of fifty Army divisions and the full strength of the Air Force, it would be impossible to carry on war against the Soviet Union for more than a year as liquid fuel supplies would be exhausted within that time.
2. At the present rate of progress of the China Incident, it will take us about four years to win. But if we carry military operations as far as an advance on Chungking we will have to employ about twenty Army divisions for three years, and our resources will be exhausted before the end of that time.
3. If we go to war with Britain and America, using the full strength of the Navy and Air Force and fifteen Army divisions, at the end of one year it should be possible to utilize the resources already developed in

the southern countries. Furthermore, it would be possible to hold out in a protracted struggle so long as we could maintain our transport shipping. The effective strength of the Navy would be the determining factor.

The report concluded: "So long as the Navy approves, the southward advance is the most desirable course."

Reports from the Chief of the Naval General Staff were discussed frequently, but there seemed to be very powerful pacifist influences in inner naval circles. Yamamoto, the Commander-in-Chief of Combined Sea and Air Forces, believed that every endeavor should be made to avoid war. His opinion appears to have been, "If we are ordered to fight we will be able to achieve a runaway victory for six months or a year, but towards the end of the second year the Americans will so increase their strength that it will be very difficult to fight an even battle."

Finally, after long discussion, agreement was reached on the general situation and the Naval General Staff determined to fight rather than sit down to die by starvation, stating firmly that it was in agreement with the policy of moving south, but that it was definitely opposed to war against Russia and extension of the China Incident operations to an advance to Chungking. The Naval Staff said, in effect, "Now is the time to begin the war as we can commence hostilities on even terms, but in two or three years' time there will be no chance of victory."

Many have since argued that the Navy's reluctant agreement to war was the result of coercion by the Army, or of a decision by the government to go to war regardless of naval opinion. It seems that a section of the Navy has tried to shift the responsibility for war onto the Army, but it is certain that the Navy of that time was not so obedient to the government that it could be forced to agree to high-handed demands by the Army on matters of policy.

At Army and Navy headquarters the final decision was that, apart from war against Britain and America, there was no other way to ensure "the preservation and defense of the nation in the atmosphere which thickens day by day." We could not overlook the fact that on the battlefields of Europe the Soviet resistance was gradually increasing and the speed of the German advance slowing down. "Many advocates of the northern movement insisted on striking at the Soviets, not because they relied on the superior efficiency of their armies, but because they thought, according to the Hitler godhead, that at any moment Stalin would die mad.

Our candid ideas at the time were that the Americans, being merchants, would not continue for long with an unprofitable war, whereas we ourselves, if we fought only the Anglo-Saxon nations, could carry on a protracted war; that after we had achieved some great victories in the south the Republic of China would be willing to conclude an unconditional peace treaty based on the principles of an East Asia Co-Prosperity League; that Russia would break away from her Western allies; and that after conclusion of peace with China, it would be possible for us to move a million troops from that country to Manchuria, which would be sufficient to deter Russia from any further adventure in that direction or to deal with any attack which might develop there.

A group of clever people stood at the crossroads without making it clear whether they favored attack to the north or to the south. When we won in Malaya, occupied Manila and the Dutch East Indies, and captured Rangoon, they claimed they had always advocated the southern movement. But today, when we are defeated, they boast of their foresight, saying, "We were against the war at the time." It is probably true that there were many intellectuals who opposed the war, but they lacked the courage to risk their lives or their liberty by open opposition to the outbreak of hostilities.

While we were engaged on our "desk maneuvers" in the General Staff office together with members of the Naval Staff, General Sugiyama, Chief of the General Staff, asked me, "What is your estimate of the rate at which the operations can progress?" I replied, "If we commence on Meiji Setsu* we will be able to capture Manila by the New Year Singapore by Kigensetsu,** Java on Army Commemoration Day [10 March], and Rangoon on the Emperor's birthday [19 April]." This estimate proved close to the results subsequently achieved.

Tojo, the Minister for War, who had attended the meeting, listened silently and gravely. He asked repeatedly, "How do you believe the war against Britain and America will end?" No one could reply with confidence to this question. All that could be said was, "We hope the war will be brought to a conclusion as rapidly as possible by coordination of political and military strategy." All present predicted that a protracted war might end unfavorably.

Today, thinking over the reason for defeat, I agree that Japan was mistaken in its judgment of national resources when contemplating opposition to Britain and America. I have no doubt that this is the correct view of the whole situation. But since I must speak candidly, I would prefer

* 3 November, the anniversary of the birthday of the Meiji Emperor, whose reign began in 1867.
**Anniversary of the coronation of Japan's first Emperor, 11 February 600 B.C.

to conclude by saying, "Japan gave exaggerated credence to estimates of the real power of Germany."

Perusing historical annals of defeats from ancient times, it appears that many writers who study causes of defeat are prone to close their eyes to the methodology of the conduct of war, and because of the shame of defeat they tend to ignore or distort the real reasons for beginning hostilities. Past history shows that force of circumstances inevitably gives rise to this attitude in defeated countries. Today, as I write, in the present world situation we are not trying to find a correct and impartial answer to this question.

From the beginning of our operations in the south, we were confident of victory, but many problems arose later. One of the most important was to develop a plan for the administration of the occupied territories which would meet the demands of a long, drawn-out war. A particular dilemma was whether it would be desirable for us to assist the development of independence of the Oriental nations which for centuries had been controlled by Britain, Holland, and America. This question should have been settled in advance, even in the face of opposition from the Navy. After much investigation and discussion between Army and Navy chiefs, the essentials of military administration in the occupied territories were determined. All was to be under control of the Army, including adjustment of operations and frictions in the rear services. Such administration was to be under the supervision of the Minister for War.

The role of the Navy was the guaranteed seizure of the islands, including the oilfields in eastern Borneo. All the rest was under control of the Army. But promotion of the independence of the occupied territories was not considered until too late for effective action.

Hasty Operations Orders

THE ALL-IMPORTANT FIRST STAGE of operations to the south was the attack on Pearl Harbor. For this stroke the authorities assembled the best men and equipment available to crush at one blow the main forces of the American Pacific Fleet. The project was secretly termed the "Z" military operation. The Malay Army Operations Section ranked equally with the "Z" group.

Singapore, Gibraltar, and Suez were the keys to Britain's control of the seven seas. Ten years in construction, the fortress of Singapore was completed in February 1938 at the enormous cost of ten million pounds sterling. Success or failure of the attempt to capture it would completely decide the fate of our campaign in the southern areas.

It seems that selection of personnel for operations to the south was secretly commenced at the beginning of September, and it was unofficially decided that I was to be Staff Officer in Charge of Operations and Planning in the Malayan sector. My selection for this position was a realization of my personal plans for the capture of Singapore, which I could not forget even in dreams, for it had been the subject of my continuous thoughts since the formation of the Taiwan Army Research Unit. I was not unconscious of the complimentary gesture paid me in my appointment to this important mission.

I state beyond doubt and without fear of contradiction that not until September 1941 did we begin active preparations for military operations to the south. This is proof that the Pacific hostilities were wholly and hastily prepared on the "Doro Nawa" model. The extent of improvisation required in such hasty preparation is indicated by comparison with the thorough planning for war against the Soviet Union, which extended over a period of years, and formulated a detailed operations plan for one year. The mobilization plans for the Soviet campaign were prepared in times of peace, and the battle formations and army commanders and staff were selected at leisure.

Lieutenant-General Tomoyuki Yamashita was unofficially chosen as Commander-in-Chief of the 25th Army to operate in Malaya, with General Sosaku Suzuki (Chief of the Third Department, General Staff Headquarters) as his senior staff officer. Colonel Ikegaya (Head of the Shipping Section, Headquarters General Staff) was also one of the first men to be appointed to the staff of the 25th Army. Other selections included some of the ablest officers in the Army at that time. Major Kunitake was appointed Officer in Charge of Southward Operations at Imperial General Headquarters. Major Asaeda, who had come to light again in Taiwan, was appointed as Auxiliary Assistant of Military Operations. Lieutenant-Colonel Sugita, who had studied in America, was selected as Intelligence Officer, and staff was also chosen for shipping and transport, signals, railways, lines of communications, and so on.

It must be specially mentioned that in the selection of personnel Malaya was given priority over Burma, the Philippines, and the Dutch East Indies sector. I who had been unofficially chosen as Staff Officer in Charge of Operations, drew up the draft plans for military operations.

After many years of fighting, and preparation for further fighting in Siberia and Manchukuo, the Army units which had been trained to confront Soviet troops were to change direction 180 degrees and prepare to fight a long war against British and American forces in the torrid zone.

The crisis was near at hand, and it was necessary to let the commanders know in writing about the peculiarities of operations in the south. Tactics used against Soviet forces had to be radically revised for fighting in the southern terrain. Transportation of troops over long distances had to be undertaken; and at the end of the sea voyage the men had to be disembarked on open beaches in the face of the enemy, and then move through dense jungle in sweltering heat, repair destroyed bridges, smash the resistance of an inflexible foe, and finally capture an impregnable fortress.

The plan to accomplish this objective had been pondered over during and ever since the Taiwan period. Now the necessary adjustments were made, and as "The 25th Army Operations Instruction Plan" the document was completely written out in one night.

In compliance with the opinion of the staff, which had made some unofficial decisions, the plan was presented to the Army Commander and approved by him about the third week in November. At that time the American Pacific Fleet was being reinforced and two British battleships—the *Prince of Wales* and *Repulse*—had been moved to the Far East. The British Army for the defense of Malaya was also being strengthened day by day.

Although I had prepared the operations instructions, the Army formations to be used in Malaya had not yet been chosen. The troops were finally selected, and it was decided that urgent measures should be taken to re-form the equipment and organization of the Army corps for operations in the south on the basis of the results of the small-scale exercises which had been carried out on Hainan.

Whirlwind to the South

ON 5 SEPTEMBER 1941, I received my written appointment as staff officer to the forces stationed in Indochina. Now that I had received my orders and had to leave for my new post without a moment's delay, I decided that our emergency preparations would have to be hastened. Packing the small trunk which I had kept prepared in anticipation of an unexpected move, I left the following morning without informing my wife and children of my destination. I see to be thinking only of travelling from one place to another. The innocent faces of my children, who bowed their father off in the entrance hall, remained in my eyes for a long time. Passing through the gate, I glanced over my shoulder at our small rented house—how many times my wife and children will never know. I thought perhaps we might never meet again.

I had passed safely through my first battle in the Shanghai Incident and through desperate fighting in central and southern China and on the battlefield of Nomonhan. Among piles of corpses and in rivers of blood I had miraculously survived until I was nearly forty years of age. But now perhaps my family and I were going to be separated for ever.

The passenger plane on which I was travelling left Haneda airport in the morning, stayed overnight at Taihoku, and flew to Indochina the following day, arriving at Hanoi just after noon. Our troops there were enjoying their siesta under the shade of trees in a peaceful village in a land of everlasting summer. That evening I arrived in Saigon, and again found the troops there stretching themselves in the cool after-sunset air. Except for the guard at Headquarters the whole staff had retired to their quarters—a palatial country villa taken over from the French. They were all in bathrobes, drinking their fill of cold beer, and each with the exclusive use of a motor car. There were constant goings and comings, to and from the wilder parts of town.

The Army Commander, Lieutenant-General Iida, a serious-minded person, bitterly deplored the frivolous atmosphere. After I reported to him that the international situation had become acute, he vacated his country house, which was located some distance from Military Headquarters, went to his business office, spread a rush mat on the floor and stayed there overnight. The day after my arrival saw the commencement of intense activity. Staff Officer Hayashi and Asaeda arrived a little late and slept on mats on the floor of the hotel in which I was quartered.

Lieutenant-Colonel Haga, the chief of General Iida's administrative staff, a friend of mine from Manchurian days, gave his wholehearted cooperation in speeding up preparation for active operations. First of all, he moved all officers from their villas and lodged them in an apartment house close to Headquarters. He then set them to work on Operation No. 1: the campaign in Malaya.

All were caught up in the whirlwind and there was no time for enjoyment of the everlasting summer. The use of cars was prohibited to all without exception, and evening banquets paid for from secret funds were completely cut out. From daylight until ten o'clock at night the whole Headquarters was a hive of activity. On the pretext of business negotiations with the French, all staff officers had been wearing long hair and smart uniforms with open collars and knee breeches. This was promptly changed to field dress and the inconspicuous shaven head.

The most urgent business was preparation for the forthcoming operations, so we at once got ready for use the aerodromes in French Indochina.

But Tokyo restricted the funds available for the work, which slowed down progress, and we were further delayed by negotiations with France. Consequently we were able to proceed with construction of only a few new airstrips. At Saigon and Phnom Penh, aerodromes were in operation and others were under construction at Tani, Kampong Terashu, Kampong Chuang and other places, but Tani aerodrome was not expected to be completed until the end of November on account of the damp ground.

The work was wholly dependent on coolie labor—not even one motor-powered machine was available. Crowds of lazy, gregarious Annamese coolies wielded shovels, and thousands of them were not a match for even one bulldozer. Several times I accompanied the Army Commander on tours of inspection to see the condition of the work and the progress being made, but the spiritless operations were not at all satisfactory. They were in fact a failure.

Staff Officer Nishioka, in charge of aerial navigation, who was nicknamed the Zen Buddhist priest, and was an unworldly, unconventional personality, was given the important task of overseeing aerodrome construction. Day and night, sweating profusely, he urged the work forward.

Sufficient aerodromes were needed in southern Indochina to accommodate that part of the Air Force which would be operating in Malaya—particularly the fighter planes, which would be required to cover the disembarkation of our forces in southern Thailand and to protect the large convoy in which they would be travelling against the danger of attack from the enemy air force.

It was our paramount duty to ensure protection of this convoy, and somehow or other we had to prepare the necessary aerodromes in the area immediately to the west of Saigon. In particular it was desired to establish one on Phuoquok Island—which it was believed might decide the success or failure of the whole operation. Staff Officer Nishioka took personal charge of this job, and as Staff Officer in Charge of Operations I must express appreciation of the work he did.

When I urged him too eagerly, the "Zen Buddhist priest" became angry. "I have more knowledge of aerodrome construction than you have," he used to say, fuming with anger. "Completion of this work is a matter of life and death for our soldiers." Becoming anxious and seeing no other way to secure the resources he required, he went on official business to Tokyo. During his absence, surreptitiously boarding a small plane, I made a reconnaissance, flying low over the island. When I saw a suitable aerodrome site—in French territory on a grassy field—I rejoiced as if I had taken an ogre's head. In the absence of Staff Officer Nishioka, and without his leave, on my own responsibility I hurried two thousand coolies to Phuoquok Island without waiting for an answer from the French authorities in Indochina to our formal request for permission to proceed with the construction of the airfield.

Furthermore, I kept the work secret even from Tokyo. If we waited for permission through diplomatic channels it would be several months before we got a decision, and it was also certain that the financial authorities in Tokyo would regard this work with hostility and quibble about finding the funds necessary for its completion. The work was quite unauthorized, and I might have been punished for pushing forward with it, but I willingly assumed all responsibility and was prepared to suffer any consequences arising from my action, as this work could conceivably be the deciding factor in the successful invasion of Malaya.

About a month later two splendid aerodromes were completed on the island. They later proved a mighty mainspring in accomplishing perfect protection of our convoy of transports and aircover for the landing of our troops at Singora, Patani, and Kota Bharu. When Staff Officer Nishioka returned from Tokyo I said to him, "During your absence I have been meddlesome; but don't get angry." And we both laughed. He was delighted at the unforeseen progress of his work. I was deeply impressed with the excellence of this man.

Staff Officer Asaeda, in disguise, went on unofficial duty in southern Thailand, and on his return reported as follows:

1. Disembarkation on the coast in the neighborhoods of Singora and Patani will be under the strong influence of the northeast monsoon about the middle of November. Seas approximately three meters high break against the shore. Because of the danger the local fishing craft do not put to sea, and if we decide to use these beaches we must make up our minds to accept some sacrifice as inevitable.

2. There are scarcely any Thai troops defending the coast and the authorities do not appear to be anxious. Fixed defenses consist of a skirmishing line only, without wire entanglements, and there are no pillboxes in the neighbourhood of our proposed disembarkation points.

3. The Singora and Patani aerodromes are poor and crude and in no way comparable with the enemy aerodromes at Kota Bharu and in Kedah Province. It will therefore be of the utmost importance to seize the enemy aerodromes as soon as possible.

4. The road from Patani which passes through Betong to the upper Perak River valley is not good and can be used by motor transport

only with difficulty. It will, however, be suitable for conduct of operations by a detachment of all arms of the service with one infantry regiment as nucleus.

This report gave us very important information for use in the opening phase of the Malayan campaign. With innate courage and wide military knowledge Staff Officer Asaeda had penetrated deep into enemy territory and had been able to quickly appreciate and record everything of military interest on his journey. He and Staff Officer Tadahiko Hayashi, both of the same Military Academy period, emulated Dr. Kyoshi Hiraidzumi; Hayashi, a man of noble personality and handsome appearance, and Asaeda, a daredevil fighting man, both displayed superb activity and balanced each other's merits and faults.

Disguised, they slipped into Thailand, the one following closely upon the other, and returned after reconnaissances of the areas on which the Army required information. Sitting cross-legged on mats in the military operations room, with maps spread out between us, day and night we worked unceasingly over the plan of operations.

Previously it had been customary when a telegram arrived in the dead of night to deliver it to the officer concerned on the following morning; but now at whatever time a telegram arrived it was delivered to the appropriate staff officer immediately. Consequently we were frequently wakened two or three times a night.

After about a month of this heavy work I somehow caught a chill, lost my appetite, and developed a very high temperature. I thought I must have either dengue fever or malaria. If I reported to a doctor I would be sent to hospital, which I was above all anxious to avoid at this time. Unaccustomed to the climate, particularly to the damp and humid atmosphere, fagged out with work, and without sleep or rest, I was almost completely exhausted. One day, however, against my inclination I forced myself to take an anti-febrile which was close at hand, and persisted in eating bananas. About a week later I found that I had recovered from this mysterious tropical disease.

About this time the Imperial Guards Division, commonly called "The Prince's Forces," moved into the environs of Saigon. The commander, Lieutenant-General Nishimura, had been presiding judge of the court-martial on the incident of 15 May 1932.* The Chief of Staff, Colonel Imai, had been Instructor in Military Tactics at the Army College. The Imperial

---

* A reference to the assassination of Premier Inukai by young Army officers. The assassins were given very light sentences at the court-martial.

Guards conscripts were specially selected from the whole of Japan, and the physique of the men made them the best division in the country from the physical standpoint. It was, however, deplorable that they had seen no active service since the Russo-Japanese War at the beginning of the century. Over a long period of years they had been trained in elegant traditional ceremonies, but they had no taste for field operations and were unsuitable for them. Their staff officers had a tendency to disobey their superior Army Commander.

When they were allotted to 5th Army, the Army Commander indicated to the divisional commander that his troops required more training, which however was undertaken in such a half-hearted manner that Army Headquarters staff was doubtful whether the division would be able to stand up to its important task. The officers in charge of each detachment in the division nevertheless reported that their troops were up to fighting standards.

The best battalion of the division appeared to be that led by Major Hidesaburo Take-no-Uchi. He was one of the few intimates among my many classmates at Ichigaya Military College, and later he became an instructor at the Toyama Military School.* For many years he trained in the martial arts and won high honors—seventh grade in fencing, fifth grade in bayonet exercises, fifth grade in judo, fourth grade in dagger exercises—twenty-odd grades in all. Such a veteran was known as the Miyamoto Musashi** of the Showa period. Occasionally, in the evenings, he would come to Headquarters, sit cross-legged on the rush mat, and discuss the campaign with me till a late hour. It was the pleasantest time of the day for us busy men.

The only maps we had for operational purposes were very inaccurate small-scale publications. In the preparations for war against Russia we had printed enough very accurate 1:100,000-scale maps to meet all requirements. There was all the difference in the world between them and those on which we were now working for the Malayan campaign, but there was nothing we could do to better the situation.

During the research period, however, we had learned by heart the topography of the region from southern Thailand to Kedah Province, from the crossing of the Perak River to the capital city of Kuala Lumpur, and from there to Johore Bahru and Singapore. Now, studying our

---

* The Toyama School taught the military arts of judo, jujitsu, and kendo.
**Miyamoto Musashi—a famous fencer of the early Tokugawa period (1600–1867).

small-scale maps, all we had learned came to mind—topography, distances, local place names, key positions, etc.—and I was able to draw up the operations plans even without needing to consult these maps.

Confronted as I was with strategic problems which would be continually changing throughout the campaign, my operations plan had to provide for defeating enemy resistance in positions which he chose to hold, and at the same time be flexible enough to deal with enemy counter-measures in such a manner as to leave no doubt of the issue.

I took no interest in food, clothing, or housing, much less in entertainment. I even became conceited, feeling that it depended upon me whether we would win or lose the war which would determine the destiny of the nation.

How many times, daydreaming, did we spring to our feet to consult the map and work over the plan! The greatest sufferers from my fanatical activities were the non-commissioned officers and men, some of whom became very fatigued; among them the number who suffered from night blindness and nervous prostration increased. It may have been unbearably cruel, but nothing could shake my belief that the small sacrifice of one or two persons in this arduous preparatory work would later save the sacrifice of hundreds of men in the front line. The fact that all the officers and men of Army Headquarters accepted the difficulties and overwork of this painful period of preparation without complaint, dissatisfaction, or irritation is attributable to the personalities and initiative of Generals Yamashita and Iida.

Army Commander Yamashita

WHEN THE ORDER OF BATTLE of the 25th Army was gazetted on 6 November, Lieutenant-General Tomoyuki Yamashita was formally appointed Army Commander. Up to this time Lieutenant-General Iida had put heart and soul into the work of preparation under the impression that he would be given command of the military operations in Malaya. However, when General Yamashita was appointed to the position, Iida was appointed Commander of the 15th Army and ordered to attack Burma.

In the sweltering heat of Saigon, for two months he had studied the map of Malaya, planning a campaign there, without any speck of selfish motive, without any political anxieties or maneuvering, and without ambitious aspirations; but as he worked he grew tired of waiting for a clear definition of his sphere of activity. When General Yamashita was appointed to the Malayan sphere he finally became discouraged, and it was intolerable for us to see

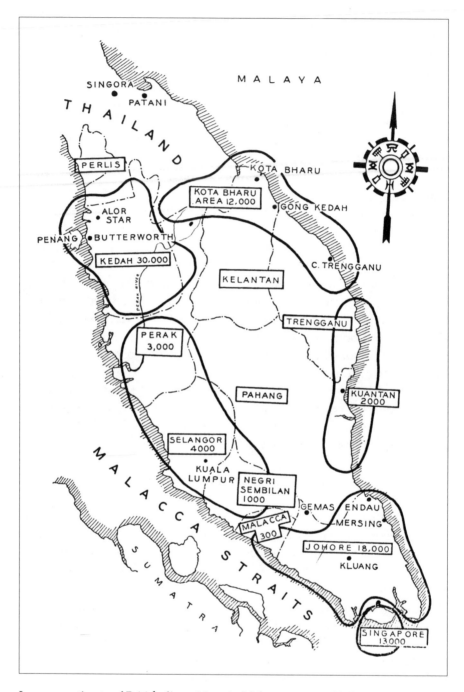

Japanese estimate of British dispositions in Malaya, autumn 1941.

his disappointed face. It appears that in the selection of personnel General Iida was not as highly regarded by Army Headquarters as was General Yamashita but his capacity for generalship was certainly not inferior.

General Yamashita was of dignified physique and commanding mien. His previous career had been brilliant, and at home and abroad his dignity was acknowledged. For many years he played an active part as the pivot of military administration, giving thorough attention to the fine points of this work. Quite unlike a hero in appearance, perhaps he was at that time the most clear-headed type of politician.

Suzuki, the Chief of Staff, was a man of great talent who had been top of his classes from the cadet school to the Military College. He was a bright, cheerful person, who harmonized well with tens of thousands of people. He was the Central Department (Tokyo) type of man, well informed in the conduct of business.

Below, I compare our strength in Malaya with that of the British Army as stated in Mr. Churchill's memoirs. The original enemy forces turned out to be far stronger than we had judged at first. Mr. Churchill estimated the strength of the attacking Japanese forces at five divisions—which in the beginning was in fact the number which Imperial Headquarters contemplated using. After discussion, however, the number was reduced to four divisions. Later, General Yamashita, after consideration of the fighting capacity of the British Army at the beginning of the campaign, decided that three divisions were sufficient and sent one division back to Imperial Headquarters. Needless to say, such voluntary reduction by a general in the strength of the troops placed under his command is rare in the military history of countries outside Japan. Was it possible that General Yamashita had blundered? Subsequent events showed he had not.

The essential features for a comparison of the strength of both sides were as follows:

JAPANESE FORCES

Army
Commander-in-Chief of Southern Armies: Field Marshal Count Terauchi 25th Army (which carried out the Malayan campaign):
    Army Commander: Lieutenant-General Yamashita
Imperial Guards Division: Lieutenant-General Nishimura—
    Strength roughly 13,000
5th Division: Lieutenant-General Matsui—
    Strength roughly 16,000
18th Division: Lieutenant-General Mutaguchi—
    Strength roughly 13,000

56th Division—never joined 25th Army; transferred to 15th Army
   for Burma campaign
3rd Tank Brigade—roughly 80 tanks
Artillery: Independent quick-firing guns—44 guns
Independent Mountain Gun Regiment—24 guns
Two regiments heavy field guns—
   48 15-centimeter howitzers
   16 10-centimeter guns (as distinct from howitzers)
Anti-aircraft gun detachment—68 guns
Three regiments independent engineers, totaling 9 companies
Army Communication Corps—
   4 telegraph and telephone companies; 8 wireless platoons
Railway Detachment—4 regiments
Close-quarter attack troops
   (trench mortars, mine throwers, bomb-guns)—2 battalions;
   24 mortars of various types
Bridging train—3 companies; 3 companies river-crossing troops
Supply troops

TOTAL STRENGTH:
Officers and men—approximately 60,000
All types of guns, including trench mortars—400
Tanks, including armored cars—about 120

Air Force
Army planes—459
Naval planes—158

Navy
(the Southward Squadron)
Cruisers—1
Destroyers—about 10
Submarines—about 5

BRITISH FORCES
(Far Eastern Section*)

Commander-in-Chief: Lieutenant-General Wavell
Army Commander, Malaya: Lieutenant-General Percival

*See Appendix 3.

Army
3rd Army Corps: Lieutenant-General Heath
9th British Indian Division
11th British Indian Division
8th Australian Division (2 brigades only) and 2/4th Machine Gun
   Battalion: Lieutenant-General Gordon Bennett
28th British Indian Brigade
44th British Indian Brigade
45th British Indian Brigade
53rd British Army Brigade
54th British Army Brigade
Malay Volunteers—2 brigades
Heavy fortress guns—about 100
Anti-aircraft guns—about 150
Anti-tank guns—about 200
Other types of guns and mortars—550

TOTAL STRENGTH:
Officers and men—approximately 120,000
All types of guns and mortars—about 1,000
Armored cars—about 250

Air Force
Fighter planes—about 100
Bombers—about 130
Reconnaissance planes—about 50

Navy
(Far Eastern Squadron)
Battleships—2
Cruisers—1 (?)
Destroyers—5 to 7 (?)
Submarines—4 or 5 (?)

SUMMARIZED COMPARISON

	Japanese	British
Total personnel	1	2
Artillery	1	2
Tanks and armoured cars	1	2
Airplanes	2	1
Ships	1	1

According to military science, in an attack on a fortress it is a principle that the attackers should outnumber the defenders by three to one. In the Malayan campaign we estimated the British military troop dispositions before the outbreak of hostilities as shown above; for our initial assaults we planned to have the same strength as the British at the points of attack (i.e. at Kota Bharu and the Jitra line).

The reason for our ignoring the principle that in attack on a fortress the attackers require very substantial superiority of strength over the defenders was based on my estimate of the quality of the troops concerned rather than on their respective numbers—a most important point which could not be overlooked.

The British forces throughout the years of peace had been, for the most part, stationed on the actual ground on which the fighting was to take place, and had trained there under their Army Commander.

Japanese troops preparing for war against Russia had been in the same position, stationed and trained on the Manchurian frontier where the fighting was anticipated. Their army and divisional headquarters were permanent organizations. The armies operating in China were in the same position. As a result, the divisions in those areas were composed of units of well-trained officers and men, many of whom had had actual battle experience, and all of whom had developed the spirit of unity which permeated from battalions right through to divisions and Army Headquarters as a consequence of long and continuous association in the same Army formation. This spirit was particularly noticeable in the 5th and 18th divisions, which were specially selected for the operations in Malaya from among all the troops on the Mainland because of their high quality. The Imperial Guards Division, as I have already said, had seen no active service, and had not had the advantage of the training and formative experience of the troops serving in China.

The staff of the 25th Army, on the other hand, had been hastily formed for the particular purpose of the Malayan campaign from officers specially selected from the whole of the Japanese Army—from Japan, Manchuria, China, and so on. It was a scratch team, many of whose members did not meet the Commander-in-Chief and the rest of the staff until immediately before the outbreak of hostilities. Some of the officers selected for the staff, engaged on important duties in Canton, Shanghai, Formosa, and other places, had not actually joined the staff at the time the Malayan campaign ended. The members of the staff, however, were knit together by the Order of Battle. The handicap of operating with a hastily assembled staff was dealt with by the Army by launching all its officers into immediate battlefield preparations, and by the readiness of each individual to risk his life for the success of the campaign.

Sitting on a rush mat, I vowed to the gods that, day and night, I would abstain from wine and tobacco. I forgot instinctive desires and worldly passions, to say nothing of lust and appetite and even life and death. My whole mind was concentrated on gaining the victory.

We will win. We *must* win.

A Secret Reconnaissance

FOR SIX MONTHS WE HAD gathered all the information possible, after which we began to put the finishing touches on the operations schedule with some knowledge of our enemy and much more of our own relative strengths. The basis of our plan of campaign was a three-point estimate of the enemy's plan of defense, which was as follows:

1. There was no doubt whatever that the British would defend the sea-front of Singapore with all their resources, and their position there was very strong. The rear of the fortress was very unprotected, however, and the enemy would in all probability use every resource to make good this defect by strengthening the rear defenses and obtaining reinforcements from their homeland while using delaying tactics against our advance through the 1,100 kilometers—the length and breadth of the Malay Peninsula—which separated the Japanese forces from Singapore.

2. The enemy forces were disposed mainly around the central portion of northern Malaya, particularly in Kedah Province and around Kota Bharu. This might mean that they intended to resist our forces near the Thai frontier and possibly to attack during, or counterattack after, our disembarkation.

3. The enemy air force was weak. Could it be that the enemy believed there would be no Japanese attack between November (1941) and March (1942)—the period of the northeast monsoon?

Judging this to be the enemy's plan, our Army had to devise a plan of operations to ensure that the British would be defeated. With all the talent of the Headquarters Staff and the Navy gathered together there were many discussions, and matters were not easily decided. The major points at issue were as follows:

1. Should we make a surprise attack with a section of advance troops at Singora, and another at Patani, carrying out disembarkation under cover

of the Air Force, and subsequently landing the main strength of the Army with the advance parties and the Air Force protecting the landing?

2. Or should we, from the very start, land a large force—at least one division—in a surprise attack on Singora and Patani simultaneously without any supporting forces whatever, after which the rest of the Army would disembark? And should we, after capturing Singora and Patani, then land at Kota Bharu?

3. Or should we land simultaneously at Singora, Patani, and Kota Bharu, forcing their capture by weight of numbers?

4. Should we, after disembarkation, secure the neighborhood of the frontier, make preparations for and wait until the landing of the rear forces and supplies—particularly ammunition, provisions, and fuel—and then begin the assault on northern Malaya?

5. Or should we, immediately after disembarkation of the first-line units, without waiting for troops from the rear, break through one section of the frontier by a surprise attack on the enemy, and then penetrate deep into Kedah Province?

6. Should we rely on previous conceptions of military science and prudent leadership, or should we, from the commencement of hostilities, take advantage of surprise and audacity in our attack to smash the enemy resistance?

Such were the new and opposing ideas which came under discussion, and opinions differed according to the personality of each individual expressing them. The strength of the convoy and its escort was limited by the concentration of our main naval forces for the "Z" operation [the attack on Pearl Harbor]. On the one hand, caution in conduct of the campaign was urged; on the other, boldness and simultaneous attacks on Singora, Patani, and Kota Bharu were strongly advocated. It was natural for the General Staff to desire a plan based on caution and established military principles in accordance with their responsibility, but it was difficult to limit discussion when considering these operations.

From the point of view of the Air Force, the problem was to provide fighter cover from distant air bases in southern Indochina in sufficient strength to enable disembarkation from a large number of transports under the nose of an enemy air force with its bases close at hand. Could this be accomplished with orthodox tactics—the establishment of strong, well-defended forward bases before making further advances? Perhaps they might not succeed! Nevertheless, in a plan to disembark a large force in one swoop and without warning, there was danger of the whole Army's being destroyed if one false step was taken or one mistake made.

We had done everything possible to formulate our plan of operations by studying the map, and there was only one way to settle the arguments which had arisen. Gambling with human life, one must risk one's own. There was nothing for it but to make a personal reconnaissance of the projected battlefields, and I immediately set about arranging it.

Captain Omuro, an Air Force man attached to the Army, was completely worn out, having been continuously engaged for over a month in secret reconnaissance work. I was at my wits' end on the evening of 19 October when suddenly a young captain in Flying Corps uniform appeared in the Operations Section. He introduced himself saying, "I am Captain Ikeda from the Kanto Army, just arrived to take command of the One-Hundred-Type Reconnaissance Plane Squadron." He was overflowing with high spirits. "Dear me, have you come?" I said to him. "Thanks for your trouble."

I went on to say, "Tomorrow I wish to go flying over the southern part of Thailand and northern Malaya, but will you be able to do it?" Pondering the matter for a while, the captain replied, "Yes, I can do it. If you, Mr. Staff Officer, can go I shall manage it." The expression on his face was full of confidence and goodwill. "Well then," I replied, "I ask you to make preparations immediately to set out at five o'clock tomorrow morning. By way of precaution, have the Hi-no-Man [Japanese flag] painted off the plane."

Captain Ikeda was in the 49th Class at the Military College. I noticed his self-possessed attitude and thought to myself that there was no need for anxiety with this man. But, be that as it might, he had just put in an appearance after a very long flight under difficult navigational conditions over the sea all the way from Manchuria; and without any rest whatever he was now called upon to fly deep into enemy territory in an unarmed reconnaissance plane. Though my request appeared merciless, the hardship had to be endured for the sake of the campaign.

The Hyaku shiki Shitei (Reconnaissance 100 Type) was an up-to-date, powerful, two-engined reconnaissance plane. Its speed was higher than that of the British fighter planes of that time and its cruising range was approximately five hours. To leave Saigon, fly to and return from Kedah Province in such a plane would take exactly five hours. Being unarmed, the machine relied upon its high speed to escape if intercepted by enemy fighters. High speed was its only weapon; it did not even carry a machine-gun.

The cumulonimbus clouds which are a special characteristic of the southern regions are dangerous to airplanes, which, if they enter them, may be disintegrated by air turbulence. And, in the event of engine failure, the plane would crash in the jungle and be burnt together with its passengers, or alternatively it might plunge into the Gulf of Siam and disappear without trace.

It was an apparent violation of international law to make a reconnaissance over Malayan territory before the opening of hostilities, but in the strained situation of that time the secret crossing of frontiers from the air, in Manchuria, the Soviet Union, and many other places, was a mutually open secret in the international sphere.

That night I stared at the map until a late hour, deciding the points we should reconnoiter. Changing from Army uniform to Air Force uniform, I realized we would have to be on the alert to leave no evidence of our true identity in the event of an emergency. We were to carry only bread and a water flask.

The aerodrome was still in darkness with nobody about except the men servicing our machine, the engines of which made the only sound to be heard. Their purring, breaking the silence showed them to be in perfect condition. The new squadron leader, Ikeda, fatigued by his long journey from Manchuria, was about to participate in his first flight over enemy territory, with an unfamiliar passenger in unfamiliar flying conditions.

The personnel of the squadron under command of a company officer were drawn up by the side of the plane, and with strained looks and in dead silence they saw their squadron leader off. Several years previous, when I crossed the frontier into Soviet territory in a plane piloted by a former pupil of mine—Sub-Lieutenant Akiyama—I had experienced an unusual feeling of tension; but with Captain Ikeda I had no such feeling. This flight was the prelude to the opening of a great campaign. If by any chance we were to be killed, I should be happy to die, provided we could furnish information from whatever sources which would be of assistance to our plan of operations. In view of the importance of the occasion I was very concerned about being piloted by a young, inexperienced squadron commander; but once in the air with him I lost all doubts and regrets. Everything went without a hitch, which I now realized could have been expected from his demeanor as I observed it at our first meeting.

At six o'clock, with the red sun behind us, we took off from the Saigon base. The officers and men on the ground who were seeing us off and waving to us gradually became smaller and faded from our field of vision. Passing Cape Cambodia across the Gulf of Siam, we flew due west with Kota Bharu as our objective, and reached it in about two hours. The altimeter indicated we were flying at about six thousand meters, and it was so cold we were almost frozen. In the rarified atmosphere, with oxygen tubes in our mouths, we crossed the gulf, keeping very much on the alert. The weather was rapidly deteriorating as we came in sight of the Malayan coast, and we knew Kota Bharu must be close at hand. But thick, heavy clouds covered the sky and obscured all view of our destination. "Let us fly lower," I ordered the pilot. We were over enemy territory, and flying at a lower altitude might disclose our presence, but we had to take the chance. We dived into clouds like silk wadding, and lost sight of everything. We went down to two thousand meters—one thousand—five hundred. The intense cold which had numbed us changed to warmth and then heat in which we sweated profusely. When we had dropped to three hundred meters we broke through the cloud strata and discovered in the nick of time we were over the sea off Kota Bharu. I could see the waves surging on the beach and seabirds skimming, but the land was enveloped in dense fog. Several times we circled at our low altitude, hoping to find a break in the fog, but time and again, like a dense curtain of floss silk it folded over us and we were unable to see through it.

Two and a half hours after our departure from Saigon, Captain Ikeda said through the speaking tube, "We will be running out of petrol for the return trip. It is but a step to Kota Bharu, but there is no alternative. It is very disappointing."

"Very well," I said. "We shall try again."

Circling again to gain altitude we emerged from the clouds into the freezing cold of the upper air. It was about eleven o'clock when we returned to Saigon after a flight of five hours, with scarcely enough petrol to land the plane safely. Regretfully tapping Captain Ikeda's shoulder, I said, "Thank you for your trouble. Rest tomorrow and the day after." The "poor bag" expression on the faces of the Army Commander and the rest of the staff indicated they were very disappointed at our having returned without any information.

Fine weather was predicted for the 22nd of the month. Again, early in the morning we hurried to the airfield. There was an expression of determination on Captain Ikeda's face. "We'll do it today," he said. We had had a hasty lesson in the method of taking aerial photographs. We took off at six o'clock, and selected Singora as our first objective. A little after eight o'clock, with not a cloud in the sky, we could see Singora and Patani as clearly as in a drawing or a photograph. To the south the coast in the neighborhood of Kota Bharu was visible. The mouths of the Kelantan River, which there divides into several channels, shone in the sun, each branch of the river appearing like a silver thread.

It seemed that from the Kota Bharu airfield the British undoubtedly aimed a dagger at the flank of Singora, and that the British torpedo planes were keeping a vigilant eye and would be prepared at once to attack any convoy attempting to land troops at Singora or Patani.

I immediately came to the conclusion that if the British made good use of the Kota Bharu aerodrome, then disembarkation at Singora would be impossible, and that therefore, come what might, we would have to capture Kota Bharu simultaneously with our landings at Singora and Patani. This at any rate was one request I would press upon the Navy, as the necessity for simultaneous landings was immediately firmly fixed in my mind.

Before long our plane passed directly over Singora and we found ourselves looking down upon the Thai airstrips—they were indeed poor affairs. Through a sea of trees stretching as far as the eye could see, an asphalt road and a railway were visible running north and south. The only discordant note in the entirely peaceful atmosphere was the sound of our plane flying on its secret mission.

For about a kilometer on each side, the road was lined by rubber plantations. On this frontage alone would movement be possible for troops of all arms of the service. Even an army possessing superior numerical strength would find the road the center of its battlefront and its flanks extending not more than a kilometer to right and left. There was consequently no need to worry about the superior numbers of the British troops. The narrow frontage on which battles would be fought limited the number of troops who could be effectively engaged on either side.

It seemed to me that without waiting to concentrate our forces after disembarkation we would be able to make an immediate thrust at the enemy, and that one efficient battalion alone could open up a line of advance through enemy defenses; the units which, after successive landings, would overtake the advance guard, could easily alternate with each other as the troops in the lead became exhausted. Furthermore, in the rubber forest and jungle, "the authority of the naked sabre would be conclusive." For us the terrain provided ideal fighting conditions.

With this impression half finished on the dry plate of my mind, I excitedly took a photograph. As I opened the window in the floor a piercingly cold wind entered through the aperture for the camera, almost freezing my breath and forming icicles on my eyebrows and beard—which formed again as fast as they were wiped off. We were so busy—and so cold. At such a time we grudged each second. Forgetting the possibility of being attacked by an enemy plane, we kept our eyes on the ground. A little later we flew over the mountain range on the Malayan frontier.

The western part of Malaya was shut in by storm clouds and concealed by heavy rain which occurs on the west coast at the same time as there is fine weather on the east coast. This is a characteristic atmospheric phenomenon of Malaya. We dropped to an altitude of two thousand meters, and suddenly, through the rain, right before our eyes we saw a large and well-equipped aerodrome.

"There's the British aerodrome of Alor Star!" we both cried involuntarily. Fortunately for us it appeared that because of the rain the British Air Force was resting, and, unperceived, we rose to a higher altitude and continued flying south. Soon we saw another large aerodrome—Sungei Patani—and still farther on at Taiping [southeast of Penang Island] yet another.

On the map the whereabouts of these aerodromes was plainly shown, but the impression gained from the map was entirely different from that gained from the air. They were just large openings in the jungle through which the various runways could be. Comparing these well-developed aerodromes with the miserable airstrip at Singora was like comparing adults to children. Obviously our enemies would be able to deploy all their available air strength on these airfields.

Even if after disembarkation we were to stop in the neighborhood of Singora for a month, waiting for the rear troops to arrive, the idea of our Air Force having to operate from the Singora airstrip against the enemy force based on this group of large aerodromes seemed to hold out little chance of success. There was therefore no other way for us to win except by rushing in immediately to attack Kedah Province by any means whatever as soon as we made a landing, in order to seize the enemy airfields. At any sacrifice we had, first of all, to capture the enemy aerodromes at Kota Bharu and Alor Star, for use by our own Air Force.

A very brief study of the position will show at a glance that because of the dissimilar weather conditions on the east and west coasts—rain on the west when it was fine in the east—it would be extremely difficult for planes based at Singora to cooperate effectively with ground forces operating on the west coast.

All discussion of this and that about our plan of operations was foolish. The first stage of our objective, in defiance of all difficulties, should be to advance to the left bank of the Perak River and at one stroke seize the three bridges across the river, forestalling any enemy attempt to destroy them.

Before us the silvery belt of the river lay at full length, meandering to the distant south. It is impossible to ford this large stream, which can only be crossed by bridges or boat. If the enemy destroyed the bridges, our advance would be held up for at least a week. This was the conclusion we reached in the plane.

We wished to fly farther south, but our petrol was running out. We had reached the limit of our range from Saigon. "End the reconnaissance. Turn back," I called out regretfully.

Changing course to the east and flying over the central mountain range at three thousand meters, before long we emerged into fine and clear weather over Kota Bharu. Climbing to six thousand meters we looked down and saw two large aerodromes in an advanced state of preparation.

Then we started on our homeward journey with the final impression that the British Army had its greatest bases of operation on the western seaboard. These alone were fully prepared with fully equipped aerodromes, but they seemed to be occupied by very few large machines. It looked as if we might have to pay dearly for the capture of these bases.

In the plane we heaved a sigh of relief when we passed Cape Cambodia at the extremity of southwest Indochina. There was no particular reason to fear death; but after one has discharged one's duty, life becomes strangely precious. At that moment, although there is no fear of death in the heart of a man whose emotions are strained at going and returning, his thoughts again turn to the craving for life.

We reached Saigon at ten past eleven, exceeding by ten minutes the maximum endurance of the plane. The last drop of petrol was gone, and we landed with difficulty by gliding down onto the airfield. If we had been five minutes later our position would have been hopeless. Captain Ikeda seemed to be utterly exhausted. His feelings on the latter part of the journey had probably been very painful—flying under the orders of a staff officer who, absorbed in the work at hand, disregarded the limits of the plane's capacity. Nevertheless, he had cheerfully and bravely carried out his orders without question. On landing I expressed my heartfelt gratitude to him. "Many thanks for your trouble and assistance. I saw all I wanted to see—please go and rest."

Without delay the many photographic plates I had so carefully brought back were developed; but the rapid instruction in aerial photography we had received just prior to departure proved quite useless. Not even one of the photographs was any good. The image of everything I had seen, however, was so strongly printed on the living retina of my eyes and on my mind that there was no need for photographs. Even after all these years I can still see clearly everything I saw on that flight.

Orthodox or Unorthodox Tactics?

STILL WEARING MY FLYING UNIFORM, I reported the results of the reconnaissance in detail to the Army Commander and the whole of the assembled staff. Following my report, the operational plan I suggested was accepted without a dissenting voice. It was as follows:

1. Land the main strength of the 5th Division simultaneously and without warning at Singora and Patani, and at the same time land a powerful section of the 18th Division to attack Kota Bharu.
2. The troops disembarked at Singora and Patani to press forward immediately to attack the line of the Perak River and capture its bridge and the Alor Star aerodrome.
3. The troops landed at Kota Bharu to press forward along the eastern coast as far as Kuantan.

The plan drawn up by Imperial Headquarters was according to orthodox tactics, and its implementation would have involved heavy sacrifice. The Malayan campaign was, however, to be a fight which could not be won by orthodox tactics. Among both Army and Navy staffs at Imperial Headquarters there had been considerable indecision regarding the tactics to be adopted, and the matter had finally been handed over to the 5th Army in the field for determination.

At Imperial Headquarters there were many frank discussions between Army and Navy on questions on which they differed, in which each side, making light of responsibility, sought to ensure that it would gather the laurels of the campaign. This was unfortunately a rather common thing. The Navy and Army frequently engaged in an ignoble struggle to reap the credit for operations. This could only be cleared up by frank and sincere discussion by representatives of the Army and Navy forces which were to be actually engaged in the campaign.

Accordingly, I visited Naval Headquarters of the Southern Squadron, which had moved to Saigon, and inquired for Commander Terasaki, the naval staff officer for operations there. He received me cordially and I was able to discuss fully with him the decisions arrived at as a result of my aerial reconnaissance, telling him it was the earliest desire of the Army to land simultaneously at Singora, Patani, and Kota Bharu. Terasaki was a real sailor, who put on no airs of dignity or ostentation, and he had been able to work closely and amicably with the Naval Staff. Speaking of Vice-Admiral Ozawa, Commander-in-Chief of the Southern Squadron, Terasaki said, "He is the best strategist in the Navy and will probably combine well with General Yamashita and carry out the wishes of the Army." After discussion he finally said, "As your plan is based on conclusions you have formed from direct observation of the enemy positions, the Navy will make the most strenuous efforts to comply with any wishes you express."

Vice-Admiral Ozawa, a man of wide understanding, was well able to compare arid evaluate the operations plans formulated at Imperial Headquarters in Tokyo with those drawn up at Saigon Headquarters by the men who were to be directly engaged in the campaign. In the early morning of 24 October, I flew to Tokyo aboard a naval bomber. During the previous month the situation and atmosphere at Imperial General Staff Headquarters had completely changed. Konoye's Cabinet had fallen and been replaced by General Tojo's, and the opinion that war was inevitable had become overwhelmingly pronounced. This opinion was endorsed by the General Staff, which soon afterwards reported to the Throne a plan for the Malayan campaign based on orthodox tactics.

This made it extremely difficult to present a different plan based on unorthodox tactics in which surprise attack and rapidity of movement were the principal elements. It had to be done without causing any loss of face to the General Staff. But Colonel Hattori, Chief of the Operations Section of the General Staff, viewed the matter dispassionately, adopted the opinions of the Army in the field, and curbed the opposition of subordinates. "This plan," he said, "is the result of Colonel Tsuji's own inspection in the face of danger, so we cannot help matters by opposing him. We can manage the documentary procedure for presentation to the Throne of the altered plan of operations."

Acting on Colonel Hattori's advice, the Chief of the General Staff and his subordinates not only willingly adopted the 5th Army plan, but supported it positively and with goodwill. This was all due to Colonel Hattori's disinterested personality, which was as bright and clear as a mirror or calm water. Without mutual confidence "in that man" or "by that man," this great military operation could never have achieved such substantial results.

When I discussed the matter with him later, Colonel Hattori said to me, "However excellent your opinion might have been, I would have hesitated to agree with your intention to modify the plan determined by the Imperial General Staff according to your own judgment based only on maps. But as the modifications were suggested as a result of your own observations in the face of danger, no opposition could be raised."

In putting these extensive modifications into practice the Headquarters General Staff encountered extraordinary difficulties. In the first place it had to transfer a number of ships to the 25th Army which had been assigned to the 14th Army for the attack on the Philippines.

To make shipping arrangements, all parties concerned were assembled at Uzina. I had to fly to Tokyo for a period of barely twenty-four hours, during which I did not have sufficient free time to visit my home. On the 27th there was a conference at Uzina to allocate the shipping in accordance with the revised military requirements. It was attended by the commanders of every Army corps to be engaged in operations southward, and by all the staff officers in any way concerned with the transport of troops. All assembled at the Transport Department Offices, and ultimately the assignment of the vessels was decided.

The Commander and staff officers of the 14th Army at the conference willingly acknowledged the superior importance of the Malayan sector, and gave up to the 25th Army several excellent vessels which had been previously allotted to the Philippines operation. I could not help expressing my gratitude. Both General Headquarters and armies operating in other areas struggled with all difficulties to find solutions advantageous to the 25th Army, and this cooperation was really the foundation of its success.

Colonel Kawashima, senior staff officer of the 3rd Air Group, which was to support the 25th Army, had been a squad commander in the Staff College, where he was an intimate acquaintance from whom I had received great kindness. Taking advantage of the opportunity of a passage in the ships allotted to the landing force, the Aviation Group loaded into the freight space large quantities of ammunition and gasoline required for the attacks on Singora, Patani, and Kota Bharu, and in addition brought a colossal quantity of supplies which was far beyond all expectations. Loading all this meant very cramped conditions for the troops and possibly a reduction in the number which could be carried, but we willingly complied with Colonel Kawashima's request to load all his cargo.

Throughout the Malayan campaign from start to finish the cooperation between Army and Air Force was ideal, and the success of the campaign was largely due to the mutual confidence felt and the mutual concessions made by each of these arms of the forces.

When the Uzina conference was over, we flew to Shanghai before going on to Fukuoka. The 5th Division, composed of specially selected troops, concentrated in the suburbs of Shanghai, had already received secret orders and was training near the city. Promptly we called on the divisional commander, delivered to him the instructions of the 25th Army, and reported to him and his staff on the general situation, carrying on the discussion until late at night.

41

This division had fought heroically in North China and Shansi under the supreme command of General Itagaki in the first stage of the China Incident. At that time I was staff officer of an Army group which for over two months was engaged in desperate fighting at Chojosen, Sekkochin, and Taigen [all in north China]. We were all old acquaintances. The divisional Chief of Staff Colonel Kawagoe and I were old friends, and I also knew by sight the Staff Officer in Charge of Operations, Lieutenant-Colonel Ogata, with whom I agreed very well. For over twenty years this division had been a specialist force, trained in disembarkation operations. It had, moreover, an illustrious tradition. Its officers and men took precedence in battle and were brimming with self-confidence.

On the following day, 29 October, we left Shanghai by plane for Canton. The 18th Division was stationed there, and the divisional commander and his staff were very old friends, especially the Officer in Charge of Operations, Lieutenant-Colonel Hashimoto, with whom I had formed a close friendship while in the Kanto army. He was then Adjutant to the Commander-in-Chief, Ueda.

The 18th was a thoroughly reliable fighting division. Its troops included many soldier coal miners from northern Kyushu. They were fond of rough work, but were quarrelsome and apt to commit acts of violence and plunder; yet there was nothing to be said against all that, for the division was a very strong and strictly disciplined formation, ideally suited for the capture of Singapore.

We sat up nearly all night working, and left early the next morning for Saigon. The only time we slept and rested was in the airplane. In a period of approximately seven days we had called at Tokyo, Uzina, Shanghai, and Canton, in each place settling very important and urgent business and accomplishing the Army Commander's plans in the way he expected. I had been a long time in staff service, and had never had such exceptional success as at this time.

When I reported to General Yamashita and to all concerned, there was a look on every face as if each had said, "It is already certain. There is no need for anxiety."

The Army and Navy Operations Agreement

TO COOPERATE IN THE MALAYAN campaign the commanding officer and staff of the 3rd Air Group arrived in Saigon at the end of October. The Group Leader, Lieutenant-General Sugawara, a man of high reputation in the Air Force; the Chief of Staff, Major-General Kumabe; the Senior Staff Officer, Colonel Kawashima; and Officers in Charge of

Operations Colonel Sasao and Lieutenant-Colonel Miyako, were all old acquaintances of mine, particularly Lieutenant Colonel Miyako, who came from my birthplace and had been a very intimate friend since our Army Preparatory School days in Nagoya. The Intelligence Officer had also been a classmate of mine at the Military Academy. The gathering together of such a group of acquaintances under the circumstances in which we found ourselves appeared to me a remarkable coincidence.

When aerial and ground operations do not proceed satisfactorily there is nowhere to go to air grievances. It is therefore essential to settle beforehand all details of cooperation. The Air Force agreed whole heartedly with the basic Army plan to disembark, advance rapidly along the Perak River, and seize possession of the enemy aerodromes. They were particularly pleased with the aerodrome on Phuquok Island, which the Army had developed on its own responsibility, and which came to the Air Force as a completely unexpected gift at which they rejoiced from the bottom of their hearts.

The Air Force expressed the opinion that after disembarkation of the 5th Division at Singora and Patani it would be desirable to consolidate and expand the airstrips at those places, and asked that a battalion of infantry and a platoon of engineers be left behind for this purpose.

Charged as he was with the responsibility of advancing to cross the Malayan frontier immediately after landing, and then carrying out a further advance to the Perak River—a total distance of about three hundred kilometers—it was not easy for the Commander of the 5th Division to agree to leave behind him about a quarter of his infantry landing force. But it was obvious that the use of Singora and Patani airstrips for our fighter planes was necessary to enable them to cover disembarkation of the remainder of the troops in subsequent convoys. Closing his eyes, General Yamashita agreed to the request.

Another point raised by the Air Force officers was the desirability of allotting them a share of the cars which would be captured in Thailand and Malaya. They asked for many other things as well, such as war supplies, fuel, ammunition for the landings and for the defense of airstrips and aerodromes, camp equipment, and so on. Without exception all their requests were granted.

The Air Force repaid the understanding attitude of the Army by its desperate cooperation in the almost impossible task of providing perfect cover for the ships of the convoy during the period of disembarkation, and thus contributed very materially indeed to the success of the landing operations.

In appointing Vice-Admiral Ozawa as Commander-in-Chief of the Southern Squadron the Navy showed that it recognized the Malayan campaign as second only in importance to the attack on Pearl Harbor. He was one of the bravest admirals in Japan, and was appointed to his new position after having been President of the Naval University. He arrived in Saigon towards the end of October.

Both General Yamashita and Vice-Admiral Ozawa were relying on agreement between Army and Navy at Imperial General Headquarters in Tokyo in respect to the Malayan operations. But, notwithstanding previous discussions, General Headquarters had not yet reached unanimity of opinion on the question of simultaneous landings at Singora, Patani, and Kota Bharu. General Yamashita and Admiral Ozawa felt that the matter must be decided.

On 15 November a conference of the commanders of land, sea, and air forces concerned in the Malayan campaign was held at Saigon. It was attended by General Staff Officer Lieutenant-Colonel Prince Takeda, representing Field Marshal Count Terauchi, the Commander-in-Chief of all Japan's Southern Armies. The conference discussed the assignment of responsibility and collaboration for the plans of 25th Army. General Yamashita expressed his hopes for carrying into effect the largest military operation of the century. When he referred to the difficulties associated with simultaneous disembarkations at Singora, Patani, and Kota Bharu, Vice-Admiral Ozawa opened his thick, heavy lips for the first time and said, "I shall do everything possible that is desired by the military forces. I will be responsible for protection of the convoy of ships and of the disembarkation at Kota Bharu." A hush fell over the whole gathering and everyone present looked on with bated breath as this final decision was given. It was a tragic and grim resolution.

The forces in the field, by mutual trust between the Army and Navy commanders actually engaged in the operations, had concluded a history-making Army and Navy Operations Agreement, which Imperial General Headquarters had not been able to decide without complications and haggling. This agreement rejected all previous ambiguities, and announced to the Navy only the Army's definite requirements for disembarkation at specific times and places if conditions were favourable for the Navy, with agreement on methods of protection against either sea or air attack and for anti-aircraft and anti-submarine warning.

The Army proposals embodied in this agreement had been determined only five or six hours before the conference assembled, and although these could give rise to most difficult problems from the naval standpoint, agreement was reached without development of any awkward situations. The final allotment of tasks was that agreed upon by the Naval Aviation Corps and the land forces' 3rd Air Group.

Such unparalleled cooperation between Army, Navy, and Air Force authorities will probably not be found elsewhere than in the Army and Navy Operations Agreement for the campaign in Malaya.

The heart of a mighty army assigned to the important task of capturing Singapore pivoted upon the combined-operations base at Saigon, to which it was welded like a piece of heated iron. It is little wonder that the fortress, with its display of impregnability, collapsed tragically in face of the attack by assailants from land, sea, and air acting in such harmonious relationship.

The eleven essential points embodied in the agreement were as follows:

1. At the commencement of hostilities, the Army, in cooperation with the Navy and Air Force, should land its main forces in areas south of the isthmus of the Malay Peninsula, crush enemy resistance, and attack across the course of the Perak River. Next, continuously increasing the strength of the attack, it should, without pause, in cooperation with the Air Force, carry on its advance to Kuala Lumpur and from there to Johore Bahru and the line of Johore Strait. After adequate preparation the assault should be launched on Singapore. The division disembarked on the east coast of Malaya should advance south along the coast. (It was considered that with air superiority the completion of all these Army operations should be a comparatively easy matter.)

2. The troops of the main force, the nucleus of the 5th Division, to assemble at Samah Harbor (Hainan) and, under protection of the Navy, were to set out on X - 4 day [4 December] for the assembly point from which they were to disembark at Singora on X day [8 December] at half an hour after midnight (0030 hours), with one section landing at Patani at the same time. These forces were to seize airstrips and break through the frontier without loss of time to crush enemy positions in the Alor Star and Betong districts, assault the line of the Perak River, and endeavor to seize the Perak River bridge.

3. The Takumi Detachment of troops of the 18th Division were also to assemble at Samah Harbor together with the main force on X - 4 day, and to leave at the same time under protection of the Navy, and on X day at midnight (0000 hours) to land at Kota Bharu, attack the enemy position, seize the adjacent aerodrome, and then advance south through Trengganu Province to Kuantan, seizing all airfields on the way, and later joining the main Army for the assault on Singapore.

4. The Imperial Guards Division, which at the commencement of hostilities would be under command of the 15th Army (in Indochina),

were to move into Thailand by land or sea as appropriate and then advance across the Malay frontier and concentrate in rear of the 5th Division, and then, according to circumstances, push forward the advance of the 5th Division, or attack with it in leapfrog tactics. The leading detachment of approximately three battalions of infantry was to be concentrated immediately in rear of the 5th Division by X + 15 day. The rest of the division was to follow as closely as possible.

5. Until X - 3 day, 3rd Air Group was to deploy in southern Indochina, entrusting to one section the duty of protecting the convoy of transport vessels and operating in conjunction with the Navy. The rest of the group at the beginning of hostilities was to attack enemy aerodromes in northern Malaya, shoot down hostile planes, and protect the landing of the Army's main forces. Thenceforth the main strength of 3rd Air Group was to engage and secure domination over the enemy air force. One section was to cooperate with the Army in ground operations.

6. The second disembarkation force was to assemble in Camranh Bay (Indochina) by X + 3 day and to disembark about X + 8 day at Singora, Patani, and Kota Bharu and reinforce the first landing detachments. The rest of the Army was to assemble in Taiwan and Canton, to depart at the proper time, about X + 25 day, to join the main forces, landing at Singora and Patani to overtake the 5th Division.

7. After reaching the line of the Perak River and consolidating, the main force was to cross the river about X + 15 day and then attack towards Kuala Lumpur. After seizure of Kuala Lumpur, the main force was to maintain continuous pressure on the enemy and push forward to Johore Strait. Throughout all these operations one section of small boats was to be used in seaborne movements on the west coast in support of the operations of the main Army.

8. The 18th Division was to operate on the east coast of Malaya and also prepare for an attack on Sumatra.

9. The 56th Regiment (Takumi Detachment, 18th Division) was to land at Kota Bharu at midnight (0000 hours) on X day and after capture of the town and aerodrome to move south along the east coast of Malaya, keeping step with the movement of the main Army. The remainder of the 18th Division was to later disembark in the area between Kuantan and Mersing and from there thrust into Johore Province to Johore Strait.

10. The whole Army was to concentrate on Johore Strait, and, after completing preparations, attack Singapore from the area west of the Causeway, crossing Johore Strait in boats.

11. On about X - 15 day the Army Combat Command Post was to leave Saigon for Samah and embark on the Ryujo Maru together with the first disembarkation units of the 5th Division to commence landing at Singora at 0030 hours on X day; afterwards, in accordance with development of the situation, it was to move on in succession to Taiping, Kuala Lumpur, and Kluang.

After my appointment to the position of Staff Officer in Charge of 25th Army Military Operations, I had, as I have said, vowed to the gods that I would abstain from wine and tobacco until the fall of Singapore. The plan of operations upon which I had concentrated with heart and soul for a period of three hundred days since the New Year, pondering over it and carefully considering its contents over and over again until I became exhausted, had finally become the standard which unified the whole strength of land, sea, and air forces. "Yes," I thought, "I would like a glass of wine," and then, "No! From now on I must remember my vow and think only of the war." Looking at a colleague's glass of beer filled to the brim, I made a gurgling noise in my throat, and, restraining my instincts, forced down at one gulp the coarse tea which was the same color as the beer.

A Dream Plan

DOZING OFF ON THE RUSH mat, with my shoulder bag as my pillow, I had a dream. Mingling among Thai forces I crossed the frontier and surged forward, receiving a warm welcome from the British Army when I arrived at the foot of the Perak bridge. Just as I was about to drink from the beautiful stream, scooping the water up in my hands, I woke up.

Was it a true dream or a false dream? When I analyzed it according to tactical theory, it did not appear impossible. Even with prospects of success of about one percent, it was worth planning its materialization and directing all our faculties towards it as a military operation.

Once, during a civil war* in Japan, a group of warriors had approached the enemy officers, felled their commander at one blow, and disappeared in the mêlée with his decapitated head as a "caller's present." Ever so many of these episodes lie hidden in the subconscious memory, and probably were linked together in this dream.

The upshot of the matter was that the realization of the dream was seriously considered and the following six-point plan evolved:

---

* The author is referring to an incident in a civil war between the Taira and Minamoto clans that occurred during the twelfth century.

1. A death-defying volunteer force would masquerade in the uniforms of Thai troops, camouflaging their attitude towards the Thailand Army.

2. On landing at Singora, by bribery or cajolery we would win over the Thai troops, bring over to our side a number of officers and men, and then persuade them to advance at the head of our raiding unit.

3. Our disguised troops, immediately after disembarkation, would board cars which they had seized on the Thailand side of the frontier, and, as if confused, with a simulated, sorrowful expression, seek help from the British Army. After deceiving the frontier barrier guard and getting through it, they would dash at full speed towards the Perak River through the unconsolidated British defenses and seize possession of the Kuala Kangsar bridge.

4. To deceive the enemy for the purpose of getting his sympathy, our troops should feign an outward appearance like the Thailand officers and men, take refuge among Thai women by gathering up café and dance-hall girls after landing, then seize twenty or thirty trucks or motor buses and advance at the head of the Thai troops who had been won over to our side.

5. With the utmost urgency and in absolute secrecy, arrangements were to be made to acquire about a thousand Thai uniforms for officers and men.

6. On disembarkation, flags of the three nations—Thailand, Japan, and Great Britain—would be issued to the disguised troops, who would advance waving in one hand the Thai flag and in the other the Union Jack. Calling out in English, "Japanese soldier is frightful" and "Hurrah for the English," they would thus break right through the frontier line.

To carry into practice these tactics for the destruction of the enemy, we would have to thoroughly complete preparations in advance. Accordingly, we dispatched Staff Officer Hayashi to Bangkok, where he obtained possession of a Thai Army uniform. We also brought secretly to Saigon Major Osone, who was camouflaged in the dress of a clerk in the Singora Consulate, and was given secret instructions for the night previous to the commencement of hostilities.

Interpretation of the Thai language was a necessity, and in addition to a Japanese who had lived in Bangkok for many years, we were able to find several other daring and shrewd young people. It all resembled child's play. Although it seemed a breach of international good faith, for the sake of the conquest of Singapore we had to disregard this aspect. With the conclusion of a military alliance with Thailand this breach of international conventions would be satisfactorily and legally settled. Our plan was certainly reckless, but it might succeed.

If we could seize the Perak River bridge before it was demolished, we would be able to shorten military operations by at least a week. Could we find a dauntless and cautious leader who could carry out the "Dream Plan"? It was not easy to secure the agreement of the Army Commander and the Army Chief of Staff to put the plan into practice, but eventually it was approved and the 5th Division Commander was ordered by telegram to select a detachment which would brave almost certain death. Major Tadashi Ichikawa's battalion, being well qualified, was chosen. But when confronted with the problem of carrying out the plan, the more they considered it, the less easy it seemed to be. If one false step was made, the whole battalion would probably be trapped. In the accomplishment of such a reckless plan it was clear that the proposer should take the lead, and I resolved to do so. After persistent requests, I was given permission to take command of the detachment.

In two weeks the Intendance Department supplied, according to sample, Thai uniforms for a thousand men. All was ready. My attitude was: "To catch a tiger you must first put your head in the tiger's den."

Plans for the most important military operations, for which I was responsible as Staff Officer in Charge of Operations and Planning, were already finished. They only awaited putting into practice. The period for cudgeling one's brains had passed. Now there was merely the question of ability to carry out the plans. At the risk of my life I would undertake the important task of implementing the "Dream Plan." If we were to die in the attempt, let us all die together.

Towards Embarkation

AT THE HARBORS OF SAMAH and Saigon all military preparations had ended most satisfactorily, but we had to speed up our departure from Saigon and move to Samah Harbor a day earlier than intended. The 5th Division, the Army's foremost troops, who were to play a leading role at the beginning of hostilities, together with the Takumi Detachment of the 18th Division, which was to capture Kota Bharu, had embarked from Canton and Shanghai and were concentrated at Samah and on Hainan Island.

On 25 November, Army Commander Yamashita, accompanied by his staff, left Saigon for Samah by airplane. Other officers and men of Headquarters travelled by boat. Geographically, a movement from southern Indochina northward to Hainan was a move away from the projected theater of operations, but strategically it was progress towards it. This was probably a parting forever from Saigon, where for about two months we had been absorbed in urgent preparations; but, reflecting upon all this, it seemed useless to regret what could not be mended.

One evening, General Yamashita arranged for food and wine for the young staff officers. He appeared to think it would console them for their labors. Since the future obstacles lying in their path were thick and three-fold, these men could not slacken from their duties, and all concerned declined the invitation and solemnly departed from Saigon. Surveying the true motives of the general in issuing the invitation, it would appear he was in a kindly mood, for he was one who enforced upon all under his command a military and moral discipline as rigorous as the autumn frost. Removing all signs of rank, the general put on an open-necked shirt and helmet and quietly took off by airplane without one person at the airfield to bid him farewell.

Samah port is indeed a naval crossroad of cherished memories where I once assisted for one night in our torrid-zone maneuvers. Army Headquarters were installed in one of the barracks in a coconut plan-tation. Shipping Transport Headquarters, under command of Major-General Tanabe, was also based there; it was at this spot without excep-tion that all final arrangements were made. The 5th Division and the Takumi Detachment were assembled, but no information at all was available about the movement of the shipping. Owing to the need for secrecy, the use of wireless had been prohibited. The twenty ships had to be raked up from every district of Japan proper, and from Dalny, Shanghai, Canton, Formosa, and other areas, and it would be difficult to avoid errors as the ships had not yet received their detailed orders.

Staff Officer Morito ran about without sleeping or resting. Staff Officer Kera, Chief of Army Shipping, steam rising from his bald head, franti-cally sought information; but by 2 December the ships had still not assembled as prearranged. As the departure was to be on the morning of 4 December, everyone was asking, "What has happened?"

We had never felt so impatient. Voices over the telephone grew threat-ening with excitement as staff officers telephoned without pause. The name Kera is an uncommon one, and it was not unreasonable that the signalers operating the telephone switch could not understand it easily. Staff Officer Kera, with rising impatience, beads of perspiration drop-ping from his head, would shout, "What, don't you understand yet? My name is Kera—the same as the last syllable of the word "mushikera" [meaning a worm, an insect]. I am Staff Officer Kera." The unexpected explosions of laughter allayed the tense atmosphere of the staff officers' room. Staff Officer Kera was really not a bad fellow. Judging from his bald head, he appeared an old man of sixty, but he had the childish face of a boy of seventeen or eighteen.

Loading the 3rd Air Group took an unexpectedly long time. They were loading even iron beds, bathtubs, and sofas. "I tell you it's not a joke," exclaimed Staff Officer Kera. "Baggage for the ground forces is limited and even officers are restricted to one trunk between two men. All baggage which is not immediately essential for the operation is to be dumped into the sea." And he struck his table as if driving in a nail.

Air Force pilots suffer greater strain than men of the ground forces, and so naturally require more satisfactory rest; but there should be a limit to everything. Everyone had to submit with patience to the utmost restriction of space, even so far as the allotment of three men to a mat (6 feet by 3 feet). This rough treatment somewhat wounded the feelings of the Air Group, but realizing the strict and impartial methods of the officers and men of Army Headquarters and of the infantry divisions, for the first time the airmen re-examined their consciences.

By degrees the twenty ships arrived, and by about noon on 3 December the convoy of transports was complete. "At last we are free from anxiety," we all thought.

In conformity with the Army's plan of embarkation, the units and baggage from each area were gathered together and put aboard the convoy. Changes had to be made in the loading of the ships, which was a difficult and dangerous undertaking quite impossible for the reader to understand. With no jetty inside the harbor, all loading had to be done from lighters, but by sitting up all night, the work of transhipment of men and baggage was completed just before it was time to set out. This was heavy labor, more strenuous than action on the battlefield.

On the evening of 2 December we had received an order for the whole Army to proceed southward to participate in the beginning of the operations decreed by Imperial General Headquarters. It was accompanied, however, by instructions that, depending on the result of Japanese-American negotiations, the order might have to be suspended. The order read:

1. It is predetermined that military operations begin on 8 December.*
2. 25th Army is to cooperate with the Navy for commencement of

---

*The Japanese attacks on Kota Bharu, Pearl Harbor, the Philippines, Guam, Hong Kong, and Wake Island were launched in that order and within a period of seven hours. Since Pearl Harbor lies to the east of the International Date Line, the attack there occurred on the morning of 7 December, local time, whereas the attacks on the other places occurred on the morning of 8 December, local times. The landing at Kota Bharu was made one hour and twenty minutes before the air attack on Pearl Harbor.

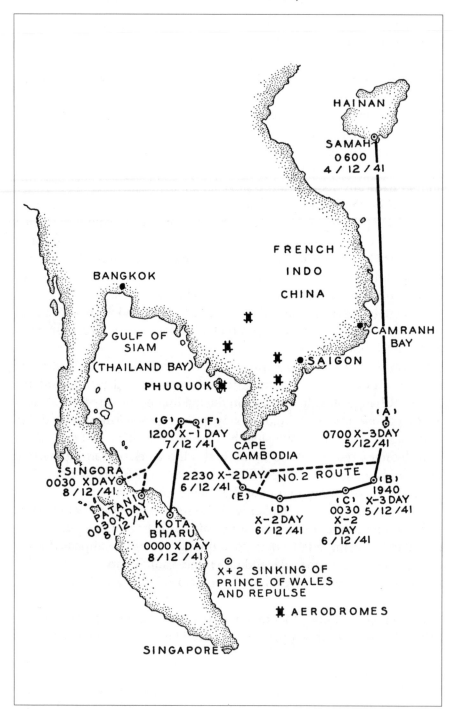

Route of the invasion convoy.

military operations for the occupation of Malaya.

3. 25th Army Commander will begin military operations based on previous orders. However, *if Japanese negotiations are concluded by the above fixed date the military attacking operations will be suspended.*

General Yamashita issued his Army Orders on the morning of 3 December. The commanders of the 5th and 18th divisions and other officers, including the commander of the Takumi Detachment, participated in an impressive address, during which there was not even a cough to be heard as all listened attentively to the voice of the Army Commander reading "No. 1 Order to 25th Army." It infused new life into our death-defying resolution for large-scale military operations upon which the national destiny was staked. It was a scene of deep emotion. Officers and men alike gave way to tears.

The Japanese-American talks were carried on by the two ambassadors, Kurusu and Nomura, in this hazardous atmosphere. In the event of an unexpected suspension of the order to attack, special instructions were to be transmitted up to the evening of 7 December. In that case, according to the Imperial command, we were to return home to Japan, suspending everything. If, however, no such instructions arrived we were to carry everything into effect as prearranged.

"To the utmost, avoiding war, seeking out diplomatic compromise, we bow to the Imperial Will."

This order was an ambiguous one such as weakens the resolution of officers and soldiers on their way, not to the trading markets, but to the battlefront at the risk of their lives.

Such a war was unheard of by former generations and will not again be paralleled in the future. This situation is explained eloquently by Mr. Tojo's statement in the International Court of Justice, where, after expressing his belief that "the war activities of Japan were really unavoidable for self-defense," he was sentenced to death.

I, too, firmly believe that it was a war without preparation and a war which was forced upon us.

Part Two

The Threshold of Fate

WHEN THE SHIPS WERE ASSEMBLED at Uzina, the choice of those on which Army Headquarters and 5th Division Headquarters were to travel became a problem. In previous landing operations there were many precedents of the senior headquarters staff boarding a prestigious warship and exercising command from it. For the Malayan operation, however, the whole Army Headquarters Staff, including General Yamashita, felt very strongly that they should participate in the fate of the front line and take the lead of the convoy in a transport ship.

Transport Headquarters had arranged for the *Kashii Maru* to carry Army Headquarters, with 5th Division Headquarters on the *Ryujo Maru*. Both were excellent ships of ten thousand tons, but the *Kashii Maru* was a luxury liner which had formerly sailed on European and American routes, and the *Ryujo Maru* was a rudimentary transport specially built for the Army. She carried no armament, but in external appearance resembled an aircraft carrier. One of her features was that about thirty large and small boats could be carried on board. Every inch of space had been considered, even that allocated for wireless equipment. She was a ghost ship resembling a warship. She could carry a large number of men, but the accommodation for them was uncomfortable and cramped. She rolled badly and pitched violently and was not a pleasant ship in which to travel. The meals served on board were boiled rice, barley, *miso* soup [bean paste], and pickled radish. She was far from being a luxury liner, and travel on her would not be welcomed by those with foreknowledge of these matters.

From its many years of training in landing operations the 5th Division knew everything there was to know about the characteristics of these ships. At the meeting of the Shipping Conference, the Operations Section of 5th Division Staff offered to exchange ships with Army Headquarters. At that time I did not know anything about the great differences between the two ships, and accepted the 5th Division offer, much to the glee of its Operations staff officers. When I got aboard the *Ryujo Maru* I understood their willingness to change ships and realized the importance of experience in such matters. Army Headquarters accepted responsibility for the discomfort and meager food on the ship and was determined to share them and take the lead of the convoy in the landing operations. But, as might have been expected, there were some below the rank of Army Commander who did not like the poor food and could not sleep in peace because of the discomfort, and who grumbled accordingly.

Prior to the sailing, the Army Commander issued an instruction in these words: "I will be aboard the *Ryujo Maru* and will land with the officers and men of the 5th Division. In the event of the *Ryujo Maru* being sunk I will take command of all units of the 5th Division as well as of the Army." The men of the 5th Division disliked the idea of Army Headquarters being aboard the *Ryujo Maru*, but we appreciated General Yamashita's desire to share the fate of the frontline troops at the landing, of which the whole Army was informed. The spirit of leadership thus displayed by General Yamashita was, from that time on, one of the causes of the success of the units under his command.

On the early morning of 4 December the moon, like a tray, was sinking in the western sea, and the deep-red sun showed its face to the east. Samah Harbor, shimmering with gold and silver waves, was as beautiful as a picture. The men on the convoy of twenty ships, confident of victory, looked towards the bows of their ships, with the radiant sun behind them and the light of the sinking moon ahead, as the Navy formed in two lines to right and left of the convoy as it ploughed through the waves heading away from the harbor. This was surely the starting point which would determine the destiny of the nation for the next century. "The die was cast." Everything humanly possible to ensure success had been done, and officers and men alike believed that "Japan's fate is the fate of East Asia."

As I stood on the bridge of the *Ryujo Maru*, gazing at Samah Harbor vanishing astern, flashes of the face of my old mother, whom I had left behind in my birthplace, and of those of my wife and children, came and went. Regrets like those are not cowardice. The convoy sailed in silence.

Not a voice was heard from the two thousand officers and men aboard the ship. All was peaceful.

During the voyage, every man concentrated intently on trying to detect enemy planes or submarines, and everyone's nerves were stretched. During the day, everyone, from the Army Commander to the private soldiers, was tense in the clear weather. Never had I wished so earnestly for heavy rain as I did then. The food on the ship was certainly not good. There was only bean soup, pickled radish, and buckets of boiled rice and barley to be shared alike between officers and men. But, driving every erroneous idea from their hearts, all offered prayers for victory, and ceased to complain of the food. Taking from their haversacks the dried eels they had brought from Formosa [Taiwan] the men baked them in the field kitchen, sprinkled salt on them, and chewed them as a supplement to the shipboard ration. Until victory we must eat sufficient to keep us perfectly fit.

Commander Taro Nagai, who was dispatched by Headquarters as Navy Liaison Staff Officer, Operations Section, was a man of commanding appearance and tall in stature, worthy of his name ["Nagai" means long]. Bright, cheerful, honest, and broadminded, he was one of those people who, when met for the first time, immediately attract goodwill, and to whom it is possible to talk as freely as if with a friend after ten years' separation. The close cooperation between Navy and Army in Malaya owed much to Nagai, whose tact and common sense made it possible.

The 5th and 6th December passed without incident. On the morning of the 7th the convoy passed Cape Cambodia and altered course to the northwest as if proceeding to Bangkok. Even though by a ten-thousand-to-one chance we should be discovered, we were now so close to our objective that no one could feel apprehensive about the completion of our plans.

The Aviation Group, which had moved all its strength to southern Indochina, was able to provide adequate air protection for the convoy from the aerodromes there. The weather became worse, and from my heart I was grateful to our planes, which lightheartedly flew through the clouds above us. Our heavy work in constructing those airfields was now well rewarded.

Shortly after noon on the 7th a message came from the signal office: "We have brought down an enemy patrol plane." We thought to ourselves, "It is a blood offering to the ground forces; but we must not be negligent; there may be other hostile planes which were not shot down." Everyone unconsciously held his breath. The discovery of the convoy sailing to the northwest we could bear with patience, but from two o'clock in the afternoon our change of course to the west must be concealed even from the gods.*

What good fortune! At about noon the weather suddenly worsened. Fog and dense clouds hung low over the Gulf of Siam, but it seemed as if the plan directed against Singora might be an airtight one. According to reports, the enemy planes which had escaped when the first one was shot down might be their reconnaissance planes; they were now appearing and disappearing among the clouds.

From noon on 7 December our fighter planes based on southern Indochina were continually diving through the breaks in the clouds and flying protection against air attack. Every moment as we approached the coast of southern Thailand the activity of our fighter planes increased. In the evening, however, the situation was particularly dangerous. To land us under the nose of the enemy air force based on Kota Bharu and in Kedah Province [Alor Star], our Air Force would have to fight to the limit of its ability.

Dusk approached. The last fighter planes covering the convoy would soon depart, leaving it unprotected until moonrise. These planes would have to land in the dark.

Even in the daylight over the Gulf cumulonimbus clouds whirled around everywhere, and fighter pilots had to take care not to get caught in their down-draft, in which case they would certainly end up as shark food. It goes without saying that planes flying and trying to land in the dark were in considerable danger.

The officers of the Kato Fighter Squadron who carried out this last daylight flight had exchanged cups of water before setting out. Prior to their going into action, their squadron leader, Lieutenant-Colonel Tatsuo Kato, said, "Leave here [at the aerodrome] the necessary personnel and ammunition, so that even if none of us return, the squadron will still be able to operate. All others come with me. Senior officers of each squadron are requested to stay here. If I do not return, Major So-and-so is to be my successor. He will reorganize the squadron and carry on the fight!"

The officers who were to be left behind flared up. They wished to share the fate of the commanding officer. "Pools!" he stormed at them. "If we do not return, then indeed you will follow later. At least just wait until then."

Leading the squadron, and braving what appeared almost certain death, just before dusk he and those chosen to follow him took their machines into the air for the last important task of the day. Attached to them, to act

* The convoy had been sighted by R.A.A.F. aircraft from Kota Bharu.

as a guide on the return flight, was a heavy bomber, but owing to the fog and dense cloud it was impossible for the planes to maintain formation.

On their return, unable to locate the Phuquok Island aerodrome, the fighters dispersed, and exhaustion of their gasoline ended in the unfortunate sacrifice of several planes, which came down on the waters of the Gulf of Siam in the darkness and sank. Squadron Commander Kato barely escaped with his life, but finally managed to land on Phuquok Island. This gallant officer was killed on the Burma front, during the second year of the war.

Under cover of darkness the convoy moved safely to the west. During a break in the heavy rain, the flagship *Chokai** flashed a signal: "The main business from now is to proceed to Kota Bharu to cover the landing of the Takumi Detachment. Pray for the success of the disembarkation—Vice-Admiral Ozawa." These were his words of farewell.

Turning towards the enemy air base the admiral took the lead towards the objective with the main forces of the fleet. His attitude at the Saigon meeting at which agreement on Army-Navy cooperation had been reached floated before my eyes. Gambling with life and death, from our hearts we trusted him to give all possible assistance to the task in which we were engaged. Following the main strength of the fleet, three transport vessels quietly turned their bows to the south and their shapes disappeared in the night.

For the success of the landing we were much indebted to the valuable and revered assistance of our friends in the Navy and the Air Force, who gave their cooperation at the sacrifice of their own lives.

Singora's Waves Are High

THE CONVOY ADVANCED ACCORDING TO program. On the way, it was fortunately free from interference from either sea or air. Only the weather would now determine the success or failure of the disembarkation. Concealed by clouds, the moon shone dimly on the surface of the sea. The northeast monsoon harmonized with the ships' course and there was scarcely any inconvenience from rolling and pitching. But would the god of the wind stay on our side? About midnight the three transports of the Ando Detachment, which was to disembark at Patani (42nd Infantry Regiment), diverged to the southeast. The fourteen ships carrying the main forces of the division, under the escort and guidance

---

* The *Chokai* was one of a class of eight cruisers of between 12,000 and 13,000 tons, completed in the late 1920s and early 1930s. Each mounted ten 8-inch guns.

of Navy destroyers, dropped anchor at 2 a.m. on 8 December in line confronting Singora beach.

Suddenly a light appeared and disappeared. As the coast could not yet be seen, we wondered what it was. Could it be a flash from an electric torch? Or possibly an alarm signal? We all strained our eyes looking at the mysterious light, which flashed on and off regularly. "Ah," someone shouted, "it is a lighthouse! It is Singora lighthouse." We felt relieved. It was evident the enemy did not yet suspect anything. The ship was pitching and rolling in the heavy sea, but as our eyes became accustomed to the darkness we saw another electric light shining bright as a firefly at Singora crossroads. "Excellent!" we said. "Our surprise is complete."

Our large transport was rolling heavily, and just as the anchor was lowered the northeast wind suddenly freshened. The question was, would it be possible to launch the boats in such heavy seas, and even if it were, could the troops laden with their equipment climb down the rope ladders from the ships' decks and transfer into the boats? The officers and men of our engineer detachments, standing at the rail, watched the seas dashing against the side of the ship and said with scolding voices, "It's useless, isn't it? What fools to think of disembarkation in such heavy seas!" This was really the sincere opinion of the men responsible for handling the boats. The seas were at least three meters high—possibly higher. In peacetime maneuvers men would not have been exposed to the danger of transhipment in such circumstances. It seemed as if the boats would be swamped as they lay alongside.

As if to efface all uncertainty, a light signal was displayed at the masthead of the *Ryujo Maru*. "Lower the boats," was what it meant. In succession the signal was repeated from the *Kashii Maru* and the other transports. When the boats were lowered the engineers, with the agility of monkeys, climbed into them. Soon nearly a hundred motor boats were floating beside the transports, tossing up and down on the waves like the leaves of a tree in the wind. With poles the engineers desperately kept them from bumping the sides of the transports. In the dim moonlight the launching of the boats had somehow proved easier than had been thought possible. Soon the next signal light appeared. "Commence transhipment." The order was passed on inflexibly as if to whip up faltering hearts. Staff Officer Hongo (Railways), Staff Officer Hayashi (Intelligence) and I, accompanied by an orderly, led the way, and climbed down the rope ladder from the deck of the *Ryujo Maru*.

In such a heavy sea it was not easy to get into the boats, encumbered as we were with our equipment. The problem was to let go the rope ladder at the right time. If one let go just as the boat commenced to fall from the top of a wave one landed in the boat safely and fairly comfortably, but if one let go the ladder as the boat was rising there was danger of breaking a leg.

Suddenly a voice shouted, "Ouch!" It was Staff Officer Hongo. The two officers following him were heavy men, each over twelve stone, and they both fell on his head. Even with his helmet on he found it painful, I dare say. There was an explosion of laughter from the troops, who were highly amused to see staff officers treading on each other. The laughter lessened the tension of the moment.

It took less than an hour for the descent, one by one, of the signalers and orderlies who were to land from our boat. Making provision for all eventualities, the wireless section had linked together a number of life-belts to act as floats for their heavy equipment, which had been wrapped and sealed in strong oiled paper packages so that salt water could not damage it. Heavy and light machine-guns were transshipped by being passed down from hand to hand.

The men who had got into the boats first became uncomfortable as they tossed and pitched, and many were very seasick, but eventually all the launches were filled with their quotas of troops and with some difficulty formed in line ready to move off towards the shore. We were getting very worried about the time everything was taking, as we wanted all in the boats landed before daylight, and the night was drawing to a close. Then, on the gunwale of the *Ryujo Mara*, three red lights appeared. It was the order to set out.

The boats were so tightly packed with men and equipment that it was impossible to move in them. From head to foot we were all drenched with spray, and we looked like drowned rats. In the heavy seas the boats frequently lost sight of each other as they rose on the crests or sank in the troughs of the waves. The sound of the boats' engines was drowned by the noise of the surf crashing on the shore. The line formation of the boats broke up as they surged forward on the crests of the breakers. Concealment and silence were no longer considered. In another second or two we would be ashore. As we approached the beach, the seas threw the boats on the sand or against each other—probably thirty percent of them were tossed bodily ashore at the water's edge or smashed into each other as they approached the land.

Everywhere soldiers could be seen holding up their weapons as they plunged into the sea. One could only pray that one's own boat would not finish like some of the others.

The time factor, however, was already causing more anxiety than the safety of the men. Daylight was approaching. Our boat was rushing towards the shore and we hoped to be stranded in the shallows. Even though we might be welcomed by a burst of machine-gun fire we felt that this would be preferable to being drowned.

As the lights of Singora's streets began to show very close at hand there was a sudden heavy jolting movement. We had run aground. Shouting to each other, "Jump!" we all leapt overboard, jarring the soles of our feet as we hit the hard sand. "The water is shallow," someone cried, and a moment later we at last trod the earth of the fighting zone. Staff Officer Hongo, who followed me, sprained his ankle as he jumped, and fell down in a sitting position. He was carried up the sandy beach on the shoulders of some soldiers. The remainder of the Headquarters Staff came ashore some hours later at the head of the rest of the Army. It was exactly 4 a.m. on 8 December when my boat landed, and our first steps ashore marked the first stage in the fighting zone which I had envisaged in a dream.

The Collapse of a Dream

THE THAI FIRING TRENCH THAT had been established as a matter of form along the sea coast was an empty shell. Our surprise attack had been completely successful. Major Osone, employed as a clerk in the Singora Consulate, should now have appeared as a guide, but nobody saw even his shadow. Hurriedly advancing along the beach, we over-took a man pulling a rickshaw. "Hold on," we said, and caught hold of him and scanned his features. He was a Thailander—exactly like a Japanese except that his color was slightly swarthier.

"Well," I thought, "there is still hope for the Dream Plan." Singora's citizens were still fast asleep.

Staff Officer Hongo could not move about by reason of his sprained ankle. Staff Officer Hayashi took command of the greater part of the officers and men already ashore, and waited for the landing of the Commander-in-Chief to select the location of Army Headquarters. With a young interpreter and the Thailander we had seized, and together with an orderly, I hurried off to the Japanese Consulate. A dog barked as we reached it. While I was pounding at the gate as if to smash it, another dog growled from the inside. At this a corpulent man, just awakened from sleep, came out and agitatedly opened the gate. It was the Consul, Katsuno. "Ah! The Japanese Army!" was all he could say—and his breath had the odor of ripe persimmons. He had probably been drinking freely the previous evening. Major Osone, rubbing his eyes, put in an appearance behind the broad-backed, white-clad figure of the Consul.

The secret disembarkation plans with full details had been purposely sent to Saigon and left there with all the information about the preparation of motor vehicles and the building up of opposition to the Military Police. But how could the Dream Plan be put into operation now? We were faced with an unforeseen situation; but this was neither the time nor the place for censure about preparations which should have been made but were not.

Without a moment's delay we had to make arrangements with the Thai police, and next with the Thailand troops. With Consul Katsuno as guide we hurried first to the police station. Four of us, the Consul, the interpreter, the orderly, and I, packed ourselves like sardines into the Consul's small car and drove off along the dark road. When we set out, the orderly carried on his shoulder 100,000 ticals of Thailand money wrapped in a large *furoshiki*,* for use in case it might be possible, and much better, to solve certain problems by paying money rather than by hurling projectiles. Shining our glittering car light on the road, we came to a large iron gate. "That is the front gate of the police station," said the Consul. Suddenly we heard a gunshot and our headlight exploded. We were plunged into darkness. There came two or three more shots in quick succession. Those shooting at us were not twenty yards away, and it was perhaps natural that they should fire upon us. In this way the morning dreams of the people of Singora were broken.

This first shot fired at the opening of the Malayan campaign was the warning signal for the emancipation of East Asia. One bullet grazed my right arm, the next passed between my hip and the Consul. At that moment, unconsciously opening the door of the car, I took cover in the drainage ditch at the side of the road.

The interpreter kept on shouting, "Don't shoot. It is the Japanese Army. Ally with us and attack the British Army."

In the darkness the white linen suit of the Consul became the target. More and more bullets flew overhead with a forbidding sound. There must have been thirty or forty people firing rapidly and at random. There did not seem much prospect of rescue from this situation. Shadows of people going and coming inside the gate of the police station gradually increased in number. It appeared as if they were going to make a sortie. We fell back to the rear, dragging the Consul and the interpreter along the drainage ditch from which they and the orderly now and again looked out to see how the land lay. None of us wished for immediate death, so we determined to start afresh.

---

* A square of silk or cotton commonly used in Japan for carrying parcels.

The 100,000 ticals of Thai money in the heavy cloth wrapper were still intact inside the car, which stood abandoned on the road, but hit by many bullets. With a feeling of resentment we withdrew helplessly along the ditch, leaving the car as a present for the Thailanders. "Mr. Staff Officer, I will go and get it said the orderly. Apparently, since he had been carrying the money, he thought it was his responsibility. Crawling from the ditch under heavy fire, he approached the car. I did not consider it was worth risking the life of even one soldier to recover the money and called to him, "Stop, come back," but as he crawled closer to the car he appeared deaf as a gecko. Strangely enough, he was not hit, and soon pulled the cloth-wrapped parcel from the car; carrying it over his shoulder, he crawled back to us in the ditch. Even now I have the impression that the enemy were pressing close on his heels. After we had fallen back about five hundred meters, the commander of a 5th Division battalion which had already completed landing heard the shooting and came hurrying along with his unit. Stopping the commanding officer, I gave him the order that two or three rounds should be fired into them. I could not help commenting later that it was like taking a sword to kill a barnyard fowl. Then I went out onto the main road.

Quietly turning over in my mind the problem of pacification of the Thai Army, I moved along the road to where their troops were camped.

The Army Commander had not yet disembarked. The battalion which had come to our rescue was the only complete unit yet ashore, and it was lining up on the road ready to move off towards the west. It was commanded by Major Kobayashi, who had been in the same term as I was at Ichigaya Military College. It was the first time we had met since we both left there ten years or so earlier. Meeting, we clasped hands. "Hello," he said. "Somehow or other we ought to come to terms and not fight the Thai Army, don't you think so?" "Yes," I replied, "but that will have to depend on events."

Then, assembling the battalion in column of fours along the road and hoisting a large white flag which could be seen even in the dark, with buglers at the head of the column, he marched his men off to the west. At the time it was thought they would soon reach the military camp, but suddenly, without warning, a machine-gun fired. Our troops were ordered to take cover, and the men quickly fell down by the roadside. Considering the position in which the enemy were established, we discovered they were deployed on a wide front and had ten machine-guns and a number of other guns covering the road along which our troops were extended in column of route. "The enemy has calculated this position," we concluded. "We will have to knock him down."

We had been patient up to this juncture, but the fighting spirit which had been restrained in us was now aroused and blazed up like fire. Turning left from the road, we struck against the Thai rear and in this manner became engaged in a violent fight, which we had wished to avoid, with the Thai Military Police. There was no room for compromise. We had to crush the resistance without delay.

Hurriedly I returned to the disembarkation point, and as I made my way along, the night gave way to broad daylight. Army Headquarters personnel had completed landing and were massing in the coconut trees on the outskirts of the town when I arrived. I reported in detail to the Commander-in-Chief on the progress of the landing and the situation in regard to the Thai forces.

Without losing a minute General Yamashita ordered that the resistance of the Thai Military Police be smashed immediately. 5th Division units which had completed landing got into position for a speedy attack, and within a short space of time had secured complete control of the area.

Looking along the shore, I saw thirteen or fourteen upturned motor boats floating on the waves or washed ashore on the beach. They were like the puffed-up globe-fish which gurgle helplessly after being washed up by a big wave. But there had been almost no damage to weapons or equipment during the landing. As a precaution, an inflatable lifejacket had been attached to every man and every weapon before they got into the boats, and so, when these capsized or were swamped, the men and their weapons were washed ashore, buoyed up by the lifejackets.

The airstrips were seized without resistance, but the Thai Army from a distance now and again poured shells onto the runways. As the sun peeped over the eastern sea our fighter planes, evading the shells, began landing on those airstrips, on which lay numerous pools of water from the previous day's rain. The planes often landed in clouds of yellow spray, and several turned somersaults as they taxied along the strips.

But the heroic thrust of the Kato Squadron was decisive. The previous evening the fighter planes which had moved out to protect the convoy saw the remains of enemy planes which had been shot down lying in coconut groves.

The Thai Army's resistance continued until about noon. Our artillery which had disembarked had opened fire on their fortified positions along the road, and presently the white flag was hoisted along the entire front. "At the command of Premier Pibul," it was announced, "the resistance of the Thai Army is suspended for the time being." This half-day was a valuable one to us, because of the possibility of a sudden counterattack by the British Army.

As the tumult which immediately followed the landing subsided it became obvious that the Dream Plan, by which it was intended to break through the frontier with our troops dressed in Thai uniforms, had broken down and no longer held prospects of success, although the Thai people in the frontier region had welcomed our troops with gifts of food. Casting aside the Thai uniforms therefore, they changed back into their own Japanese dress. Our immediate need now was to launch without a moment's delay the strongest possible attack on the frontier, so as not to give the enemy time for preparation.

Major Osone, who had been dispatched to work as a clerk in the Consulate in order to make arrangements for action immediately following the landing, had been given a letter of instructions which included a secret code for deciphering telegrams that he was ordered to destroy at the appropriate time. He had burnt the letter too soon, and consequently had been unable to decipher the telegram informing him of the time and date of the landing. Thus he had been unable to make the last-minute arrangements with the Thai police and army. In plain clothes, with bowed head he accepted the rebuke of a senior staff officer for his error. But it was in fact questionable whether his blunder had not actually contributed to the success of the Army's operations. If he had handled the situation correctly and made preparations as instructed, the Thailanders might have become suspicious and information of our intentions might have got through to the British. The inactivity and lack of initiative of the Thailand forces was quite possibly due to the fact that, owing to Major Osone's error, they had no suspicions of what was to happen. The Major's consternation when, after being awakened by the barking of a dog, he saw us at the gate of the Consulate, was paralleled by the panic and disorganization of the Thai forces and authorities, which indicated that the concealment of our intentions was one of the reasons for the success of our surprise attack.

Shortly after the issue of Premier Pibul's order, a Thai Army messenger reported at Army Headquarters. General Yamashita welcomed him with a cordial bow, with correct military etiquette. The envoy looked exactly like a Japanese. He was in fact believed to be the secret child of a Japanese nobleman, Nagamasa Yamada, and he was received without hostility. He immediately entered into negotiations to prevent further delay in the implementation of our plans.

It was essential for us to break through the frontier without loss of time. This task was given to the troops at the head of the 5th Division, who were, already moving along the road to the west. I followed them as fast as possible, and en route picked up three medium tanks which were waiting by the roadside for reinforcements. Together we made rapid progress. Farther along the road I collected a number of soldiers and a field gun—the artillery was being landed with difficulty and had not yet received orders to advance—but I took the gun and its escort forward with me because of the danger that the enemy troops might counterattack, in which case it would have been important to meet them as soon as possible, with the greatest strength available to prevent their attack reaching our beachhead.

As Staff Officer in Charge of Operations, I did not wait for orders, but substituting for the Commander-in-Chief, in the interests of the whole Army I promptly speeded up the advance of every unit.

Shortly afterwards one of our planes flying low overhead dropped a message. It said: "Large enemy mechanized force this day at noon passed through Changlun moving north."* If this powerful British mechanized force crossed the frontier ahead of us it would certainly launch a heavy attack on our disembarkation point. Feeling uneasy, I hurried forward and before long overtook the leading troops of the 5th Division. They were a detachment under command of Lieutenant-Colonel Shizuo Saeki, who had been ordered to deploy and protect the disembarkation of the main forces of the Army. When it was explained that the ships had not yet finished unloading, Saeki expressed his willingness to attack the advancing enemy column.

Lieutenant-Colonel Saeki was a strong old man who had been at the Military College at the same time as Lieutenant-General Suzuki, the Chief of Staff; but it appears he was a poor hand at making his way in the world. The more able of his classmates had become lieutenant-generals by the time he was a lieutenant-colonel commanding a regiment, yet his intrepid fighting spirit was stamped on his face. He was by instinct a fighting commander.

With the three tanks and the field gun I had picked up en route, Colonel Saeki, on his own responsibility, urged that there was no time to rest and that the assault on the frontier should begin immediately. With the three medium tanks in the lead, followed by one light armored unit, two squadrons of mechanized cavalry, and the field gun—a total of about three hundred men—he ordered an advance to meet the enemy mechanized force.

---

* Evidently motor transport and Bren-gun carriers.

There was only one road through the area, but on account of the contours of the land, the relative military strengths did not appear to be the decisive factor. Alertness and daring would decide the issue at this beginning of the war.

After the rain there were pools of water here and there on the road. As night fell, the dense growth of the luxuriant forest shut out the light of the moon and it was difficult to see even what lay under one's feet. We hurried along as fast as we could. Near midnight, as we approached Ban Sadao village on the frontier, we heard rifle shots and gunfire at the head of the column. Our advance guard had come into collision with the British. The moment had arrived to launch our surprise attack, and the order was issued for an assault.

Before sunset the enemy commander appeared to have made preparations for fighting and to have disposed his troops accordingly. From an extended front they were in position to fire on any troops moving along the road. Their tracer bullets were dragging red tails through the night. Jumping from their lorries, two companies of our men, like hunting dogs, swiftly dispersed into the rubber plantation on both sides of the road, and our field gun opened fire on the enemy front. After fighting for about an hour the British weakly crumbled to pieces and retreated to the south, leaving a blood-stained armored car and a sidecar. Inspecting these first trophies of war, we discovered a blood-smeared map in the armoured car. It was accurate and showed clearly in colored pencil the enemy fortifications and dispositions around Changlun and Jitra. Such a map would obviously have been in the possession of a senior officer.

As we did not possess even one accurate map of the area, we were extremely happy to have captured this one. It was a gift for which we expressed our gratitude—especially for the penciled marks on it showing the disposition of the British troops. I at once reported the prize to the Commander-in-Chief and set out to return to Singora in the captured sidecar, calling in passing at 5th Division Headquarters, where the news had just been received of our successful attack on Pearl Harbor. It was a good omen, and the faces of officers and men alike showed unrestrained pleasure.

Army Headquarters had set up business in some houses among the coconut trees near the beach. On the afternoon of 8 December, three enemy bombing planes which had attacked Singora anchorage were attacked by our fighters but escaped. One of them was later, shot down farther along the coast. The Dream Plan had fallen through, but nevertheless General Yamashita expressed heartfelt pleasure at the successful commencement of operations by the Saeki Detachment.

Patani is a small market town on the coast between Singora and Kota Bharu. The Ando Detachment of the 5th Division (42nd Infantry Regiment with a battery of artillery and a section of engineers) landed there at a point on a road which led into the upper Perak River valley, and which was considered suitable for movement of troops and of strategic importance. Staff Officer Asaeda was detailed for duty with the main strength of this detachment, to which was assigned an important strategic task requiring a long period of independent movement.

At the beginning of the China Incident this regiment had broken through the Great Wall of China and had received a letter of commendation for its great achievement. I personally had a strong feeling for the regiment, with which I had shared the risks and hardships of the China battlefields. The regimental commander, Colonel Tadao Ando, was a skillful and experienced leader, and had attached to him Staff Officer Asaeda, an officer of exceptional qualifications, who has already been mentioned several times in this narrative. There was not the slightest doubt as to the success of the detachment.

At early dawn on 8 December the men of the detachment began to disembark on the beach at Patani, from which they had to drive the strongly resisting Thai Army. Officers and men, chest deep in water and mud, had to fight their way ashore. Staff Officer Asaeda, half buried in the mud during the bitterly fought action, found himself in a quandary. At length our troops fought their way ashore, but the assault was far from easy. Once ashore it was found that the roads were bad and the mountains precipitous. Progress was slow, for determined resistance had to be broken down. The results of this assault were, however, remarkable; it drove a powerful wedge into the enemy's flank and made the operations on the main front much easier.

The transport ships landing troops at Patani had been ordered to withdraw to Singora during the daytime to take advantage of the air protection afforded the main landing area by our fighter aircraft, but the commander of an engineer regiment in charge of landing operations at Patani neglected this precaution. As was only to be expected he was subjected to an air raid which damaged two of our best transports—fortunately after all the men and most of the arms and ammunition had been unloaded. It was the only error in the landing operations.

The Assault on Kota Bharu

KOTA BHARU WAS THE NORTHERN gate of the British Dominion of Malaya. It was the metropolis of Kelantan Province, and was the base of operations for the Royal Air Force, which had a fully equipped and well-defended aerodrome there.* Lying about two kilometers from the coast it was protected by a triple line of pillboxes and wire entanglements between it and the beach. Topographically, Kota Bharu lies in a moat formed by the arms of the Kelantan River, which here flows in several streams into the sea. In strength, the position was second only to the fortified positions of Mersing and Singapore. We believed the beach was heavily mined by the enemy and we waited eagerly—and anxiously—for our opportunity to land under protection of our fighter planes.

The Takumi Detachment detailed to capture this strong position comprised the 56th Infantry Regiment, one battery of mountain guns, two quick-firing guns, one battery of anti-aircraft guns, one company of engineers, one section of signalers, one section of medical and sanitation personnel, and one field hospital. There was a total of 5,300 men.

At midnight on 7–8 December, the three transports had anchored offshore, and despite the heavy seas that were running, successfully transshipped their troops into the boats. Then the naval escort began a bombardment of the coast as a signal to commence the landing. The enemy pillboxes, which were well prepared, reacted violently with such heavy fire that our men lying on the beach, half in and half out of the water, could not raise their heads.

Before long, enemy planes in formations of two and three began to attack our transports, which soon became enveloped in flame and smoke from the bursting bombs and from shells fired by the shore batteries. The *Awagisan Maru* after ten direct hits caught fire; later the *Ayatosan Maru* did likewise after six hits. The officers and men of the anti-aircraft detachment, although scorched by the flames, finally shot down seven enemy planes. As the fires burst through the decks of the ships, the soldiers still on board, holding their rifles, jumped over the side. Kept afloat by their lifejackets, some managed with difficulty to get into boats while others swam towards the shore. For these men it was a grim introduction to war.

Groups of enemy fighter planes attacked our launches and poured a hail of bullets into them as they drifted on the surface of the sea, but nevertheless, by degrees, most of our men got ashore and formed a line on the beach. There, as daylight came, it became impossible to move under the heavy enemy fire at point-blank range. Officers and men instinctively dug with their hands into the sand and hid their heads in

* Kota Bharu was defended by 8th Brigade, 9th Indian Division.

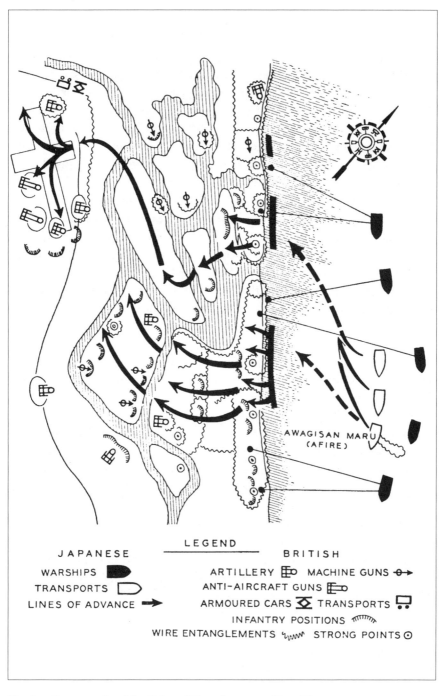

LEGEND

JAPANESE

WARSHIPS

TRANSPORTS

LINES OF ADVANCE

BRITISH

ARTILLERY   MACHINE GUNS

ANTI-AIRCRAFT GUNS

ARMOURED CARS   TRANSPORTS

INFANTRY POSITIONS

WIRE ENTANGLEMENTS   STRONG POINTS

AWAGISAN MARU
(AFIRE)

The landing assault of the Takumi Detachment at Kota Bharu.

71

the hollows. Then they burrowed until their shoulders, and eventually their whole bodies, were under cover. Their positions were so close to the enemy that they could throw hand grenades into the loopholes in the pillboxes. All the time they were using their steel helmets to dig their way farther forward, with their swords dragging on the sand beside them. Eventually they reached the wire entanglements. Those with wire-cutters got to work, but they had scarcely commenced when there was a thunderous report and clouds of dust flew up, completely obscuring the view for a time. The attackers had reached the British mined zone. Moving over corpses, the wire-cutters kept at their work. Behind them followed a few men, piling up the sand ahead of them with their steel helmets and creeping forward like moles. The enemy soldiers manning the pillboxes fought desperately. Suddenly one of our men covered a loophole with his body and a group of the moles sprang to their feet in a spurt of sand and rushed into the enemy's fortified position. Hand grenades flew and bayonets flashed, and amid the sound of war cries and calls of distress, in a cloud of black smoke the enemy's front line was captured.

Across the river was the second line. Our men did not know the depth of the water, but some who still wore lifejackets charged into the stream, sending up clouds of spray, and managed to cross the river and capture the second line at bayonet point.

Reorganizing his troops after the landing, at sunset the commander of the detachment prepared for a night attack against the enemy airfield. Heavy rain unexpectedly closed down on the battlefield, but by 8 p.m. one corner of the aerodrome had been attacked, and the whole aerodrome was occupied by midnight. Kota Bharu town was not captured until after 2 p.m. on 9 December. This victory was followed up by the capture of Tanah Merah aerodrome on the 13th, and of Kuala Kulai airfield on the 19th, which completed the destruction of the British military and air base at this northern gate of Malaya. In this action we captured 27 field guns, 73 heavy and light machine-guns, 7 airplanes, 157 motor cars and trucks, and 33 railway goods wagons.

As well as the *Awagisan Maru* and *Ayatosan Maru*, our losses totaled 320 men killed in action and 538 wounded. It was one of the most violent actions in the Malayan campaign.

I should add by way of a note of explanation that I did not personally participate in this battle. The foregoing account was compiled from reports of staff personnel, officers and men engaged in the fighting, and of press correspondents who were present.

The Last of the British Far Eastern Squadron

THE SUCCESS OF THE SURPRISE attack on Pearl Harbor had exalted Japan. The second news of a great victory came from Imperial Head quarters. Even the voices speaking through the microphones seemed to tremble with gratitude. At five minutes past four on the afternoon of 10 December, Imperial Navy Headquarters made the following announcement:

> From the outbreak of hostilities the movements of the two British capital ships have been closely observed. Yesterday afternoon they were discovered by one of our submarines carrying out a reconnaissance in cooperation with naval surface ships and the Navy Air Force. At half past eleven this morning our submarines again confirmed the position of the British ships, off Kuantan on the east coast of Malaya. Without losing a moment the Naval Air Force entered into a dauntless and daring attack and in a twinkling of the eye, attacked at about twelve forty-five. The *Repulse* was seriously damaged by the first bombs dropped and shortly afterwards the *Prince of Wales* was hit and developed a heavy list to port. The *Repulse* sank first, and shortly after, at ten minutes to three, the *Prince of Wales* blew up and finally sank.

The third day of hostilities has resulted in the annihilation of the main strength of the British Far Eastern Squadron.

This announcement, worthy of the Army, the Navy and the Air Force, caused wild excitement among the people of Japan, but of course the whole of Britain was shocked.

To encourage the men of the Army to bestir themselves in the campaign in Malaya and achieve a military record equaling that of the Navy and Air Force, I published to the troops a supplementary account of this brilliant achievement. Summarizing the newspaper reports of the time and the facts of the battle as related by officers and men of the Naval Air Force who participated in it, I issued the following report:

> On 9 December submarines reported the enemy's two battleships proceeding northward along the southeast coast of Malaya. There was no hesitation about making preparations to attack them immediately. One day's delay would be to the disadvantage of our military operations, and we waited for the troop leader's order to attack. In the midst of a strained silence a second report came from a submarine patrol. The order, "All planes prepare for immediate

departure," flew about in every direction. Early in the evening, No. 1 Squadron also sprang to its feet. It was only an hour and a half before sunset. At the destination, which was a long way off, the weather was cruelly bad. It was a stormy flight, for we struck dense clouds, fierce squalls and heavy rain. Visibility was almost zero and we flew all round the target area on what proved a hopeless reconnaissance. As soon as we returned to base we enthusiastically prepared for an attack next day. At twenty minutes to three on the morning of the tenth a submarine sent the following signal: "A battleship is in flight to Singapore at a speed of twenty knots. We hope to intercept it fifty miles south of the Anambas Islands."

Not waiting for the dawn, some planes departed in high spirits to search for the enemy. The eyes of the commanding officer shone with purpose and tension. "It is the golden opportunity of a thousand years," he said. "Let us use up all our strength." At ten minutes to eight the main bombing force and the torpedo unit set off. Providentially, the weather was good; there was not a cloud over the sea. Until a quarter to twelve there was no sign of the enemy warships. Our planes had begun to turn back with feelings of disappointment when Number Three scout plane reported five black spots under their eyes on the sea. Dropping to a lower altitude we saw the enemy ships. The radio tapped out: "The enemy's capital ships are in sight. Position four degrees north latitude, east longitude one hundred degrees fifty-five minutes. Time forty-five minutes past eleven. Morning." It was the first completely reliable report.

On receiving this communication, the aircraft of our comrades in arms flying back to base turned their noses straight to the position given. They aimed at a point fifty miles east of Kuantan. At five minutes past twelve came a second report:

"Enemy battleships are accompanied by three destroyers. Sailing in regular order, the *Prince of Wales* and the *Repulse*." Ten minutes later the bombing unit was in position to attack. Below them was a majestic sight—the superlative battleship *Prince of Wales* with the *Repulse* following and three destroyers forming a triangle around them, all steaming ahead in a single, protective formation.

At forty-five minutes past twelve the order "Attack" was given. As the bombers came down to a lower altitude, all the enemy warships opened up anti-aircraft fire. Each plane in succession dropped its heavy bombs, one of which beautifully hit the *Repulse* amidships, causing an eruption of brown fire. While the bombers were circling for a second attack, the torpedo flight flew in, half going to port of the *Repulse* and the other half to starboard of the *Prince of Wales*. They came in low over the water and launched their torpedoes. Several colossal columns of water rose beside both battleships, showing that we were hitting the mark.

The *Prince of Wales* had three twenty-five-barrel 20-millimeter pom-poms and one twenty-barrel, four eight-barrel 40-millimeter quick-firers, and sixteen secondary-armament guns as well as four 4.7-inch anti-aircraft guns. Each minute these could discharge 60,000 shells and bullets. The ship was putting up a desperate defense with every gun firing to the limit of its power. The question was, would such a barrage be able to stop our attack?

Yellow powder smoke filled the sky. The falling projectiles set up a lurid spray as if sand was being hurled all over the surface of the sea. At 1:45 a large formation of torpedo planes located the battleships, and with the commanding officer's plane in the lead began a ferocious attack on the *Prince of Wales*. Almost immediately from her hull a column of water rose higher than her mast. She had been hit again. Their torpedoes discharged, every plane flew over her bridge and machine-gunned her decks.

At this moment another unit began to attack the *Repulse*. Thunderously, a column of water rose over her stern. As it released its torpedo, the second plane of the flight exploded over the sea, a mass of flames, but at the same instant its torpedo hit the *Repulse* amidships, and for the second time a huge column of water rose beside her. Without a break from bow to stern, a deep red line of flame trailed along her deck.

As the third plane flew in with machine-guns firing, the sailors of the *Repulse* collapsed or deck before the hail of tracer bullets, which blinded even the anti-aircraft gunners. There were marines too on board who covered their faces with their hands as if to escape the sweeping fire. Shrouded in black smoke, the *Repulse* suddenly developed a heavy list while the *Prince of Wales*, some distance away on the port side, came almost to a standstill. At this moment a destroyer blew up and sank.*

Another bombing unit appeared in the sky above the bewildered battleships, which were trying to escape. Battered as the ships were, they kept on fighting in the true British naval tradition. As our attack changed to further bombing and the planes came in at lower alti-

---

* This statement is incorrect. The three destroyers accompanying the battleships, H.M.S. *Electra*, H.M.S. *Express* and H.M.A.S. *Vampire*, all survived the action.

tude, one plane made a noise as if it was being scraped with a straw broom. It had been hit by an anti-aircraft shell. The rest of the planes carried on their attack on the *Prince of Wales*. A bomb hit her afterdeck and brown flame rose from a tremendous explosion. The *Repulse*, slowly turning and circling, was on the point of sinking. Suddenly, jet-black smoke enveloped her huge hull and she disappeared. On the surface of the sea, brown oil spread among the floating debris and the two destroyers moved in to pick up survivors. The *Prince of Wales*, vomiting dense black smoke from her stern, was steaming slowly at about eight knots and listing heavily to port. Gradually her speed dropped. A destroyer pulled up close as if to lie alongside the battleship. At that moment there were two huge explosions almost simultaneously, and the great battleship—boasted unsinkable—began to go down slowly by the stern. Less than half a minute later she had sunk, and the bright southern sun shone dazzlingly on the oil spreading over the surface of the sea.

Next day, one bombing unit again flew over the scene of the bloody battle, where the waves now undulated tranquilly. A large bouquet of flowers was dropped on the spot where several thousand British seamen* who had fought so bravely were now sleeping quietly.

This is the account of the battle as reported by the units of the Naval Air Force which participated in it.

At the time of the Japanese-American negotiations immediately prior to the outbreak of hostilities, Admiral Sir Thomas Phillips had been Vice-Chief of the British Naval Staff. Just before the outbreak of war he had been appointed to the command of Britain's Far Eastern Squadron, whose flagship, the *Prince of Wales*, together with other vessels reached Singapore on 2 December.

Little more than a week later, off shore at Kuantan, this British naval commander lay at the bottom of the sea. His fate—and that of his ships—was an elegy on the fate of Singapore.

I set out below an account of the battle from a British newspaper of that time.

The British squadron was led by the flagship, the *Prince of Wales*, on a cruise up the eastern coast of Malaya. Admiral Phillips issued orders, "We are about to attack a Japanese convoy which is pro-

---

*The number of officers and men lost in the *Prince of Wales* and the *Repulse* was actually 830.

tected by ten warships. I expect you to do your duty." On the evening of 9th December he received a report that the Japanese fleet was approaching. Altering course on the morning of 10th December the *Repulse* was given the task of opposing the enemy. That day, just after noon, an undisclosed number of Japanese planes at an unknown height appeared without warning and made a dive-bombing attack on both ships. The *Prince of Wales* was hit on deck and her airplane hangar smashed to pieces. The bomb penetrated the deck, and burst in the tweendecks, enveloping them in flames. The whole crew were engaged in fire-fighting, but without success as the ship quickly began to sink. Notwithstanding the terrifically heavy anti-aircraft fire, the Japanese aircraft dropped torpedoes or perhaps repeated their bombing attack, and finally the *Prince of Wales* sank. Just before she disappeared, the crew, all of whom were covered in crude oil, were ordered to abandon ship, and jumped overboard singly and in groups, each struggling in a different direction. In the water they clung to life rafts and pieces of wood drifting about, and at length when some distance from the ship they saw a dense cloud of smoke rise to the sky as she sank, and there remained only the oil and the men floating on the surface of the sea. Several hours later some survivors were picked up by a destroyer.

The *Prince of Wales*, the British Navy's superlative new battleship, had been completed in April 1941. She was 739 feet long with a displacement of 35,000 tons and a speed of over 30 knots, and her main battery comprised ten 14-inch guns firing shells each weighing about 1,900 lbs. The range of the guns was longer than that of the previous largest 15-inch guns used by the British Navy, and their destructive power was greater.

A distinctive feature was her anti-aircraft power. She carried four airplanes and was equipped with three anti-aircraft machine cannon, each with twenty-five barrels mounted in five rows of five—the first of their kind in the world—and one other of twenty barrels. She also carried four anti-aircraft pompoms, each with eight barrels, which could fire eight hundred rounds a minute. When all these guns were firing, 60,000 bullets and shells a minute were poured into the air and fell like rain.

The *Repulse* was a battle cruiser of 32,000 tons displacement, 794 feet in length, armed with six 15-inch guns, eight 4-inch anti-aircraft guns, and eight 21-inch torpedo tubes. She carried four aircraft and had a speed of twenty-nine knots. She had been built in 1916, but had been completely modernized in 1936–39.

Sir Thomas Phillips entered the Navy in 1903 and served in the First World War. At various times he also served as an instructor at the Royal Naval College, and as a delegate to the League of Nations Land, Sea and Air Commission. In 1938 he was in command of a destroyer flotilla, and in 1939 he became Vice-Chief of the Naval Staff. In 1941 he was appointed Commander-in-Chief, Eastern Fleet, and was killed in battle only a few weeks after taking up his appointment.

A Death in Bangkok

JUST PRIOR TO THE OUTBREAK of hostilities, the policy of the Thailand Premier, Mr. Pibul, was subtle. In a dispute which had arisen over the Thailand—Indochina frontier about the time of our advance into southern French Indochina, Japan had acted as an intermediary and showed friendly solicitude towards Thailand. But it was natural that the Thais should be apprehensive about the possibility that Japan might be defeated by Britain and America. If, by any chance, Thailand allied herself with Japan and became an enemy of Britain and America, what would be her destiny? To refuse an alliance merely because of such doubts would be unworthy, but on the other hand, Thailand's support could not render any very substantial aid to Japan. From the history of Nagamasa Yamada, and the fact that they supported Japan's claims at League of Nations conferences after the First World War, notwithstanding the unfavorable atmosphere expressed in the voting of forty to one against Japan, we could understand Thailand's sympathy for Japan.

The common Buddhist religion created a deep feeling between the peoples of the two countries, and moreover the mutual advantage that lay in the exchange of Japan cheap manufactured goods for Thailand's surplus resources was of considerable importance to both countries.

The most important factor governing the attitude of the Thai Government was the desire of the Thai people to become completely independent of British influence. "Thailand for the Thailanders" was a slogan which could perhaps be achieved by the strength of the New Japan, and a demand which would strengthen daily from the time the first shot was fired in the Pacific war.

If we had entered into diplomatic negotiations before commencing operations we would have exposed all our war plans. It was better to make a bloodless advance on Bangkok with one army corps at the beginning of the hostilities, seize the capital, and then persuade the Thai Government to join our camp. The advance against Thailand was planned in accordance with this overall policy, and the responsibility of putting it into practice was given to Lieutenant-General Iida of the 15th Army. The Konoe Imperial Guards Division was then under command of that army. The plan was that this division would advance as far as possible into southern Indochina, and at the appropriate time cross the frontier and march on Bangkok. It was expected that by that time full information would be available on the position in the Thai capital. As the Imperial Guards Division was comprised of carefully selected men, there were no misgivings their behavior towards the Thai people. In addition to these considerations the fact that the division was already in Bangkok would render it easily available for the second stage of operations in Malaya, as it would be possible for the troops to catch up with the divisions already there by use of rail and motor transport.

Before dawn on 8 December the Konoe Imperial Guards Division was ready to cross the Indochina frontier at the same time as the commencement of the landing of the 5th Division at Singora. It broke through the frontier without encountering resistance of any importance, and by noon on 9 December its leading units had arrived at a position a few kilometers from Bangkok. The Iwaguro Regiment at the head of the column, and from it the Take-no-Uchi Battalion, was chosen by the regimental commander. "Select a brave and discreet officer to ascertain the state of affairs in Bangkok," he ordered. Major Take-no-Uchi had secretly anticipated such an order and immediately volunteered for the task himself. "As this duty is very important, please let me do it," he said. There was some concern about permitting the battalion commander to undertake the task—he was regarded as a Miyamoto Musashi—and on this venture there was some prospect he might be killed. However, the regimental commander, even though he regretted it, had no option but to accede to the wish of the Major.

Before long the Major and his secretary were driving south at full speed. When they reached a point close to Comuan aerodrome, just outside Bangkok, a hostile group of excited and panic-stricken Thai soldiers and civilians blocked their way. A crowd began to rock the motor car and then attacked it. The passengers in the car could not free themselves from their assailants, who were hanging to the vehicle in clusters. They tried driving at full speed, stopping suddenly and then accelerating quickly again. Every time some of the rioters were shaken off, some more jumped on. Eventually, even the veteran Take-no-Uchi had to abandon the vehicle. The swarming mob hemmed in the Major and his orderly and finally killed them.

The Iwaguro Regiment brushed aside the crowd which had blocked the path of its envoys, and ended all opposition by a bloodless advance into Bangkok.

The Major's dead body with sabre and revolver still grasped in his hands was picked up later, covered with wounds. A worthy man had been lost for a wasteful purpose. At least he had, in opening the decisive battle for Singapore, made perfectly clear his capacity for sacrifice, and thus he conquered, although he lost his life.

Twenty years had passed since Take-no-Uchi and I had shared our joys and sorrows at the Nagoya Preparatory School. He had now become one of the first victims of the Malayan campaign. That one man's death is better than the death of a thousand is a consolation to the spirit, but I found it hard to resign myself to the loss of my friend.

On 11 December, Thailand Premier Pibul and Japanese Ambassador Tsubogami reached agreement on a Thai-Japanese Treaty, and on completion of the necessary procedure it was formally signed and announced in Bangkok on 21 December.

Its terms were as follows:

For the Governments of the Empire of Japan and the Kingdom of Thai the establishment of a New Order in East Asia is the only road to the prosperity of Eastern Asia.

This agreement is made in the belief that the above-named governments have the firm will and the ability to eliminate all sources of trouble between them and that restoration of unconditional world peace is an essential matter.

Article 1. An alliance is established between the two countries, Japan and Thailand, as the foundation for respect of sovereignty and mutual independence.

Article 2. If either party is involved in military dissension with a third party, Japan and Thailand as allied powers agree to help each other by every kind of political, military and economic means.

Article 3. Matters which become operative under Article 2 shall be determined by a conference between the government agencies in Japan and in Thailand having power to deal with the matters in question.

Article 4. In the event of Japan and Thailand becoming involved in collaboration in hostilities no peace or truce shall be made except in accordance with mutual agreement.

Article 5. This Treaty becomes effective simultaneously with signatures on behalf of the two powers and it will, remain valid for ten years. The contracting countries will consult each other about renewal of the treaty at an appropriate time before the expiration of the aforesaid period.

Part Three

Breakthrough on the Jitra Line

THE MOST URGENT WORK AFTER the landing at Singora was to establish and organize Army Headquarters. Next, without delay we had to attack towards the Perak River in Kedah Province. On the evening of 9 December, after driving off an enemy detachment I caught up with the front line of the Saeki Detachment for the second time.

The Kawamura Brigade, which had completed its landing, was ordered to join the Saeki Detachment that evening, and with it break through the frontier.

Major-General Sanro Kawamura came from my native town. He had achieved a consistently high reputation from Junior Military School right through Staff College. He had shown himself courageous on the battlefield and was credited with the ability to quickly see through the general situation in battle. By chance I met him in Sadao village when he arrived there.

About an hour previously, the Saeki Detachment had moved towards the frontier for the purpose of searching out the enemy positions. Hurriedly we pursued them, and on the way twice heard heavy explosions ahead of us. We hurried on, traveling by night, and formed the opinion that the enemy was blowing up bridges. When we came to the first bridge, on the Thailand side near the frontier, we found as we expected that it had been blown from its foundations. A very powerful charge of explosive must have been used. "The British must have munitions to spare," we thought as we surveyed the damage. Our mud-stained engineers were hurrying to make repairs, but there was no time to wait for them to finish. Leaving our vehicles, we went forward on foot and started to cross the frontier. At the end of an hour we ran into the gate across the road at a customs inspection post.

Undoubtedly we were at the frontier, but there was not so much as a puppy in sight. "This is suspicious," someone remarked. "Where can the Saeki Detachment have gone? Why is there no sound of firing? Is the enemy attempting a ruse of some kind?"

It was extremely improbable that the Saeki Detachment would have detoured far off the main road, for it was impossible to move through the jungle in the darkness. The situation seemed ominous. It was quite inconceivable that an armed force could be blocked by such a crude obstacle as the gate across a frontier. It would be a relief to hear even a rifle shot.

It was in the dead of night on 9 December when I passed through the gate and stood alone at the ominous frontier. I intended to go as far forward as I could until I met with friend or foe. Watchful and sharp as a needle, I zigzagged south along the asphalt road, crossing from left to right as I advanced. When I had gone about four or five hundred meters I heard someone squirming along the roadside. I approached with stealthy footsteps, lowering my right hand to my sabre. Friend or foe? Shortly afterwards I vaguely discerned some soldiers holding rifles and wearing steel helmets. "Is that the Saeki Detachment?" I asked. "Yes, it is," came the answer.

"Where is the detachment commander?"

"Hello, Mr. Tsuji, I'm here, I'm here," replied the kindly voice of Lieutenant-Colonel Saeki from among the rubber trees nearby.

Finding that his vehicles could not cross the smashed bridges, the detachment commander, leading barely two hundred men on foot, had on his own responsibility crossed the poorly guarded frontier. He had been ordered to stop at the frontier and investigate the enemy's positions. "But," he said, "as the enemy was not there I could not investigate him."

He was as calm and self-possessed as if on maneuvers. "This man knows what he is doing," I thought, and smiled to myself. "He can certainly carry on."

Before long the detachment started to move forward. The adjutant, Captain Oshima, a young officer of the 1935 period at the Military Academy, advanced at the head of the column with two men. They walked about five hundred meters without meeting any obstacles they could not tackle. The road, which had become a trench twenty or thirty meters in depth and more than a hundred meters in length, had been blown up from its foundations. For such large-scale demolition how much explosive must have been used? "Is it the enemy we must fear?" we thought. "No! What we have to worry about is the quantity of gunpowder he has available for use."

Enemy shells began to drop behind and in front of us, and we were involuntarily fascinated by the frequency of these bombastic explosions. "Yes! It is the blind shooting which obstructs repair at the demolition points. But the range isn't too accurate, is it?" Hearing these comments by their young captain on the enemy artillery fire, the men nimbly rushed out in the intervals between the firing to look into the shell holes. "Let us go on until we meet them." Advancing southward for another thousand meters, they found their way to a small bridge about twenty meters across. It had also been so badly smashed that little trace of it was left. Crying, "Oh, again!" they crossed to the southern side of the stream, splashing through the water. We were impressed by the behavior of the men ahead. "Ah! Mr. Staff Officer, it is the enemy!" said the adjutant in breathless expectation, pulling my sleeve to attract my attention. Immediately from about ten meters in front of us doubtful voices could be heard. At finally encountering the enemy, we actually felt relieved.

The adjutant and I proceeded to take cover in the ditch on the left-hand side of the road and the enemy's machine-guns opened heavy fire. Bullets beyond count flew, dragging tails with green and blue lights overhead. "They are firing high, but will soon drop a little lower." Strange, whispering voices were heard in the rubber trees, as if a patrol lay motionless, cautiously repressing all movement while seeing how the land lay. Enemy soldiers in some strength were apparently right in front of us. Were they perhaps coming to make a sortie? Tightly grasping the handles of our sabres and unfastening the safety catches of our pistols, we stood on guard. Shells began to fall to right and left, to front and rear. A record-breaking number of blue or green signal flares were being sent up from the enemy lines—continuously, two rounds, three rounds. There were sounds of engines starting, apparently motor vehicles or armored cars of which the enemy seemed to have a large number.

Soon, one platoon of the Saeki Detachment rushed to the scene. "I say, get into that rubber plantation from the right; look sharp, the enemy is escaping." Forty or fifty soldiers, flashing their swords, charged like shepherd dogs into the darkness among the rubber trees. Voices cried out and groans could be heard sporadically amidst the reports of firearms. Meanwhile the sounds of engines appeared to move away and they gradually became fainter. Under the eyes of the sentry, and of the adjutant and his orderly concealed in the ditch, the enemy was escaping without even making a sortie, although he had many cannon and machine-guns and was menaced only by one small section with a handful of guns.

We now understood the fighting capacity of the enemy. The only things we had to fear were the quantity of munitions he had and the thoroughness of his demolitions. Some people might think it inadvisable for the Staff Officer in Charge of Operations to move at the very head of the advance guard, or perhaps they might condemn such action on his part as merely a search for glorious deeds. The adverse criticism and comments are entirely mine, and they weigh on my mind, for a moment earlier with my own eyes I had seen the skill of the enemy.

The enemy had the choice of the battlefield, and our whole plan would have to be thought out in accordance with his movements. The accurate estimation of the tactics and efficiency of the enemy and the fearless devising of measures for their defeat on the actual ground are the most excellent means for the achievement of victory. Subsequently, our tactics and leadership for the Malayan campaign were determined according to the observations made at the commencement of hostilities.

After the skirmish, one armored car and a small number of corpses and weapons were abandoned. The first prisoners of war taken were all Indian soldiers, short of stature like the Japanese. They were probably Gurkhas. However, not showing any particularly hostile feeling or sign of fear of Japanese soldiers, they were reconciled to their defeat by being arranged before the camera. It appeared that these prisoners typified the mentality of the Indian soldiers who would be fighting against us, and that they were the British Army's "goods for consumption." We heard about the situation of the enemy from these soldiers, who chattered to the extent of their knowledge. The enemy immediately ahead of us was the reconnaissance unit of the 11th British Indian division, the main forces of which were holding fortified positions between Changlun and Jitra.

Extraordinary Tactics

OUR EXPERIENCE OF BARELY MORE than one day and one night indicated that the enemy's tactics involved the complete destruction of communication points by demolition and the employment of concentrated destructive firepower from his rear positions. It was beyond doubt they would gain time by obstructing our repairs. From the frontier to Johore Strait it would probably take half a year to cover the distance of eleven hundred kilometers. Somehow or other we would have to outwit the enemy's design by baffling his tactics.

On the morning of the 10th we received a report from the engineers saying that it would take them more than half a day to repair the bridge satisfactorily. While waiting among the rubber trees for the repairs to be completed the commander of the detachment and I discussed the tactics which should be adopted from now on. As a result of this discussion we devised a plan according to the appended tactical map [on the following page]. There were some who thought that these tactics considerably underestimated our opponents, as they were such as could only be applied when the enemy was despised. However, judging from our observation of the fighting capacity of the British troops we had already encountered, it seemed quite possible to apply them.

After discussion with Major-General Kawamura, who was in command of the detachment, we decided to put the new tactics into effect. I had at once driven off in a vehicle to the rear and reported to Kawamura. His feelings on the matter were identical to mine and those of Lieutenant-Colonel Saeki. It was our opinion there was no other way, and that it should be left to Saeki to try out the method when he attacked Changlun.

This village, according to reports, was the gateway to the northern part of Kedah Province, and lay about twelve or thirteen kilometers from the frontier; it was believed to have powerful defenses. At the frontier the enemy had shown no resistance worthy of the name.

Orders for an attack on Changlun according to the tactics outlined in the diagram were received from the brigade commander, the gist of which is shown on page 89: while protecting the Changlun bridge with the advanced infantry while the engineers were completing repairs, the remainder of the Saeki Detachment, awaiting orders in the rear, would attack through the advance guard at night and in the darkness would penetrate the enemy line and throw him into disorder, then follow the retreating enemy to the south, rushing forward in the one action to the Perak River.

The strength of the Saeki Detachment was as follows: 5th Division Reconnaissance Unit (light armored and light tank units, one company each; two companies motorized cavalry), commanded by Lieutenant-Colonel Saeki; one company of medium tanks (about ten tanks); two mountain artillery guns; one platoon of engineers; one section of signalers; one section sanitation (medical) unit—grand total about five hundred men. The 21st Infantry Regiment protected the artillery unit by deploying its main strength in the rear of the front-line troops who attacked Changlun.

I had not yet witnessed the enemy's pretense of resistance, and so, accompanied by an orderly, I moved out of the rubber plantation at the north end of Changlun to observe the progress of the battle from the front line.

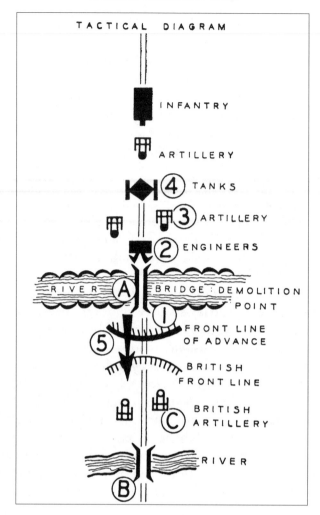

Diagram of special tactics.

Explanation:

1. The infantry, occupying forward bank at the point of demolition (A), cover repair operations.

2. The engineers, covered by the infantry, repair the bridge.

3. The main concentration of artillery neutralizes the enemy artillery (C) impeding the operations of engineers and infantry.

4. Tanks, a section of artillery, and infantry muster for a sudden attack.

5. With work on the bridge completed, the infantry advance suddenly upon the enemy positions. (For this, as far as possible, advantage should be taken of darkness or heavy rain.) After the commencement of the infantry attack, the column in readiness (4) advances quickly under cover of darkness or heavy rain, breaks through the midst of the enemy, and occupies bridge (B) before demolition can be effected.

The enemy artillery which had opened fire had, to say the least of it, about twenty guns. With the bursting of the shells among the rubber trees the enemy were covering the fighting zone with smoke, casualties were following close upon each other, and it seemed that even withdrawal would be difficult. Suddenly, heavy shells of the 10-centimeter (25-pounder) class fell close by. Yellow smoke ascended from their bursts and a strange offensive odor greeted my nose. Scarcely knowing from where it came, the troops, on hearing a voice calling "Gas!" were confused. Without a moment's delay they put on their gas masks. Such alertness and such skill! Even at a special drill display by order of the Emperor one would not have seen anything like it. "Heavens!" I exclaimed to my orderly. "We haven't even an anti-gas mask or helmet." Immediately soaking towels in wet mud we covered our mouths and nostrils. Enveloped in choking bursts with their offensive smell, we became anxious about the anti-gas gear of the whole army. We were asking ourselves, was it asphyxiating gas or tear gas? After some time had passed and our eyes and respiration were not painful, we decided that the shells were probably not gas shells. Nevertheless it was rash and exasperating not to have a gas mask. Suddenly a loud voice called out, "It is not gas." There was no reason for thinking otherwise, and all the officers and men removed their masks as if relieved from anxiety. "Just as we thought," they said. "They were not gas shells."

The engineers were bravely plunging up to their chests in the river amidst the violent shellfire, which caused their bodies to dance as they repaired the destroyed bridge. The enemy fire was concentrated on the river crossing-point. Although supported by our artillery we could not get close enough to locate enemy guns concealed among the rubber trees. After the fierce battle of destruction and restoration had continued for two or three hours, a puffy summer cloud appeared in a corner of the sky. It quickly widened and heavy rain began to fall on the combat zone. During the rain, "repairs completed" was announced, and the order "Saeki Detachment advance" was given. Enemy shells luckily deadened the noise of our tanks, and the torrential rain concealed us. It was not yet evening, but the heavy rain like a dark curtain restricted the field of vision.

Ten medium tanks cut ahead of the Saeki Detachment, crossed the bridge which had been repaired, evaded shells while enemy machine-gun bullets rebounded from their armor, and advanced like angry cattle running amok. Lieutenant-Colonel Saeki in a black motor car captured from the enemy followed immediately after the medium tanks. I had been responsible for suggesting these extraordinary tactics, and to assure myself of the results achieved by the raiding party I requested a drive in Colonel Saeki's car. The broad, level asphalt highway was not even damaged. The rain flowed like a river. Before long, while splashing along behind a tank, bullets came flying from left and right. The sound of metal striking against the car body drowned the noise of the engine and had a violent effect on one's eardrums, but it was impossible to stop—increased speed was the only way to safety. I could not see anything in the tank or even its commanding officer. It seemed that every enemy soldier had his eye on the black car in which I was driving and that they were all firing at it. We could do nothing but drive along as if with our eyes shut. After we had travelled about two kilometers we came upon a mystery. Ten guns with their muzzles turned towards us were lined up on the road, but beside them we could not find even one man of their crews. The enemy appeared to be sheltering from the heavy rain under the rubber trees but the fire issuing from sentries' huts or from tents gave the impression of coming from a formidable adversary. "It's just like a surprise attack at Okehazama,"* I thought.

Suddenly, immediately in front there were reports of rifles and hand grenades. Our tanks were ready on the road, and the twenty or so enemy armored cars ahead were literally trampled underfoot. It was a hand-to-hand fight which seemed to overstep the bounds of common sense. On each side of the road there was a deep drainage ditch and a high embankment. The enemy armored cars could not escape by running away, and were sandwiched between our medium tanks. The distance of enemy from enemy was so close that cannon and machine-guns could not be brought to bear against one another. It was speed and weight of armor that decided the issue. Excitedly we poked Colonel Saeki in the back and pointed to an enemy armored car that had turned upside down in the drainage ditch. The top was embedded four or five inches in the earth wall, and in that position the car was burning. We seized it and turned it right side up again. Risking the exposure, our troops leant over and threw hand grenades at the enemy soldiers inside who were bewildered and at a loss to know how to escape.

Blood fell as rain, flowing profusely and spreading thinly over the road surface.

Probably between two and three thousand enemy troops had taken shelter from the rain under the rubber trees on both sides of the road, and through this slight negligence they suffered a crushing defeat which by degrees they seemed to understand. Soon darkness descended on the battlefield.

---

* Okehazama—Japanese Army training ground.

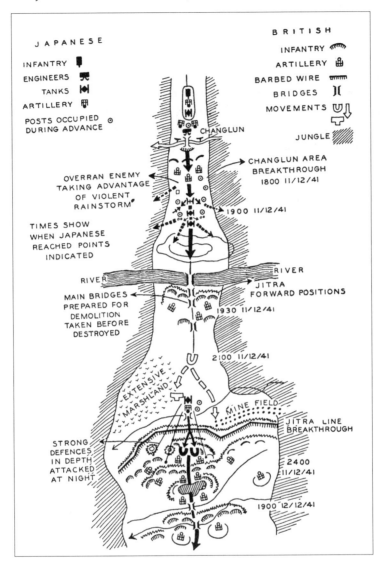

From Changlun to Jitra—map of the Saeki Detachment's breakthrough.

The enemy seemed to regard the black-painted car as easy prey. Fire was concentrated on it and at one time it appeared likely to be captured by enemy troops firing from behind the shelter of thick rubber trees. As they approached we fired at them with revolvers.

The main strength of the division realized from the gunfire in the distance that something unusual was happening. During the evening, the column which was to support the Saeki Detachment took up its position in the rear of the detachment. The detachment commander, however, following up his victory, had the will and purpose to attack as far as the Perak River.

Without casting a glance at the remnants of the enemy among the rubber trees on both sides of the road, for the second time the medium tanks were rushed to the head of the column. Everything was now pitch-black. The rain at last stopped, but it was still three or four hours until moonrise. In the darkness of Nubatama [Stygian blackness], one could not see even a meter ahead. With only the faint glimmer of the lamps of the tanks shining immediately in front on the track of the advance, we came across several bridges. At each of them we alighted from the car and made an inspection by the light of a pocket torch. Without exception, preparations had been made for their demolition—the explosive charges were laid and the electric wires connected. Promptly cutting these wires with our sabres, we hurried on the advance, thus nipping in the bud the destruction of about ten bridges. Both to our front and rear there were signs of movement of enemy troops and cars.

It is extremely unlikely that the Japanese troops were aware of the distance to which they had penetrated the enemy line. Hurrying south, to advance even one extra meter without delay, the troops did not thoroughly understand where they were going. Since the days at Saigon I had been zealously learning the map by heart, but with the rubber plantation on both sides of the road I could not see far or use my judgment as to our position. Reckoning it by the speed and running time of the car, it seemed I must be only a short distance from Alor Star, the metropolis of Kedah Province. The spirited column of our troops was watching and pouncing upon its opponents as if in a blood-crazed bullfight.

A Chance Exploit

IN THE DEAD OF NIGHT a signal shot was suddenly fired in the path of the column. A shot in answer to a shot. Identical red flares ascended to right and left, to front and rear. As if in answer to this signal, a barrage fell in front and rear of the column and for a time held up its advance. The medium tanks, which had made their wild and disorderly attack, were blocked at the approach to a demolished bridge and brought the closely packed column to a standstill on the road. This was resistance in earnest. In daylight it would be dreadful to be held in such a position by superior enemy artillery.

Lieutenant-Colonel Saeki alighted from his car on the left side of the road and walked about among the rubber trees to stretch his legs. "We will have to break through this evening," he said. I agreed with this opinion, and a number of patrols were sent out to locate the enemy guns.

Before long, one returned. "The line of advance through the enemy fortified position is not difficult," the patrol officer reported. "There are wire entanglements, but there are gaps between them, and the enemy troops are not yet in position. It seems as if a night attack would be possible." This was a most important matter. The young second lieutenant who gave us this report was a handsome youth of rather feminine appearance, as we could see by the glow of his electric torch. His name was Oto. It appeared he had crept into the enemy line and on the way back had killed a sentry who was posted at the other end of the bridge. His coat was stained with the enemy's blood. Judging by the artillery fire, the resistance we had encountered came from a fairly powerful force, but according to the report of the second lieutenant there was a chance of making a successful night attack, which was just what we wished to do. One way or another, by break of day we would find a way out of the position in which we found ourselves.

Our troops were rather uneasy, but this report was as good as a boat for the crossing. Perhaps there was even a possibility of success. Without delay the order for a night attack was given to the Nagai (No. 1) Company, to be led by Second Lieutenant Oto. The Nagai Company moved along the road in the darkness, turning towards the sound of the guns. The enemy artillery became exceedingly active. We retaliated by moving towards the enemy's position from the road front, and a violent battle developed extending all along the line. Judging from the sound, the enemy seemed to have forty or fifty guns. Would it be possible to do as we hoped and break through his line with the Saeki Detachment of barely five hundred men? Had not Second Lieutenant Oto treated the enemy rather lightly?

Shortly afterwards the enemy shellfire became concentrated on the rubber plantation around detachment headquarters. The enemy appeared to bombard this area at night as a precautionary measure irrespective of whether or not there was an objective to be fired on. The big rubber trees set up a frightful sound as one after another they were split. The position of headquarters had to be changed frequently. Clearly the military situation was not developing at all.

Just before dawn the reserve unit, No. 2 Company, was thrown into the battle line. We had no more reserves. Day dawned gradually, and with daylight it seemed that the worst possible had happened. Keeping such a matter to oneself makes one depressed in spirit. More than half the rubber trees had been mown down and the places in which one could take cover were gradually being narrowed down. About five o'clock a soldier from the front line returned to report. The upper half of his body was blood-stained. Standing motionless before the detachment commander he said, "The company commander, sir, has been killed in action, there are many casualties, but all is well." As he came to the end of his report, he fell. The surgeon examined him and found he had been wounded through the chest. He had faithfully returned with his report and collapsed, seriously wounded.

It was an astonishing position. It would be fatal to assault based on the optimistic but half-doubted report of Second Lieutenant Oto. Although knowing intuitively that the enemy was a tough one, we had forced the night attack because of our fear of becoming involved in difficulties after dawn; but the night attack had been unsuccessful and dawn had come without waiting for us. Furthermore, the main strength of the division was in the distant rear. There might not be time to prepare for this emergency. There would have to be a little more careful guidance. Thoughts of self-condemnation overwhelmed my heart. Our lives would have to compensate for our errors.

Searching everywhere for the enemy's weak point, we grew increasingly impatient as full daylight came. On the line of the road, our ten medium tanks and the light armored vehicles had become the target for the superior enemy artillery. The number of blood-covered wounded in retreat along the drainage ditch had increased. Before long there came an officer smeared with mud and blood. As he came closer I recognized him. It was Second Lieutenant Oto, who had given us his first report the previous evening. "Hello," I called. "It's only a slight flesh wound. Cheer up." Unconsciously breaking into a run as he drew near, he came up and grasped my hand. "Staff Officer, sir, it is inexcusable. Oto has made a mistake in his estimate of the enemy's strength." His tears were falling like rain. Was the wound on his right shoulder from a hand grenade? The flesh, deep red like a pomegranate, was swollen. His face was pale as if all the blood had drained out of it.

"Don't worry," I said, "we can win this battle." While sympathizing with the second lieutenant and increasing my own excitement I put into his mouth a broken piece of chocolate which had been left in the bottom of my map pouch. The second lieutenant's hot tears trickled down and fell on his mud-covered hands. "Everything is all right," I assured him. "Get to the rear quickly and get well." Putting him on a hastily constructed stretcher, some men carried him away, threading their way through the lull in the shellfire as they moved towards the rear.

There had been no report whatever from the two companies which had penetrated the enemy line the previous evening. They might have been counterattacked by superior enemy forces and perhaps annihilated.

Somehow or other we had to find a way out of our difficulties. From our left wing I walked alone into the rubber trees and saw a strange ghostly circle like scale on a grassy thicket. Looking at it carefully, I saw it was a land mine area with its front covered by wire entanglements and surrounded by two or three lines of them. How far would this strong line extend? It seemed to stretch without limit. The section on which we had made our night raid was a narrow front less than a hundred meters across the main road. The position in front seemed to be a solid, deep fortress capable of holding out for several months. It seemed absolutely beyond our power to break through.

With impatient feelings I returned to the original detachment head-quarters, and Lieutenant-Colonel Saeki, with a grave expression, said to me, "Mr. Tsuji, as commanding officer I cannot live. By my error in estimation of the enemy's movements I have made a lifelong failure. A great many of the men under my command have been massacred. I will now leave for the front line. I mean what I say."

I replied, "This is a battle conducted by the Chief of Army Operations Staff. If there be a failure, the whole responsibility falls on me. But the position is not yet desperate. Let us try to break the deadlock. Please wait a while." And thus with difficulty I consoled him. If Colonel Saeki were killed, I felt that I could not go on living. Without a moment's delay we would have to bring forward the main strength of the division, but under such heavy bombardment it seemed there was no passage through for either telephone message or orderly. "Kindly lend me your car," I said to Lieutenant-Colonel Saeki. "Mr. Tsuji," he replied, "through this shellfire, how. . . ?" Seeing he was doubtful about the prospects of the car getting through the barrage area, I pushed him back, jumped into the car with the driver, and drove off at full speed, safely breaking through the barrage. Shells burst close to front and rear, to left and right, and often the body of the vehicle rose from the ground, but mysteriously, no shells hit the car or us in it.

About four kilometers to the rear, Major-General Kawamura, although uneasy about the artillery fire so close at hand, had not yet accelerated the move forward of the main body of our troops.

It was a little after noon when we arrived at the rear headquarters of the Saeki Detachment. Taking a survey patrol in my car, I again drove through the barrage after passing on the alarm to Colonel Okabe, com-mander of the Okabe Regiment, who had just paused for lunch among the rubber trees. We urged the artillery regimental commander to get his guns into position speedily. Our party suddenly became filled with enthusiasm. The survey patrol—the eyes of the artillery—moved to a point just behind the front line, and under their direction the guns began to rain well-aimed shells into the enemy position. Gradually it appeared we had extricated ourselves from a critical position.

Soon afterwards the Okabe Regiment deployed a battalion to the left of the Saeki Detachment and then made a detour to the rear of the enemy. We were now perhaps evenly matched with our opponents. However, as a daylight attack was difficult, the divisional commander decided to wait until sunset, meantime putting our full strength in order for a night attack.

The sun was sinking and preparations for the night attack had been completed when, unexpectedly, there came a report from the front line: "Enemy soldiers retreating."

Rapidly advancing, with not a hair's breadth between the regiments ahead of us, we rushed in over the heads of the crumbling enemy. From reports of prisoners we knew we were at the Jitra line, and that this position had taken roughly six months to construct. It was defended by one division, which it had been believed would be able to stem the advance of the Japanese Army for at least three months.*

The casualties of the Saeki Detachment had been twenty-seven killed in action and eighty-three wounded—a total of one hundred and ten men. The enemy retreated, leaving behind as souvenirs about fifty field guns, fifty heavy machine-guns, about three hundred trucks and armored cars and provisions and ammunition for a division for three months. Casualties suffered by the enemy were not clear to us, but over three thousand surrendered after having thrown away their arms in panic and taken refuge in the jungle, from which they were driven out by hunger after several days. The majority of these were Indian soldiers.

The breakthrough of the Jitra line was due to extraordinary tactics and to an error in the report of our first patrol. If we had judged this well-fortified position correctly, launched a full-scale attack with the whole strength of the division, and become locked in the struggle, it would have taken more than ten days to break through, and we would have had to be prepared for over a thousand casualties.

The much-bragged-about Jitra line, which was to have been defended by a division for three months, was penetrated in about fifteen hours by barely five hundred men.

---

* The Jitra line garrison comprised: *main road*, 15th Brigade (1st Leicesters, 2/2nd Gurkhas, 2/9th Jats); *main road to west coast*, 6th Brigade (2nd Battalion East Surreys, 1/8 and 2/16th Punjabs).

If the handsome, pitiful Second Lieutenant Oto had not reported wrongly, even the courageous commander of the Saeki Detachment would not have been expected to make such a reckless attack. Undoubtedly it was a glorious exploit. It could not even be considered common sense. But often actual conditions on the battlefield determine hazardous issues. Our success was due to the intangible belief in victory resulting from scores of insubstantial factors.

The thoroughly equipped forces which we had seen on our way to the attack caused fears which even now, after so long a time, I can still feel. The wire entanglements were spread in several lines, the innumerable trenches were deep. Shells were piled up like mountains, as too were gasoline, provisions, ammunition, and so on. However, all this only exaggerated the strength of the Jitra position.

Our officers and men who since embarkation had been living on dry bread and salt and had been fighting for several days found tobacco, cakes, and tinned foods piled up chock-full in a storehouse in the rubber plantation. They were, however, disappointed. There was no time to waste, so, with rifles slung over their shoulders, and with as much food and tobacco as they could carry in their hands, they hurried along the road to the south. "Churchill's allowance is a delicacy, isn't it?" they commented as they continued their advance, forgetting even that they were tired. Before long this storehouse was taken over by our communications unit. Considering things from the practical angle, the communications unit could not wait at the landing point at Singora for the unloading of ammunition, provisions and gasoline. So without waiting for transport, each man had been moved to the front with dry bread and rice sufficient for only a few days in accordance with the plan: "Depend upon the enemy for rations."

We had to be grateful to General Percival, not only for provisions for the men but also for cars and gasoline abandoned in abundance. If such tactics as these could be kept up, then our fighting officers and men would not go hungry. Speaking to an English engineer officer taken prisoner, I asked, "How long did you think this fortified position would hold out?"

He replied, "Held by the full strength of the 11th Division, I believed it would hold out for three months at the least."

"Your reason?" I asked.

"With the jungle and swampy ground as natural obstacles on both sides of the road, northern Malaya was made into a defense zone with three lines of entrenchments which took our engineers six months to construct. As the Japanese Army had not beaten the weak Chinese Army after four years' fighting in China, we did not consider it a very formidable enemy."

Asked what roughly was the disposition of troops in the Jitra line, he replied, "In effect there were three lines. Utilizing the swamp as the front line, we obstructed the approach of the Japanese Army by blowing up the bridges and thus caused delay. This was called the Atan line. For the second line as the principal position we used the jungle to the full, equipping it with wire entanglements, land mines, and anti-tank trenches. This line was constructed very solidly. Building the third line deep in the rear, we used the contours of the land to the fullest extent."

"What was the reason for the feeble breakdown?" I asked.

"God alone knows," he answered. "To attack this position you should have had more than one division. It seems that knowing a large force was already landing, the Japanese Army rushed in to the attack, and I thought they made a detour to our rear."

I said, "We really made a night attack with less than five hundred men."

"That was very foolish," he replied.

"What about your divisional commander?" I then asked him, but all he could say was that his whereabouts were unknown.

Second Lieutenant Oto, whose report had launched the attack, was sent back to the rear to Saigon Field Operations Hospital, but he developed gangrene and died. I had the feeling that the flower which had just bloomed was shattered in the storm of one night. When I returned to Japan at the end of the war, Oto's brother one evening paid an unexpected visit to my small house. He looked exactly like the second lieutenant. He owned a large wine shop at Mihara in Bitchu, and brought me some homemade wine as a present.

"I am extremely worried that my younger brother while on patrol misjudged the enemy's position and so caused the sacrifice of many of our officers and men. Please tell me the truth," he said, with an anxious expression on his face. Unconsciously I straightened myself. The newspaper article which reported my talks just after my return had reported incorrectly and thus caused much suffering. "No," I said, "this report was surely not the correct one, but that was because he was too brave and crept into the enemy's position so easily that he judged their strength was much weaker than it was. If at that time he had reported that their position was unusually strong, even the Japanese Army might not have made such a reckless night attack. However, the division brought the matter to a conclusion with the loss of a hundred men."

Afterwards I met Oto's mother. I have deep feeling for the children of this mother—the elder brother and the younger brother. I feel sorry even today for the loss of a valuable youth.

The Churchill Supplies

ALOR STAR IS THE CENTER of Kedah Province. It should have been well worth fighting for by the enemy as it was also the center of the defenses of northern Malaya, but the nearby Jitra line, which should have held out for three months, collapsed in fifteen hours so that any delays in our advance were transitory. Even the bridges across the large river flowing on the north side of Alor Star, because of incomplete demolition, were crossed by our motor cars in less than an hour.

We pushed forward with the advance party, heading towards a large, paved aerodrome which I had observed during my trip in the reconnaissance plane before the outbreak of hostilities, and unexpectedly found that it was scarcely damaged. Here was a gift of bombs piled high, and moreover in one of the buildings hot soup was arranged on a dining room table: Among the surrounding rubber trees one thousand drams full of high-grade ninety-two-octane petrol were piled up. About noon that day our planes successfully made their first landing at Alor Star. Completing their preparations that evening, one squadron of fighter planes and one squadron of light bombers pushed forward and carried further our brief attack over the heads of the retreating enemy, using the enemy's abandoned gasoline and bombs. To our fighter groups who had risked their lives protecting our convoy of transport ships these were most acceptable gifts.

When Major-General Kawamura arrived in the city of Alor Star, the enemy, who had been slow to escape, were firing from houses everywhere, shooting from second-story windows. Mopping up was proceeding throughout the town. Standing at a street corner in the dead of night among the flying bullets, Major-General Kawamura, hardly pausing for breath, urged the troops, "To the south! To the south!" But he was taking a great risk.

There were a road bridge and a railway bridge across the large river flowing by the southern side of the city. We attempted to seize these before the enemy could destroy them. A daring raid by a party of eleven men under Lieutenant Asai attacked the road bridge. Riding in sidecars they pushed ahead of the infantry and arrived at the bridge at 10:10 a.m. on 13 December. Under heavy fire, with Corporals Kaneko and Nakayama, the lieutenant immediately charged across to the southern end of the bridge. They cut the electric wires leading to the demolition charges with their sabres, but just as they did so there was a tremendous roar and the whole bridge and fragments of flesh flew into the air. All that was left was the remains of the bridge foundations. Corporals Kaneko and Nakayama penetrated the enemy line on the south side of the bridge and killed a number of men, but they were outnumbered, and Nakayama was killed and Kaneko wounded. The enemy, perhaps expecting an immediate attack in greater strength, stampeded and retreated to the south.

Another raiding unit, moving abreast of the Asai patrol, proceeded to attack the railway bridge higher up the river. By great good fortune they were able to make a perfect seizure and cut the electric wires before the demolition charges were exploded. By spreading thick boards along the bridge decking it was possible for motor cars to cross the bridge soon after.

The subsequent pursuit made great gains. By high-speed assaults on Taiping and Sungei Patani, the four large military aerodromes in Kedah Province were captured almost undamaged—we were able to repair them and put them into use in half a day. We called these "the Churchill aerodromes." They were provided with abundant equipment, ammunition, fuel and provisions. We were pleasantly surprised.

Our hurriedly constructed air base in southern Indochina could not be compared in equipment with these new airfields. Possession of twofold numerical air strength was one reason for our superiority over the Malayan theater of operations, but the decisive factor was that we were able to take immediate advantage of the captured "Churchill aerodromes."

Advancing with the Calendar

THE DAY AFTER THE CAPTURE of Alor Star, Army Headquarters moved into the city. It was barely four days since we had left them at Singora, but it seemed a long time. Extending a heavy hand, General Yamashita said, "Thanks for your trouble. You have done well," and he was good enough to entertain us hospitably. We forgot the fatigue of our several days' unceasing activity, and our tears flowed. The face of Second Lieutenant Oto, who had apologized by saying, "There is no excuse for making a mistake in the enemy's movements," and that of Saeki, the detachment commander, as he excitedly exclaimed, "Already it is the end," floated before my eyes. It was our thanks to the revered victims.

Staff Officer Hongo, who had sprained his ankle when disembarking, had not received any medical treatment. Now, getting about with the aid of a pine walking-stick, he hobbled along at the head of the railway unit, hastening repairs of the line where it had been smashed. The young staff officer Kunitake, who was to carry out attacks with small boats along the west coast of Malaya, zealously prepared transport by road and rail to

Alor Star for the motor boats from which we had landed at Singora. Staff Officer Asaeda was fighting in the jungle with the Ando Detachment. Staff Officers Sugita and Hayashi were making desperate efforts to ascertain the enemy position by interrogating prisoners of war and inspecting captured documents. Thereupon, while avoiding any interference in matters which concerned the Staff Officer in Charge of Operations, they drew up an operational plan which worked perfectly, like the cogwheel of a watch. Basing their ideas on experience, they modified a section of the operational plan approved by the Army Commander and suggested the following five-point course of action:

1. The main strength of the Imperial Guards Division and the 5th Division would rapidly push forward to the Perak River line while a section of the 5th Division seized Penang. Preparations for the seizure of Kuala Lumpur would next be made.
2. The Takumi Detachment would as rapidly as possible capture Kuantan, moving overland, and after putting all aerodromes in working order would move towards Gemas or Kuala Lumpur. If the situation so required the detachment would be reinforced by two additional infantry battalions from the 18th Division landing at Kuantan.
3. Headquarters and remaining units of the 18th Division would be landed in the neighborhood of Mersing to cut off the retreat of the enemy.
4. To the south of Kuala Lumpur the Imperial Guards Division, the 5th Division and the Takumi Detachment would attack the main enemy forces retiring from the north towards Johore and isolate them from Singapore.
5. The Imperial Guards Division, the 5th Division and the 18th Division would assault and swiftly occupy Singapore.

While painstakingly picturing the strength of the enemy to be encountered, the extent of the demolitions to be expected, the time necessary for repairs to roads, bridges and railway, topographical features of probable enemy defense positions, and our own strength for attack, I made an entry in my diary of anticipated dates:

1. Crossing of Perak River, approximately 15 December.
2. Occupation of Kuala Lumpur, 14 or 15 January.
3. Arrival at Johore Bahru, 31 January.
4. Occupation of Singapore, 11 February, the anniversary of the coronation of the Emperor Jimmu (660 B.C.).

As our subsequent progress demonstrated, this forecast almost hit the mark. Kuala Lumpur was occupied a little earlier and the reduction of Singapore was four days behind the date estimated. The paper plan was realized almost as if the pages had been torn off a calendar. Our success was an unsurpassed pleasure, but the making of that calendar was a task so laborious that it might have been engraved on my bones. Fully recognizing the fighting power of the enemy, we had to analyze our own effective strength.

Our plan to capture such an important enemy position as Singapore on the anniversary of the coronation of the Emperor Jimmu was made the precedent for the whole Japanese Army; yet subsequently, on battlefields other than those of Malaya, attempts were made to repeat our performance without due regard for the condition of the frontline troops concerned, and examples of failure were not few. One conspicuous case of failure was in the operations against Imphal in the Burma theater. The staff there did not reconnoiter carefully, and working only on an academic desk plan they pushed forward their front line without proper preparation to capture the well-fortified position of Imphal on the anniversary of the Emperor's birthday. The attack was a complete failure.

To believe the Divine Wind* will always blow for us on this National Celebration Day is a desecration of the gods.

The Okabe Detachment (21st Infantry Regiment) took over from the Saeki Detachment the lead of the 5th Division in pursuit of the retreating enemy, and pressed hard on their heels for the next twenty-four hours, never slackening pressure. When the head of the column arrived at Gurun they found the enemy strongly entrenched there.** The position was more easily defended and more difficult to attack than Jitra. In front of the position was a wide expanse of paddy fields affording an excellent field of fire for the enemy. Only one road passed through the area.

After the enemy's defeat at Jitra we expected a desperate resistance, believing that the enemy had been strongly reinforced with newly arrived troops. On the afternoon of the 13th, fierce fighting commenced, and by evening it appeared as if the enemy were not going to be easily driven from their positions. Our frontline battalion was fighting a bit-

* The Divine Wind (*kamikaze*)—a typhoon which in 1281 destroyed the fleet of the Mongol emperor Kublai Khan, foiling his invasion of Japan.
** Gurun was held by the 6th and 28th Gurkha brigades, with the 15th Brigade in reserve.

terly contested battle. It was commanded by Major Kobayashi, an old classmate whom (as I have mentioned) I had met again on the morning of the Singora landing.

In the dead of night Major-General Kawamura, the brigade commander, gave me the use of a car. To observe a night raid, he and I hurried to the front line and ran into enemy shellfire, which was concentrated on the road. We stopped and jumped out. In my mind was the fear that the brigade commander might be injured. After taking cover in the ditch by the roadside for some time, we again returned to the car. There, amid the flashes from bursting shells which dazzled us and the noise of the explosions which shook the ground, I suddenly felt as if I had been stabbed in the buttocks with burning chopsticks. Blood poured down my thigh and began to seep through my trousers. The stains, which looked black in the moonlight, gradually spread. The wound was in a soft part and it bled freely. No bones appeared to be damaged. The wound was slight, but it was not in a good area. I felt small while being bandaged. By degrees, pressure of the bandage on the wound stopped the flow of blood. It was the fourth time I had been wounded since my first battle. As time passed, the blood congealed and my trousers became stiff. Next morning, when we began to advance on foot, I felt a pain as if I were being stabbed high on the inside of my right heel. Pulling off my long boots to investigate, I found a shell splinter in my little toe; the blood which had oozed out had stiffened like starch, causing the boot leather to cut into my foot above the heel as I walked.

On the early morning of the 14th we penetrated to an important crossroad. At this place vast quantities of munitions were piled up like a mountain on the roadside; several trucks laden with provisions stood abandoned as if to welcome our army. Sitting in the first vehicle, grasping the steering wheel, was the corpse of an English soldier, the top of whose head had been cut off by a shell. A group of Indian soldiers who had been taken prisoner were sitting around in a circle smiling and chattering. Then a European officer, also taken prisoner, came along. He was a first or second lieutenant. At sight of him forty or fifty Indian soldiers, with a solemn expression, instinctively sprang up and courteously saluted him. Was the dignity of the Englishman who confronted the Indian soldiers that of a strong man? That instinctive standing up and saluting, which manifested itself even in the backwash of the battlefield, made those Indians seem like slaves.

Thinking I would like to thank my old classmate Major Kobayashi, who had been fighting desperately from yesterday through the morning, I inquired for him at his battalion. I found him stretched out on a six-foot bench, sleeping as if he were dead. It would be a shame to waken him. From my wallet I took some tobacco and placed it quietly by his head. Then, driving away in the car, we hurried to the head of his unit, which was attacking alternately with the Kobayashi Battalion. Here we secured booty: cars for driving purposes, and liberal provisions of gasoline. The "Churchill supplies" included tinned food and bread, but at the moment it was not convenient to stop for a meal.

The Capture of Penang

THE ISLAND OF PENANG WAS not only a commercial center, but also a fortress second only to Singapore. Even though its defenses were incomplete, we believed they were powerful.

Our first operations plan provided that Penang should be captured by the regiment of the 5th Division which was still in Shanghai at the time of the Singora landing.

If reinforcements from Britain arrived at the right time and the enemy counterattacked from Penang, it would have been possible for them to delay our thrust towards Singapore; also, with an aggressive enemy holding the island, there would have been a constant threat to our communications between north and south. From the point of view of caution it was therefore common sense to safeguard our rear by capturing Penang in the first stage of operations. If we advanced south ward without taking Penang, but only glaring sideways so to speak, we would always be worried that the enemy might plunge a dagger into our flank.

The day we unexpectedly broke through Jitra, a full-strength air attack was made on the island. From its base in southern Indochina our Air Force set out and divebombed enemy shipping moored in Georgetown Harbor and burned and destroyed the greater part of the port.

We had destroyed the Jitra line and entered Alor Star like a tidal wave. According to Malayan refugees who had fled there after the bombing of Penang, the garrison of the island* had been moved up to the front line at Jitra, but had not arrived there. Withdrawn from Penang with its morale good, it had panicked on receipt of news of the crushing defeat at Jitra. It was therefore not difficult to imagine that the British had been given a heavy blow that they would remember.

---

* The 5/4th Punjab Regiment, which garrisoned Penang, had been withdrawn to the mainland. Part of it was used in an advance to The Ledge, across the Thai frontier; the remainder to reinforce the 11th Indian Division after its losses at Jitra.

We could not miss such a golden opportunity, and the 5th Division decided to send the Kobayashi Battalion with a battery of artillery and a section of engineers to launch a surprise attack on Penang.

On 15 December in the early morning, using boats found locally, they made a surprise landing and took possession of the whole island without losing even one man. The men of the garrison who had moved out to Jitra and Alor Star, and learned of the defeat of their main forces there, were completely exhausted on their return to the old spider's web which their defense plan appeared to be, and they were welcomed by a Japanese flag flying on the wharf. The capture of Penang was an important supplementary gain to the overwhelming victory at Jitra, and it definitely removed the greatest obstacle in the way of our scheduled advance.

Penang Island is as beautiful as a painting, with coconut trees and betel palms on its sandy beach. The center of the island is Malaya's most notable scenic spot. About 2,700 feet above sea-level, in the Gokurakuji [Buddhist paradise] Temple the tablet that had been signed years ago by Admiral Togo and General Nogi* while touring the temple still hung as if to welcome our troops.

The Perak River Obstacle

THE ANDO DETACHMENT, WHICH HAD reduced the obstinate resistance of the Thai Army after landing at Patani, did not find it an easy matter to join the rest of the division at the Perak River. Their objective was to seize the Perak River bridges (both road and railway) at the first opportunity. Stealing a march on the main strength of our army, by day and night they moved rapidly south along the mountain road through the jungle.

It had been generally believed that in exceedingly dense, luxuriant jungle, with vines climbing around great towering trees, little movement would be possible except on the road. But, after crossing the Malay frontier, the Ando Detachment found fortified positions and obstructions constructed by the British Army. Judging from the evidence, there is no doubt that the British invaded Thai territory prior to our landing.

The six-foot staff officer, Yutaka Asaeda, putting on rubber shoes, advanced at the head of our column with the spearhead commander. Approaching the frontier town of Betong, a group of soldiers was seen on the high ground. Asaeda thought to himself, "Probably it is the Thai Army. I expect a truce has already been made with them. They are

---

* The commander of the Japanese Fleet and the Commander-in-Chief of the Japanese Army in the Russo-Japanese War of 1904–5.

defending their frontier against the English Army." Having come to this conclusion, the staff officer nimbly scrambled up the hill. The swarthy-colored, queer-style soldiers looked at him strangely. Laughing, with a pleasant face and without ceremony he approached them saying, "Don't worry." As he tapped the shoulder of one of these unfamiliar foreigners, the Indian soldier, who should have been a Thai, turned and shot from the hip at him with an automatic rifle. Unscathed, quickly cutting down several of the enemy, Asaeda stumbled down the hill and rejoined our spearhead. He had escaped by a hair's breadth.

After an obstinate resistance the Indian soldiers were put to flight, and the Ando Detachment, fighting on a bad road, crept through the jungle, eating fruit, and moved towards the bridge at Kuala Kangsar earnestly and without rest.

When the main strength of the division reached Taiping after the capture of Alor Star, the Ando Detachment signaled that it had been strongly counterattacked the previous day by European troops* at the mouth of a narrow defile. The report stated that the detachment was within about a day's march of the Perak River bridges, and that in one way or another they would reach their objective, but that at the moment the enemy, on high ground, blocked the advance.

After the seizure of the Taiping aerodrome, I hurried by air to visit the Ando Detachment, flying in a "Direct Contact Machine" (a small two-seater reconnaissance plane) detailed for service with the Army. Enemy fighter planes were operating from Ipoh aerodrome nearby. As a large number of enemy planes were returning to their base after a sortie over Taiping, we took off immediately after they left.

Feeling like a young sparrow stealing an eagle's eye, we flew between formations of enemy planes and turned towards the Perak River bridges. This reconnaissance was dangerous and not at all easy. Our eyes were flashing like those of a peregrine falcon. Second Lieutenant Imai, the pilot, directed his attention especially towards watching for enemy planes, while I concentrated mine on the neighborhood of Kuala Kangsar bridge, which I saw was not yet demolished.

Enemy vehicles frequently moved south across the road bridge and large numbers of infantry were marching northward. This was surely significant. We dropped to five hundred meters so that in our reconnaissance we should not miss anything. Obviously there was still a powerful force of the enemy on the north bank of the Perak River counterattacking the Ando Detachment, but it would only be a few days before the bridge

---

* Evidently the Argyll and Sutherland Highlanders.

was blown up. To ignore this position and allow the enemy to demolish the bridge would be foolish. The Ando Detachment would have to make an opportunity to send a powerful raiding patrol into the enemy rear, and without a moment's delay information on the enemy's position had to be given to Staff Officer Asaeda.

Turning towards the Ando Detachment line of advance, we flew low over the enemy rear. The battlefield was hidden by jungle and rubber trees and we could not see the enemy troops, but rising from the jungle we saw about twenty columns of white smoke such as comes from the burning of cotton waste. More than twenty enemy guns were holding up the advance of the Ando Detachment, the position of which was now becoming desperate.

It was impossible to make even the remotest guess at the location of our own and the enemy infantry lines. We dropped the plane to an altitude of one hundred meters and glared at the ground with eyes like those of an eagle watching a rabbit, but we could not see anything. Several bullets pierced the fuselage of our machine. Presently we changed course from north to south. Then we saw a Japanese soldier rushing about, and reducing speed we eventually discovered the location of the Ando Detachment headquarters. On some vacant land at the roadside by the edge of the rubber trees the Japanese flag stood out clearly, and, with this as a guide, I dropped a communication tube. My message was as follows:

Commander of the Ando Detachment and Mr. Staff Officer Asaeda from Staff Officer Tsuji.
1. Esteemed detachment, heartfelt thanks for your heroic fighting for several days in succession.
2. The main strength of 5th Division penetrated Taiping this morning.
3. The Perak River bridge is still intact and enemy infantry is moving northward over it. Pay attention to vehicles moving south. To the limit of your ability make a raid on the southern bank of the Perak River from upstream. Take possession of the southern end of the bridge before it is demolished by the enemy. Your cooperation is desired. I pray it may be your last desperate fight.

Finally I dropped some tobacco and cake to the soldiers who picked the message up. They looked up yearningly at us as they waved their grimy towels. Several officers appeared from among the rubber trees. Perhaps Colonel Ando and Staff Officer Asaeda were among them. We were too far off for them to answer if we called. Praying the detachment would stand firm now that their objective was within reach, we returned to Taiping.

But our exhortation and the strenuous efforts of the detachment were not sufficient to easily defeat the desperate counterattack by an enemy several times the detachment's strength. The Perak River, which we had long recognized as an obstacle, now appeared even more formidable. The river was more than five hundred meters wide, fast-flowing and of unknown depth. If the enemy blew up the bridges and relied on this natural stronghold, he could easily hold the position for a month.

According to information received from our Air Force, enemy reinforcements were moving northward in rapid succession from Kuala Lumpur. The 11th Division, which had been defeated at Jitra, was assembling the remnants of its troops in this natural stronghold. They seemed to have already been reinforced by about one brigade of infantry, and a detachment was obviously being concentrated in front of our Ando unit. There were some among us who urged striking, somehow or other, at the exhausted enemy on the north side of the Perak River.*

Major-General Endo, commanding the light bombers of our Air Force, shrewdly and heroically cooperated with the ground forces throughout the Malayan campaign. He was a man whose opinions were highly valued. He had made great strides in establishing his units at Sungei Patani airfield, and sought our views on a new plan for seizure of the Perak River bridges.

"The enemy's demolition charges are probably at the southern end of the bridges," he said. "Upon withdrawal of the enemy from the north bank there is no doubt the bridges will be blown up immediately. Tomorrow we should set out with all our planes concentrating with light bombs on the southern end of the bridges to cut the electric wires connected to the demolitions and so prevent them exploding. Later we can keep up continuous bombing to prevent any approaches to the southern end of the bridges."

This was indeed a new principle. Up until now, planes had been used to blow up bridges. Now they were to be used to stop them from being blown up by the enemy. We returned to Army Headquarters at dawn on 22 December, agreeing to put the plan into operation. That evening we could not sleep, praying for the success of the Ando Detachment patrol, and hoping the enemy on the north side of the river would not retreat

---

* The Perak crossing was held by the remnants of the 11th Division, and by Kroh force, withdrawn from The Ledge, together with reinforcements from the 12th Indian Brigade.

too quickly. About midnight a boom like distant thunder was heard in the south. "Ah, that's it!" we thought. It was the evil sound of the complete blasting of the two bridges over the Perak River, as I had seen it in a dream. The British Army had blown up the bridges and abandoned several thousand Indian soldiers on the north bank of the river. When fighting the Japanese Army, it is the British Army which excels in retreat; in the Japanese Army there would have been no blasting until it was certain that the last of our comrades in arms had crossed the river.

On 22 December in the early morning, the Ando Detachment charged into Kuala Kangsar. As the objective of their landing at Patani had not been accomplished, the officers and men of the detachment viewed the ruins of the bridges with anger and disappointment, but moved on rapidly to seize the pontoon bridge at Blanja farther down the river. When they arrived on the river bank there, however, they found that even the thick mooring rope of the pontoon bridge had been cut and the pontoons themselves were full of holes. The Army's plan to occupy the Perak River bridges and to forestall the enemy's demolition had completely broken down, but a counter-plan was immediately evolved to enable us to meet the situation.

Crossing the Perak River

AT THE COMMENCEMENT OF HOSTILITIES the Konoe Imperial Guards Division, which had advanced into Bangkok, had ended its mission because of the cooperation of Premier Pibul. The 5th Division had continued severe fighting and hot pursuit for two weeks after disembarkation without even one day's rest. Signs of exhaustion could be seen. Consequently it was necessary to move the Guards Division in to support the 5th Division on the battlefield. Just as the medieval champions, Takatsuna and Kagetoki, had vied with each other in crossing the Uji River, so the Guards Division and the 5th Division, lined up before the Perak River, would increase our fighting strength by their rivalry.

However, although the best brains of the Guards Division had been instructed about the Army plan before leaving Saigon, it seemed they had little enthusiasm for the idea of making rapid progress on the battlefield.

The troops of the Imperial Guards were hurried forward rapidly so that the advance guard arrived in Taiping on 22 December, but the divisional commander did not arrive until a day later. In a movement such as this it would have been proper for the Divisional Headquarters to hasten, but it seems that the leaders had a tendency towards dignity and grandeur in the execution of orders given them by Army. They moved towards Kuala Kangsar to prepare for a river crossing there and a subsequent attack towards Ipoh. It was anticipated that by the morning of 24 December the division would have concentrated its engineers, a battery of artillery, and a full regiment of infantry in its forward area.

The 5th Division was to cross the river in the neighborhood of Blanja and attack towards Kuala Lumpur through Kampar in one mighty drive. The boats used at the Singora landing were loaded on cars together with the collapsible boats (small motor launches which folded up and could be carried by a few men). Complete with engines, these were set up on the river bank as they arrived and could be used for the crossing at any hour. These preparations took time, but a week was not a long period to prepare for crossing such a large river in the face of the enemy, and thorough preparation was only a common sense precaution.

The Guards Division, earlier in the campaign, had believed it would be able to march leisurely across the bridges, and if necessary to hold consultations in the event of any delay. Their mentality was complex.

Some had formed the opinion that the 5th Division would cross the river single-handed, but the position developed that "Takatsuna" and "Kagetoki" were now indeed competing with each other in meritorious deeds. When telephone inquiries were made of General Matsui, commanding the 5th Division, he always answered, "At what time will the Konoe Imperial Guards cross?" and when any questions were asked of the Guards Division the answer came back, "How is the 5th Division?"

The Army Commander gave his decision. "We will begin to cross the river on 26 December at twenty hundred hours," he said, basing his decision on information received concerning the movements and morale of enemy troops.

General Yamashita's decision was contrary to the expectations of both divisions, each of which had believed it would be ordered to move when ready. The 5th Division, elated with its success at the beginning of the campaign, said, "We will manage the crossing somehow or other," while the Guards Division, competing for the honors, said, "We must not lose." The divisional commanders were already pawing the ground with impatience at being held up before this natural stronghold.

Having completed the issue of Army Orders, I was able to spend a full day at Army Headquarters for the first time since disembarkation at Singora. Headquarters were located in the Taiping Middle School, where, from the point of view of supplies and business, there was an atmosphere of serenity suggestive of Saigon. On their way through the rubber trees during the advance the soldiers had caught monkeys by

1 Berlin, February 1941. Lieutenant-General Yamashita presenting a sword to
Field Marshal von Brauchitsch, Commander-in-Chief of the German Army.
Courtesy of Australian War Memorial.

3 "Battered as the ships were, they kept on fighting in the true British naval tradition."

Opposite: **2** "The bombing unit was in a position to attack. Below them was a majestic sight — the superlative battleship *Prince of Wales* with the *Repulse* following."

4 "The Hyaku shiki Shitei was an up-to-date, powerful, two-engined reconnaissance plane."—The type of aircraft ("Dinah") in which the author made pre-war flights over Malaya. Courtesy of Australian War Memorial.

5 "The golden opportunity of a thousand years." —An aircraft searching for the *Prince of Wales* and the *Repulse*, 10 December 1941.

6 & 7 "Should we side with Germany just because of Hitler's and Ribbentrop's bluster?" Foreign Minister Matsuoka in Berlin, March 1941, with (*above*) von Ribbentrop, the German Foreign Minister. Courtesy of Australian War Memorial.

8 Field Marshal Count Terauchi, Commander-in-Chief of Japan's Southern Armies.

9 Lieutenant-General Nishimura, Commander of the Konoe Imperial Guards Division. Courtesy of Australian War Memorial.

10 Major-General Endo, commanding officer of Japanese light bombers during the campaign. Courtesy of Australian War Memorial.

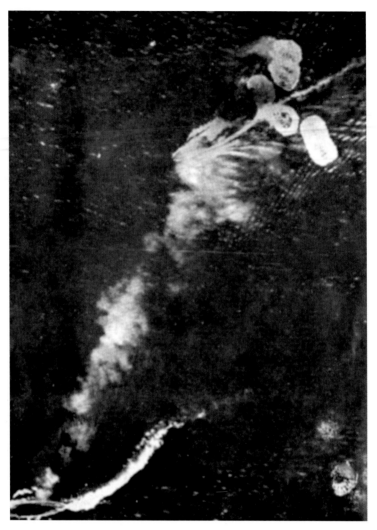

11 "The *Repulse* [*bottom*], slowly turning and circling, was on the point of sinking. ...The *Prince of Wales* [*top*] was steaming slowly at about eight knots and listing heavily to port."—The last moments of the British battleships.

12 The *Prince of Wales* leaving Singapore on her last voyage, 8 December 1941. Courtesy of Australian War Memorial.

14 Post-war photograph of the demolished Mersing bridge, showing Japanese repairs. Courtesy of Australian War Memorial.

Opposite **13** Engineers at work. "On an average our troops fought two battles, repaired four or five bridges, and advanced twenty kilometers every day."

15 The author in the uniform of a lieutenant-colonel.

This photo was taken after the campaign. At Colonel Tsuji's throat is the Order of the Sacred Treasure, 3rd class. The other decorations (*l.* to *r.*) are: Order of the Golden Kite, 4th class; Order of the Rising Sun, 4th class; Decoration of Manchuria, 4th class; Decoration of Manchuria, 5th class; Order of the Golden Kite, 5th class; Commemoration Medal of the Coronation of Emperor Hirohito; Commemoration Medal of the Census; Commemoration Medal of the Founding of Manchuria; Commemoration Medal of the 2,600th year after the accession of the Emperor Jimmu; Campaign Medal of the Chinese Incident; Campaign Medal of the Manchurian Incident.

16 & 17 Indian sappers preparing to blow up a bridge, and (*below*) Japanese troops crossing a demolished bridge. Courtesy of Australian War Memorial.

18 "Our first steps ashore." —Equipment being landed at Singora.

19 Kota Bharu. "The enemy soldiers manning the pillboxes fought desperately."

20 Army Commander Yamashita inspecting a scene of fighting. At left is Lieutenant-General Suzuki; at right is Staff Officer Nagai, the Navy liaison officer. Courtesy of Australian War Memorial.

21 Engagement at Bakri. "The Gotanda Medium Tank Company…lost its ten tanks one after the other." Courtesy of Australian War Memorial.

22 & 23 "The British Army formations were almost completely equipped with motor cars and trucks, and whenever we were able to steal a march on them. . . their soldiers had to abandon their cars and trucks and continue their retreat on foot." Photograph above courtesy of Australian War Memorial.

24 Fire resulting from Japanese air attacks on Singapore Island. Courtesy of Australian War Memorial.

25 Japanese troops attacking shortly before the surrender.

26 The "Imperial Palace," Johore, the Japanese Headquarters observation post for the assault on Singapore. This photograph, taken from the Singapore side of Johore Strait, shows the breach in the Causeway below the tower. Courtesy of Australian War Memorial.

27 Japanese troops landing on Singapore Island at the beginning of the assault.

28 "The Konoe Division completed repairs to the Causeway and pushed forward."

29 "All officers and men who did not ride with the trucks were provided with bicycles."

30 & 31 "Even the long-legged Englishmen could not escape our troops on bicycles....Thanks to Britain's dear money spent on the excellent paved roads, and to the cheap Japanese bicycles, the assault on Malaya was easy."

32 "...Crossing on log bridges held up on the shoulders of engineers."

33 Troops of the 18th Division crossing a river near Singapore.

34 Troops advancing to capture the naval base.

35 The British floating dock lying sunk in Johore Strait.

36 Oil tanks on fire at the naval base, Singapore Island.

37 & 38 Demand and consent. Lieutenant-General Yamashita (*seated*) confronts Lieutenant-General Percival, who is seen signing the surrender agreement in the lower picture. Photo below: courtesy of Australian War Memorial.

39 "These Asian peoples who were emancipated by the fall of Singapore will eternally pronounce benedictions on their benefactors." Malayans celebrating the Emperor's birthday after the campaign.

40 The remains of native shops damaged in Singapore. Courtesy of Australian War Memorial.

41 & 42 Contrasting emotions after the surrender. In the top picture Lieutenant General Yamashita (*fifth from right*) is standing with Lieutenant-General Percival. Next to Yamashita in the front row is Lieutenant-General Suzuki, the 25th Army Chief of Staff.

43 Japanese advancing across Seletar airfield.

44 Fires burning on Kallang airfield, near Singapore city, after an air attack. Courtesy of Australian War Memorial.

45 Staff Officer Sugita conducting Lieutenant-General A. E. Percival (*right*) and other British officers to the Ford factory at Bukit Timah, where the surrender took place.

46 Lieutenant-General Yamashita at a commemoration service for Japanese dead.

giving them fruit and were amusing themselves watching their strange ways. It was like a scene from a play.

A member of the staff from Imperial Headquarters was at this time visiting the battle line, and he brought news of the progress of the landings in the Philippines and the capture of Hong Kong. From our hearts we rejoiced at the success of our comrades in arms.

Staff Officers Asaeda and Hongo, who had been fighting with the Ando Detachment for over a fortnight, washed the dirt off themselves in a drum-can hot bath under the open sky, and it was possible for all to freshen themselves up for future operations.

Staff Officer Kunitake was steadily making preparations for small-boat maneuvers on the western coast while both divisions were preparing to use boats along the enemy's southern bank of the Perak River. Stealing a march on all of them, Army prepared its secret plan for the capture of Kuala Lumpur.

On 26 December in the dead of night, first from the 5th Division, and soon after from the Imperial Guards Division, came the reassuring telephone messages: "River crossing successful." With only a few days' preparation we had forced the crossing of this large river in face of the enemy. Was it by Providence or Divine Grace? Up until that time, both divisions had met with success. Thinking over matters since the disembarkation at Singora, all seemed be the continuation of a breathless scene.

According to Mr. Churchill's memoirs, there were already three Japanese divisions deployed in the front line at this time, but that was not the case.

One regiment of 5th Division infantry was still in Shanghai, barely one-third of the strength of the Imperial Guards Division had reached the front, and 18th Division Headquarters and two of its infantry regiments were still waiting at Canton. Including the Takumi Detachment on the east coast with its two numerically weak regiments, we had barely two divisions in Malaya at this date. Opposing us, the enemy had the full strength of his 3rd Army Corps (9th and 11th divisions, together with reinforcements of roughly two brigades*).

On the Perak River front the enemy was much stronger numerically than we were and, in addition, in the line of the river he held a natural stronghold. In air power, however, we were approximately twice as strong as the enemy, and had practically acquired control of the air. This is not to deny that the enemy's fighter planes were vigorously aggressive and quick to take advantage of any gap in our air superiority. At Ipoh we

---

* A reference apparently to the 12th and 28th Indian brigades.

were subjected to the first night bombing raid we had experienced since the landing at Singora.

The Imperial Guards Division encountered little opposition in crossing the Perak River and moving into Ipoh; they arrived in high spirits over their success so early in the war.

As a matter of policy, units without battle experience were, wherever possible, thrown into action against weak opponents, and this proved profitable throughout.

The 5th Division, which crossed the river lower down at Blanja, had been attacked on the flank by the newly reinforced enemy, but had itself outflanked the enemy on both sides on the morning of 25 December and driven them back; thus the division was able to complete its crossing of the river according to schedule on the evening of the 26th.

From Ipoh we began our advance on Kuala Lumpur, the capital city of Malaya, the second objective of our military operations. A group of enemy reinforcements arrived to defend the Perak River crossings two days behind time.

Our two divisions involved in the river crossing did not encounter very serious enemy opposition, but the operation nevertheless took a long time. Most of the fighting troops were ferried across in boats, but for the passage of tanks and heavy vehicles of the rear supply troops we had to repair the bridges.

After examining and verifying the damage, Major-General Hattori, commander of the railway troops, reported that repairs would take roughly three weeks. General Yamashita encouragingly replied, "Dear me, Major-General, it can be done in a week." The available strength of the division was mustered for the work, which was carried on at full pressure day and night. In barely a week the work was done and it was possible for heavy vehicles to pass continuously over this long bridge—which must have been a great surprise for General Percival.

I must write especially of Staff Officer Hongo, who, as the reader will remember, had sprained his ankle at the landing, but had avoided medical treatment for fear he might be sent to hospital. Since the beginning of the campaign he had had to get about with a stick. He was in charge of the railways, and he kept them in perfect condition, effecting repairs with extraordinary rapidity.

Part Four

Dying Wishes to a Beloved Wife

SINCE THE RUSSO-JAPANESE WAR the Imperial Guards Division had had no actual battle experience, and its fighting capacity was an unknown quantity. Yet the officers and men who received their baptism of shellfire in the fight at the crossing of the Perak River, where they unexpectedly routed an enemy of superior strength, exerted an unusually good influence in the subsequent campaign.

The road which extended to Ipoh from the Perak River was not completely destroyed, for the British were not given sufficient time to demolish it. Those in the lead of the Imperial Guards Division, after crushing the resistance of a small number of the enemy left behind, took possession of Ipoh on the morning of 26 December. I entered with the van of that unit. There was no street fighting, and one had the feeling of entering a quiet, undamaged country town.

From the aerodromes, which the enemy had occupied up to the previous day, our Flying Corps, under the command of Major-General Endo, using bombs and gasoline which as usual were left by the enemy, increased its bombing attacks on the routed British columns.

Planning to advance as far as the location of our next Army Headquarters, we moved forward with a section of the advance party to prepare an encampment in the Ipoh Middle School.

On the evening of 28 December a shrill air-raid siren pierced our dreams. It was an enemy raid. Amid the reports of the guns of our comrades, who were shooting at random, and the crash of bombs dropped by the enemy, in the twinkling of an eye the peaceful streets of Ipoh were seething; but there was not much damage.

111

Evidently the fighting spirit of the enemy air force had not yet degenerated. For the next military operation this was a factor we had to ponder. As Kuala Lumpur was the capital city of the Federated Malay States, we expected the enemy to resist its capture with befitting obstinacy.

While the staff was racking its brains to plan for the leadership of the 5th Division and to find a way to use the Imperial Guards, a senior staff officer arrived. "Look here," he said, "how would it be to scatter from the air a manifesto to the native rulers of Malaya asking for the cooperation of their people? Please have a draft proclamation drawn up by the commanding officer."

At such a busy time it was deplorable to dither about with such unnecessary and trifling problems. Had there been any certainty that the Malay rulers' cooperation could be counted on it might have been an excellent idea to draft such a manifesto; but there was no guarantee that any useful result would be achieved and perhaps that was why the Major-General would not write it. The obstruction of the work of an excessively busy staff by such simple-minded suggestions was not to be endured. The status of the Malay rulers was similar to that of village headmen; even if we dropped the written masterpiece, how much reaction would there be? Propaganda might be desirable after we had conquered the British Army, but in the meantime I argued that we could not afford to send airplanes on such futile missions.

The senior staff officer, however, obstinately demanded the manifesto, saying, "If you think it is improper to use the Army Commander's name, my name will do! Please draw up the proclamation without fail."

"Ah, yes," I murmured. "If the name of His Excellency, General Yamashita, appears, the local rulers will recognize it; but who will know your name?"

This was a fairly severe slap in the face. In the peacetime Army I would have been punished for making such a remark, but amid the stresses of a campaign, insults among officers are everyday affairs, and it was doubtful if what I said had any effect. Members of the staff showed no malice, but none of them felt any goodwill towards the senior officer who persisted in this trivial issue while the more important and urgent work of the battle was at hand.

An English major who had been wounded in the chest at the battle of the Perak River was picked up and carried into Army Headquarters. At the dispensary he received courteous medical attention from our Army doctors. It is a fine thing that enemy wounded should receive the same treatment as the wounded of one's own side. This was the policy of General Yamashita, and it was carried out. The English major was given cow's milk and soup—which of course came from Churchill's supplies. But it was too late. He was beyond help. Through the interpreter, who inquired what messages he wished conveyed to his family, he said, as tears rolled down his pained face, "Please tell my wife, who is a trained nurse in Singapore, that I am happy to die as bravely as is expected of a British soldier. The address is. . ." He had scarcely finished speaking to us when his eyes closed and he died. There is no difference in human nature between one's own side and the enemy side. We positively vowed to convey the message. After the capture of Singapore we made inquiries, but it appeared that the major's widow had already left in a boat which was afterwards sunk by the Japanese Navy. It is probable therefore that she followed her husband. When I recall that sorrowful fate—predestined from a previous life—and the promise that was never carried out because of the fortunes of war, the incident even now weighs on my mind.

At Ipoh, thinking back over the military operations which had so far overwhelmed the northern part of Malaya, and pondering the enemy's whole transport plan, I felt the existence of a contradiction which I was at a loss to understand. It was this:

1. If it was considered that the enemy would rely on Singapore Fortress, and hold out there to the last man, then the military strength that had been poured in north of the Perak River was excessive. As the 3rd Army Corps [9th and 11th Indian divisions] retreated, fresh troops were successively and continuously moved northward to reinforce it in the decisive battles in northern Malaya.

2. The enemy were increasing the strength of their field-operations army, and preparing fortified positions; yet their resistance lacked sincerity and showed a reluctance to face a decisive battle with us.

3. Viewing the war from the standpoint of the British Empire at that time, it appeared that in North Africa the British Army was in the midst of a life-and-death struggle with Rommel's German Army advancing on the Suez Canal. The defense of Suez would be considered to take precedence over the defense of Singapore. If this was accepted as a natural war principle, then in Malaya the British would have to conserve their forces. It appeared a mistake for them to exhaust successively their military strength in the unprepared fighting zone of northern Malaya. Yet the excellent enemy main force which was thrown against us in first-class condition was, it seems, proceeding northward from the Singapore Fortress district.

4. Pouring in fresh reinforcements from the British Army's main strength to support the forces destroyed in the opening battles was like pouring water on thirsty soil. While this continued there was reasonable hope for our success.

5. On the one hand it appeared best to avoid a hurried assault on Singapore Island, and to destroy the enemy outside the fortress first. On the other hand it seemed essential to capture the stronghold before reinforcements could arrive from Great Britain.

Altogether it was very difficult to form a well-reasoned judgment.

The enemy's conduct of military operations was obviously a strategy of "playing to the gallery," and it appeared they had no consistent policy. Our original scheme, decided before the opening of military operations, was to concentrate our whole strength on the prompt reduction of Singapore, and we agreed to adhere to this decision. For that reason, therefore, the Konoe Imperial Guards Division concentrated around the environs of Ipoh, and the 5th Division pushed southward as fast as possible in order to give the enemy no time to develop new defensive positions.

The British war strength was superior to that of the 5th Division, whose troops were exhausted, but preparations could be made to attack with the fresh Imperial Guards Division, which was in better condition than the 5th Division. The enemy having abandoned the Perak River, the next point at which we anticipated resistance was on the line between Kampar and Tanjong Malim. If the enemy intended to depend upon this important line and plan a serious and decisive battle, we must annihilate them there, reinforcing the Imperial Guards immediately with the right wing of the 5th Division. It was decided to open the attack with the 5th Division, which would carry the fight up to Kuala Lumpur, and then to alternate the 5th Division with the Imperial Guards to maintain the speed of the assault to the south.

Small-Boat Operations Dumbfound the Enemy

THE NAVAL ACTION OFF KUANTAN had annihilated in one blow the main strength of the British Far Eastern Fleet by sinking the *Prince of Wales* and *Repulse*, and had given us complete command of the sea off the east coast of Malaya. But Singapore remained in good condition, and the air base in Sumatra and the sea off the western coast of Malaya were still in the grasp of the British. Those who planned our small-boat operations had to take due account of these facts. Our plan, which appeared to disregard the principles of war by driving our Air Group forward to the enemy air bases in the northern part of Malaya, was based on the assumption of air–sea cooperation. The small boats to be used were roughly forty large and small motor boats used in the Singora landing, which, as I have mentioned earlier, had been taken overland by road and rail to the Alor Star River. After being launched again there they were collected in the neighborhood of Lumut at the mouth of the Perak River, together with about twenty other boats which had been captured at Penang. Altogether these boats carried a battalion of infantry—more or less—and they travelled along the coast in the rear of the enemy, ceaselessly menacing their retreat.

It was a problem what troops to put aboard the boats to increase the scale of this operation. Eventually the 1st Maneuvers Unit, composed of the main strength of the 11th Regiment under the command of Colonel Watanabe (one and a half battalions), one section of mountain guns, and a section of engineers, was selected to be ferried from point to point along the coast as required to harass the enemy's retreat.

At Army Headquarters in Taiping, the regimental commander came to say goodbye. "I wish you to keep the regimental colors at Army Headquarters in Taiping," he said. I thought, "This unit is not under the direct control of Army, and as orders are given by the division commander, being sent to him from Army, so naturally the regimental colors should be in the custody of the division commander. The colors must share the fate of the regiment's main strength, which is putting into operation these vital maneuvers from which the whole Army expects so much!"

It is natural for a regiment to protect its colors, but if I had been the regimental commander I should have wished to raid the enemy territory carrying them, for, if the boats carrying the regiment were sunk, would it not be better if the colors were sunk too? Thus the soldiers would be inspired by the thought that their cherished colors would share in their own fate of life or death.

Feelings of misgiving were apparent in the regimental commander as he said his pathetic farewell before departing. General Yamashita encouraged him. "Don't worry about the colors," he said. "They'll be all right. I shall certainly take care of them. You do your duty with all your might."

While the regimental commander was going away, without knowing why it seemed to me I could see the shadow of death at his back.

The intelligence staff officer of the division was to accompany the unit. In such a raiding action as this, success or failure hinges on the selection of the commanding officer and his staff. Staff Officer Asaeda was considered for the task, but as he had just returned after sharing the hardships of the Ando Detachment, the divisional commander had no hesitation in appointing his chief intelligence officer to the position.

During the night of 30 December the detachment put out from Lumut at the mouth of the Perak River. While they were celebrating the New Year on the open sea, they were discovered by enemy planes and swept by machine-gun fire, which they returned, bringing down one plane. A number of men of the detachment were wounded, and there was some uneasiness about the future because of the enemy's early discovery of the expedition. The infantry-laden boats nevertheless continued on their way.

On 4 January, reaching Sungkai, they were in a position to menace the enemy line of retreat in the rear of the main British forces.

The 5th Division had for many years been trained in military landing operations, and was a land force with good knowledge of the sea. There was some danger that their over-confidence might override their common sense. Everything depended on the discretion and general character of the commander, but this well-trained division had successfully carried out all maritime operations assigned to it.

By contrast, the Imperial Guards, when they took over the small-boat operations from the 5th Division, were completely without maritime experience and "rushed in like fools where angels feared to tread," though not without results. Entering Port Swettenham, which is the outer harbor of Kuala Lumpur, they landed deep in the rear of the key position of Morib, and, smashing enemy resistance, seized the strategic point of Kajang above the main road south of Kuala Lumpur. This reckless action took the enemy unawares, and was the real reason for their abandonment of the important capital city of the Federated Malay States.

In this operation the detachment of our men in the small boats had thrown common sense to the winds, but they caused consternation to the commander in charge of the units of the British Army on the spot. In face of the threat to his rear he retreated immediately and swiftly, leaving our men with their objective achieved.

Prime Minister Churchill, from London, indignantly protested to General Wavell and rebuked General Percival—which in the circumstances was not unreasonable. "Control of the western coast passed to the Japanese Army, which did not have even one naval vessel there. The failure was a blot on the history of the British Navy," wrote the old Prime Minister, who repeatedly referred to the incident. "Why didn't the Navy oppose the enemy advance with destroyers, submarines or airplanes?" he asked. That was one of the questions we also asked ourselves.

Admiral Pound, replying to Mr. Churchill's rebuke, stated that his inability to prevent the Japanese attack along the west coast of Malaya was due to the inferiority of the British airplanes, the failure of scorched-earth tactics at Penang, and Japanese utilization of the small boats left behind by the British. Those may have been some of the reasons, but even if the British Navy had shown the fighting spirit of the Japanese officers and men, it might not have been able to prevent the successful operations of the fleet of small boats.

New Year's Eve on the Battlefield

THE 5TH DIVISION, WHICH CROSSED the Perak River using alternately the Okabe and the Ando regiments, made a double attack on the enemy front from the jungle, and steadily continued its advance south. But the enemy brought up their reserves from the south in rapid succession. The 5th Division was exhausted, and moreover it was below strength, as one section was still engaged on the small-boat maneuvers, whereas the enemy forces were reinforced by fresh crack troops. The tempo of the southern advance slowed down. The enemy, based on the strongly fortified Kampar position, resisted stubbornly, and deployed for a bitterly contested battle for the last days of the old year and the beginning of the new.*

Boarding a car that had been captured at Ipoh, carrying one light machine-gun (and a mosquito net that I was never without), I left Ipoh with two men and a driver on the afternoon of 30 December. Intending to share a glass of wine with the troops in the line to celebrate the New Year on the battlefield, we drove about fifty kilometers. Suddenly we found ourselves in the midst of heavy shellfire, as intense as that experienced on the Jitra line. It was coming from enemy guns in the mountains which constitute Malaya's spinal column, and which lay across the main road to our destination. Even after the position of the enemy guns was located it was very difficult to silence them, owing to their concealment in the jungle.

Kampar had apparently been hurriedly fortified by the day-and-night labor of a large, fresh British Army group together with a large number

---

* Kampar was held by the 15th Indian Brigade (survivors of the 6th and 15th Brigades) with a field regiment and anti-tank battery. The 12th Brigade had been overwhelmed by the Imperial Guards Division at Telok Anson on the west coast; its retirement enabled the Japanese to threaten the flank at Kampar. The 12th Brigade was in action later at Slim River.

of coolies, but was evidently not a solid engineering work. Owing to the contour of the ground, our attack progressed slowly. The full strength of the Army division and the air groups cooperated for the attack on the front line, but up to the evening of 31 December there was no expectation of success and some danger of failure.

Leaving our car concealed in the rubber trees, we made our way along the main road to the front line, which was roughly three hundred meters from the enemy. On arrival there we were caught in a violent barrage and it was impossible either to advance or retire. Closely scrutinizing the enemy line, it appeared to me that our left wing was the important sector. The enemy presently counterattacked with a bayonet charge, and hand-to-hand fighting ensued; one could say that it was impossible to distinguish between attacker and defender.

By chance a company of our medium tanks under the command of Captain Ochi came charging along the main road at this moment. I called to him, "Hello, Ochi, that's it, that's it, go from this side to the left. Be careful of the artillery." The meaning of this will not be clear to the reader, but the tank company commander, knowing that the staff officer speaking to him had been surveying the position on the sector, needed no further explanation, and replied, "Yes, I understand." He went straight forward through the smoke of the barrage. Clear of the bursting shells, the tanks were soon, like snails, scrambling up the slope of the enemy's fortified position, giving great encouragement to our frontline infantry. The enemy resistance, however, remained stubborn. By the evening of 31 December, the position was beginning to look grave. We spent the night in our car, huddled under mosquito nets, just behind the front line. We were completely fagged out, and were just drifting off to sleep when a shellburst lifted our car off the ground. I told the driver to move the car a hundred meters to the rear, and we got into another position, which seemed safe. We were just dozing off again when another shell landed right beside us. I said, "Well, we had better move back a bit more." The shellfire, however, seemed to follow the car, and no sooner did we move to a new position than we would have to shift to another one. The heavy shellfire indicated the possibility of an enemy counterattack either during the night or at dawn. The divisional commander had no reserves at all, even the color parties of the regiments were in the line. The Ando Regiment, which had made a detour from the main road into the jungle on the west, failed to connect with the division. It appeared that if the enemy counterattacked us we might be forced back to Ipoh. At such a critical time it was of course impossible for me to leave the front line. It was, I may say, the first time in my whole life I had spent New Year's

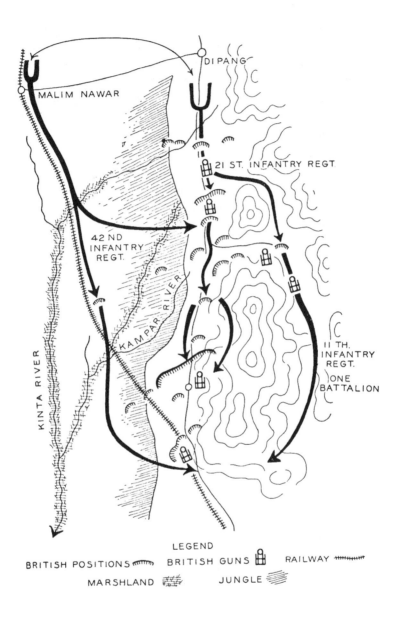

DI PANG

MALIM NAWAR

21 ST. INFANTRY REGT

42 ND INFANTRY REGT.

KAMPAR RIVER

KINTA RIVER

11 TH. INFANTRY REGT.

ONE BATTALION

LEGEND

BRITISH POSITIONS ͢ BRITISH GUNS RAILWAY ͢

MARSHLAND JUNGLE

Operations in the Kampar region.

Note: Of total enemy strength, British Indian Army 45th Brigade completely annihilated.

Eve in such circumstances, and I shall probably never do so again. In Tokyo at the end of this first year of war everyone would be celebrating the New Year with noisy greetings and dishes of soba [vermicelli] while listening to the New Year's Eve bells ringing. And here we were locked in a battle spreading over the middle section of Malaya with the issue in grave doubt. In place of bells ringing out, "All is vanity and there is nothing certain in this world," we heard only the roar of gunfire informing everyone of the certainty of defeat for the weak.

The agonizing night ended at last. The light of the sun, which began to show its face through the rubber forest, was, for some unaccountable reason, scarlet, like blood. This seemed to me not unreasonable in the circumstances. Throughout the night and all the morning a continuous stream of wounded men were making their way back from the front line, either carried on stretchers or supported on the shoulders of comrades who were themselves wounded. Casualties had been heavy, but in the front line there was not a man who did not greet his comrades with a "Happy New Year!"

"That Which One Sows . . ."

THE ANDO REGIMENT, AS I HAVE said, had been given orders to detour from the main road through the jungle on the western side. Their experiences and hardships almost baffle description. Immersed to the chest while cutting their way through the swampy jungle, they were only able to advance about two thousand meters a day. Above the level of the swamp there lay a network of thorny vines and cane through which they had to cut every inch of the way. The men were covered in leeches, and everywhere were venomous snakes, without fear of man, raising their heads and ready to strike. During the day it was an inferno of heat through which no breezes blew. At night the men were chilled to the bone. The jungle was a gruesome place at night. The men were exhausted by the ordeal of the day's march, and there was no life in the voices with which they encouraged one another. No rice could be cooked, so they had to chew dry, uncooked rice. These conditions continued for three days and three nights, but by early dawn on 2 January the Ando Regiment was in the rear of the enemy and in a position to attack their gun positions with hand grenades.

This attack on the rear of the enemy position by the Ando Regiment caused a sudden change in the situation on the whole battlefront. While the enemy attempted to deal with the threat to their rear, the Okabe Regiment made a successful frontal attack, and the enemy were soon in full retreat.

Singing triumphal songs, the soldiers of the Ando Regiment raised the Japanese flag over Kampar Fortress—and then picked off the leeches which covered their bodies.

Mr. Churchill says in his memoirs that the Japanese Army had become expert in jungle warfare. From the enemy Prime Minister this is high praise. But his comment is surprising. The 5th and 18th Divisions had had abundant experience of the Chinese Front, but they did not even know the meaning of the word "jungle." The soldiers first saw jungle only when they landed in Malaya.

The study of jungle warfare had been set down as part of the duties of the Investigation Department in Taiwan, but very little work could be done on the subject as there was no suitable jungle there. Afterwards, the advance of the Imperial Guards Division into the southern part of Indochina provided some experience, but in Indochina there was no malignant, swampy jungle as there is in Malaya.

It was not jungle experience or training in jungle warfare but the indomitable fighting spirit of the officers and men which enabled them to surmount difficulties and hardships, to make detours through the jungle, and attack the enemy rear.

In war there is a greater suffering than that of combat: the agony of one's heart. As a means to ensure the enforcement of military discipline and the maintenance of public morale by the Army Commander at the beginning of hostilities in Malaya, I was one of those who stubbornly advocated that men guilty of "plunder, rape, and incendiarism, without any distinction whatever regarding rank, should be executed before a firing squad." But, sheltering under existing laws and regulations, there were others who would not consent to this, and in the final result they got their way; the penalty for the offenses in question was to be only "heavy punishment."

During the Manchurian Incident it is a matter for regret that there were quite a number of breaches of military discipline perpetrated on civilians by the Japanese Army fighting in China and Manchuria. Yet to the bitter end there was nobody who advocated execution by shooting for these crimes, and even to this day I feel strong dissatisfaction that such an attitude should have existed. Positively, such things must not be repeated in the war that was just beginning.

After the Kobayashi Battalion had seized Penang there were many more misdemeanors than were disclosed. According to the reports of the inhabitants, three soldiers in collusion pillaged and raped, and there was not the slightest shadow of doubt in the matter. At once, the Military Police made a rigorous investigation and arrested the criminals, who were tried by court-martial. The Army Commander held the battalion and regimental commanders responsible as well, and punished them by thirty days' close arrest.*

I was ordered to convey personally the Army Commander's order to the divisional and regimental commanders, and the incident aroused painful recollections of the time when, as a cadet company leader, I was condemned to thirty days' close arrest by Inspector-General M__ of the Department of Military Training. At that time I had nipped in the bud the activities of a student of the Army Academy who had been implicated in the November Affair,** thus preventing him from becoming involved in the scandal.

To maintain discipline in an army it is necessary to impose heavy penalties for some offenses. In the middle of a desperate battle, however, I felt it was rather awkward to have to inform a battalion and regimental commander that they were under close arrest for thirty days. I wished to postpone the punishment until after the battle, for, if they were placed under arrest while it was still in progress, the officers concerned would undoubtedly be depressed and their conduct of operations might be adversely affected. I have never had such a painful duty to perform.

Of course the Army Chief of Staff, or the staff officer, assistant commandant, according to the status of the officer-in-charge of operations, must issue the order, "Relentless death by shooting," which was strongly advocated for the men in question. The feelings of the Army Commandant who had to order the punishment were well known: "That which one sows, one must reap."

Because of heavy losses in the bitter Kampar battle the enemy, who had rallied on the second day, began to retreat all along the line after the flank attack by the Ando Regiment which followed their jungle detour. This regiment now became the front line in pursuit of the enemy.

The Okabe Regiment, which had lost heavily, was ordered to reorganize as our support line. This was the only opportunity I had of speaking to the regimental commander. Taking care that the purpose of my visit would not be known to others, I called on the fatigued veteran, and said to him, "I am sorry to trouble you, and I hate to tell you, Mr. Regimental Commander, that His Excellency, the Army Commander, holds you responsible for the incident of plunder and rape by soldiers of the Kobayashi Battalion, and he has condemned you to close arrest

---

* Close arrest meant suspension from duty, confinement to quarters, and the loss of half pay during the period of punishment.

** A rebellion of young officers against the Tokyo Government.

122

for thirty days." It was an extremely painful duty for me to convey this order to the tired-out regimental commander, who had lost so many subordinates in the hard fighting, but had at last routed the enemy. I was glad I was speaking to him in the dark so that we could not see each other's face at the time.

He replied in a grave voice, "I heard of the misconduct of my subordinates, and must accept it as due to my unworthiness as a commander. There is no excuse. Respectfully I accept the punishment. Please convey my apologies to His Excellency, General Yamashita."

The misconduct of subordinates had been a cause of considerable worry to this commander. Our objective in the war was the emancipation of the Far East, and the error or misconduct of even one or two persons could give rise to much evil influence. It was necessary, therefore, that commanders should be punished if they failed to prevent misconduct by their subordinates, for, as the saying goes, "a little leak can sink a great ship."

Deep in my heart I sympathized with the regimental commander, for he was a pathetic figure and believed he should commit hara-kiri to atone for his offense. To comfort him I told him his excellent conduct during the battle would be minutely reported to the Army Commander. I also called the regimental adjutant aside and said, "Be careful of the regimental commander. Under no circumstances must you agree with him." I gave this caution in case the regimental commander discussed with the adjutant his intention to commit hara-kiri.

A Thrust Through the Jungle

THE TAKUMI DETACHMENT, LANDING AT Kota Bharu, had raided and captured the enemy aerodrome. This exploit at the beginning of hostilities was a brilliant achievement. Next day, notice of this success was communicated to Field Marshal Count Terauchi, Commander-in-Chief of the Southern Armies, at Saigon. He immediately bestowed a citation on the detachment. Normally citations were only bestowed after careful investigation of the circumstances and reports by army commanders, divisional commanders, and unit commanders. Field Marshal Terauchi's simplification of the formalities pleased the staff and indeed the whole Army.

One section of non-commissioned officers of the Independent Engineers, under command of the Takumi Detachment, had however become panic-stricken at the enemy's bombing. Without orders from their troop leader they had boarded the large motor boats, crossed to the east of the Gulf of Siam, and retreated to the open sea off Saigon. Correct Army procedure in such cases of desertion in the face of the enemy was to hold a court-martial immediately. But this was not done, and the incident was thought by many to detract from the citation of the detachment.

The Army Commander, who had some insight into this hardness of feeling towards the Takumi Detachment, issued orders that they must "seize Kuantan promptly and rapidly advance southward along the east coast." The roads were poor and supply problems difficult, but no excuses for delay were permitted.

The east coast of Malaya is not so well developed in communications and industry as is the west coast. The small rivers are mostly without bridges and must be crossed by ferry boats or by wading. Furthermore, the jungle is incomparably thicker than that of the west coast.

The Takumi Detachment, losing time in combating the resistance of small enemy groups, was the first to experience the menace of this terribly thick jungle.

Kuantan is a strategic point on the eastern coast of Malaya and is situated roughly halfway between Kota Bharu and Singapore.* It was the capital city of Pahang Province. The harbor was of no value because the water close to the shore was shallow, but in the suburbs there were fully equipped military airfields. To smash any landing from the east coast, the enemy had prepared an impressive defense with about one brigade of troops and strong air support.

The Takumi Detachment first came into contact with the enemy around Kuantan on 29 December, and on the morning of the 31st commenced the assault on the town and took possession of it. The enemy, however, obstinately defended the aerodromes on its circumference. The Takumi Detachment thereupon made a detour through the jungle, and attacked the enemy from the west, thus intercepting their line of retreat. In a night attack on 3 January our troops destroyed nearly the whole of the enemy brigade, and finally seized the aerodromes.

During this battle the enemy brigade commander, who was taken prisoner, was asked, "Why did your men raise their hands so quickly?"

He replied, "For what reason did you attack only on the front where we had not prepared to meet you?" He went on to say, "When we defend the coast, you come from the dense jungle. When we defend the land, you come from the sea. Is it not war for enemies to face each other? This

---

*Kuantan was held by the 22nd Brigade, 9th Indian Division.

is not war. There will be no other way than retreat, I assure you." This criticism was characteristic of the British attitude throughout the whole period of operations, and was common to every front.

Divergent Opinions

THE 5TH DIVISION HAD CAPTURED THE fortified position of Kampar with great difficulty, and in one day its fighting spirit was seen to decline. Nearly a month had passed since the landing, the troops had had no rest at all, and, notwithstanding heavy casualties, they had received no reinforcements. Kuala Lumpur, the capital city of the Malay States, was still far distant, and Singapore was six hundred kilometers away.

The Okabe and Ando regiments took the lead alternately, each trying to outdo the other. While hurrying to Taiping Headquarters to report the victory of Kampar, I visited the 5th Division in the rubber plantation at the roadside. Just as I arrived, a signal was received from the staff officer in charge of the small-boat maneuvers which read as follows: "Since the day before yesterday the detachment has been repeatedly machine-gunned by enemy planes, and at night considerable damage was caused by an attack by enemy warships. We are of the opinion that until the mastery of the air is guaranteed to us, future maneuvers of the small boats should be recognized as an impossibility."

This opinion was in accord with that of the divisional staff, who believed that under the conditions then obtaining, the military strength in the district was insufficient to intercept the retreat of the enemy, and wished to call into the fighting line the Watanabe Regiment, which was engaged in small-boat maneuvers in the district, and which it was believed would encounter more serious difficulties in the distant Kuala Lumpur area.

The divisional commander was strongly of the same opinion as his staff, and the question arose, "Well, what about the opinion of Army Headquarters?"

The Watanabe Regiment was not under direct control of Army, but was subject to the orders of the divisional commander. When the regiment sent a pessimistic signal saying that further satisfactory operations did not seem possible, the divisional commander decided to consult Army Headquarters before ceasing the small-boat maneuvers.

I called at Army Headquarters to discuss the position, and left believing that Army would act according to the wishes of the divisional commander. Almost immediately on my return to divisional head-quarters, however, there came a signal from a senior staff officer at Army, ordering the division to continue the small-boat maneuvers no matter how great the difficulties, and to advance to the rear of the retreating enemy. The signal concluded: "In light of the progress of the battle on the main road there is no need for fresh troops."

Division replied to the Army Commander, "We will do as Your Excellency desires!"

What had happened? The Army instruction was in direct opposition to the opinion of the commander entrusted with the conduct of operations in the area, who had a full appreciation of the strategic position. Furthermore, before visiting Army, I had just returned from the front line to divisional headquarters; the correct procedure would have been to summon me to discuss the position, and to convey any decision through me to the divisional commander. It seemed to indicate some lack of trust in him at Army Headquarters.

Throughout the whole campaign there was no incident which caused such indignation as this. From the front line to Army Headquarters was more than a hundred kilometers. Army celebrated the New Year in the rear of Taiping, beyond the sound of gunfire and where the real state of affairs was not known. It was strangely disturbing to me, an Army staff officer, to receive orders by telephone to proceed to the front line, when the order was not sent through the divisional commander. To verify matters I telephoned the senior staff officer, who replied, "Yes, His Excellency believes that operations must proceed as ordered at all costs." I replied, "If the officer who is in charge of operations in this area is not trusted, please dismiss him at once."

I was furious. Here it was, New Year's Day, and wherever one went on the battlefield one encountered a bloody procession of wounded. I had just had the painful duty of conveying to an old regimental commander, thoroughly exhausted by fighting, the order that he was to be punished by being placed under close arrest; I myself was worn out, having been rushing about for some days without sleep or even an opportunity to lie down. It seemed to me that some of those at Army Headquarters celebrating the New Year beyond the sound of gunfire must be intoxicated with toso [spiced wine].

In my indignant mood I rushed off in a car. The repairs to the Perak Bridge not being finished, I crossed on foot at midnight, and arrived at Taiping Headquarters some time after 2 a.m. Waking up the Operations Section, all of whom were sound asleep, before the whole staff below the Chief of Staff I said bombastically, referring to myself, "Please dismiss from office the person in charge of military operations!" Then I fell on a bed and went straight to sleep, completely exhausted by the shock and strain, which in truth had not ceased since the days at Saigon. I slept until noon next day.

The Army Chief of Staff, in conference with an assistant commandant and a senior staff officer, reported in detail to the Army Commander, recommending that the commander of the Watanabe Regiment should be relieved of his duties. I heard casually, at a later date, from several sources that General Yamashita would not give his consent to this proposal.

This matter of having their own way from the beginning—even to excess—considerably strengthened senior officers and their colleagues; where personal friction occurred, they thought it expedient to relieve the officer concerned of his duties. It was a state of affairs that made this entire trivial incident easy to understand, if not accept.

The small-boat operations of the 5th Division were suspended, and when the Konoe Imperial Guards Division inherited this duty, the curtain fell on this drama.

The Imperial Guards were, as I have said, completely inexperienced and untrained for landing operations from small boats. Nevertheless, taking the place of the adept 5th Division, with roughly one battalion of infantry, they made a sudden attack on the enemy's rear, deep into the distant areas round Malacca, Muar and Batu Pahat. Our strategic aim was thus accomplished, much to the indignation of Mr. Churchill and to the despondency of General Percival.

Although attacked by airplanes and devastated by naval vessels, the troops in the small boats knew they were suffering no more than those on land. Continuously outwitting the enemy, recklessly charging any opening without preparation, they achieved a success in battle beyond all expectations, and shocked the British Army. With barely one battalion of infantry, armed only with infantry weapons, they rushed on the enemy "like blind men unafraid of snakes"—and succeeded.

Two Young Warriors

THE ENEMY, BEING DEFEATED IN the neighborhood of Kampar, received reinforcements and, relying on the advantages of the ground in the locality, again resisted stubbornly in the area around Slim River.

Substituting for the Okabe Regiment, the commander of the Ando Regiment, to which two platoons of engineers and a company of tanks were assigned, mounted his infantry on bicycles and advanced south over the bridges and roads which had been destroyed. The bridge demolitions, which extended as far as Slim River, appeared so thorough that no wheeled vehicle could be expected to pass through. But the infantry, carrying their bicycles over their shoulders and wading across the streams, never paused in their close pursuit of the enemy.

The 15th Regiment, Independent Engineers, which again moved into the fighting zone, completed the repair of the bridges with phenomenal speed, enabling the heavy-vehicle units to overtake the Ando Regiment, which, maintaining its pursuit on bicycles, cleared the way for artillery, tanks, and other infantry to be brought up into position to attack the enemy around Trolak. Our confidence in the Ando commander's skill, by the end of this great battle, was justified beyond all expectations.

Our attack began at six o'clock on the morning of 7 January. We deployed a thoroughly consolidated fighting force of infantry, tanks, artillery, and engineers. By shortly after seven o'clock we had broken through the seven lines of the enemy position, advancing roughly six kilometers in length and depth.

Taking the lead, cutting their way through the break in the line, were two second lieutenants, newly appointed graduates of the Military Academy. Second Lieutenant Sadanobu Watanabe, commander of a platoon of leading tanks, headed the attack, and was closely followed by Second Lieutenant Morokuma, commander of a frontline platoon of infantry.

The tanks, trampling underfoot the net type of wire entanglements set up as obstructions on the road, were intercepted by enemy artillery, which laid down a barrage around them. The enemy anti-tank guns particularly began to open fire from pillboxes in the rubber plantation, and it seemed that Second Lieutenant Watanabe would be shot up at any moment. But the company commander's tank saved the situation by covering him with shellfire. As he advanced after piercing the enemy's front line, a white concrete bridge gleamed before his eyes on the road ahead. It had not yet been demolished because the enemy's main strength was still fighting in front of it. It was necessary above all else to capture this bridge intact. A heavy explosive charge could be seen set up on one of the piers, with the electric wire to fire it leading to the rear.

Opening up the turret cover of his tank, Second Lieutenant Watanabe jumped to the ground, rushed forward through enemy bullets which fell round him like rain, and with his sabre cut the electric wire. At this moment Second Lieutenant Morokuma killed an enemy soldier who had dashed forward to throw a grenade at Watanabe. Our ten tanks immediately sped forward and crossed the bridge. They advanced roughly three kilometers and then stormed a second bridge. Continuing on, they crossed a third and a fourth.

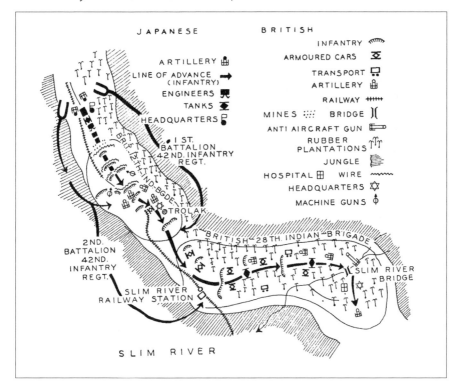

The battle of annihilation at the Slim River.

Notes:

1. Overall depth of enemy positions—about 20 kilometers.
2. Enemy strength—two brigades (of these, one completely annihilated).
3. Strength of our attacking force — one regiment infantry, one company tanks, divisional artillery, one company engineers.
4. Time—0400—1400 hours, 7th January.

Under very heavy fire from both sides of the road, and entirely cut off from our own troops, the tank company arrived at a fifth bridge, which was also mined. The electric wires to fire the charges could be seen. Watanabe had been wounded in the right hand and could no longer use his sabre, so from inside the tank he fired a machine-gun at the wires until he cut them. The tanks crossed the bridge, which was about a hundred meters in length and on the line of retreat of the enemy's main force, which was thus effectively cut.

The enemy attacked desperately to recapture the bridge, but our tanks overran their infantry, artillery, and anti-aircraft gun positions and attacked their advanced headquarters.

Single-handed fighting by the ten tanks continued for about three hours. They appeared to be encircled by several hundred—no, several thousands—of the enemy. Our small infantry force, which had kept up with the tanks, although completely encircled by the enemy and engaged in bitter and confused fighting, cut its way through the jungle and continued to advance.

Enemy 10-centimeter howitzers (25-pounders) resisted to the last from a position on the road. First Lieutenant Sato, substituting for Second Lieutenant Watanabe in control of the tanks, was attacking these guns, and when only about ten meters distant from one of them received a direct hit which smashed his own leading tank to pieces, killing his tank crew and himself. He remained sitting upright among the ruins still grasping his sword. Hasi, a first-class private, was dead at his machine-gun and Sergeant Totu had collapsed beside his gun like a dish of *ame*.*

Some tank reinforcements arrived and the attack continued, finally over-running the last of the enemy heavy-gun positions. When twilight fell, our few tanks were encircled by two enemy brigades, which still had from ten to twenty heavy guns. These counterattacked the tanks from four directions, and grenades and mortar shells were falling all around them. By midnight, however, our main body of infantry, having smashed the desperate enemy resistance, broke through their position all along the line and overtook our advanced tanks. After nineteen hours' continuous and desperate fighting, our troops had destroyed two enemy brigades and gained the greatest victory of the campaign in Malaya up to that date.

This battle was an example of close cooperation of our infantry, tanks, artillery and engineers. Major-General Bennett, the enemy commander, was killed in action.** The enemy abandoned the bodies of those killed in the battle together with several hundred severely wounded who were calling for help. Thirteen heavy guns, 15 anti-tank guns, 20 tractor-drawn guns, 6 anti-aircraft guns, 50 light armored cars and 550 motor cars were abandoned in the rubber jungle, together with ammunition, rations, forage and medical stores. These supplies—all kindly left behind by the British would enable two of our brigades to fight easily for a month.

---

*A soft, glutinous, sweet Japanese jelly, made from various kinds of grain.
** Major-General Bennett was incorrectly reported killed by a prisoner taken by the Japanese. He was not present at this battle. Neither he nor the troops under his command came into action until later at Gemas.

Roughly twelve hundred prisoners surrendered on the battlefield. Others who had escaped into the jungle—probably more than two thousand—surrendered because of hunger during the next few days.

Such a complete victory had not been expected by either general or divisional headquarters. It was considered largely due to the two young officers, Second Lieutenants Watanabe and Morokuma, particularly Watanabe, who carried out his duties like a war god. No matter how cleverly planned a scheme of military operations may be, unless the units putting it into practice are skillful and well trained, it is impossible to establish such records as were achieved on that day by those two young officers.

It is not boasting to say that the conduct of the plan of operations in Malaya was excellent, but the success of the campaign was not due merely to the plan of operations, it was mainly attributable to the front-line soldiers, who were on fire with the high ideal of the emancipation of Asia, and displayed a fighting spirit which aroused the admiration of Mr. Churchill. Everyone must acknowledge that throughout the whole campaign our soldiers without exception fought splendidly under the orders of the young officers who led them into battle.

To the rising postwar generation I say, You must bestir yourselves to action before the cold criticism of society. You are the ones who will determine the future destiny of the people and the State. There must be no change whatever from the spirit of those who reflected credit on the nation from the battlefields of Malaya so many years ago. None of us, not even the younger generation, can escape from the chaotic conditions of the changing world. The young people of today must, for the sake of the nation, develop the same spirit of altruism, self-sacrifice and purity of motive that actuated the youth of Japan on the battlefields of Malaya. I cling fast to bright hopes for the future of our people and our nation.

The Fall of the Federal Capital

THE FRONT GATE TO KUALA LUMPUR, the federal capital, was smashed wide open in the Slim River battle. As a result it was possible to use only one division—the 5th—in the direct attack on the city.

The Imperial Guards, after crossing the Perak River, concentrated the whole of their strength around the environs of Ipoh, and now had to allot duties for the fresh strategic groups of troops arriving. On completion of repairs to the Perak Bridge, Taiping Headquarters began the advance to Ipoh on 3 January.

After the battle of Slim River, the staff officers concerned returned to Ipoh for the purpose of drafting new instructions for the Army. Observations from the beginning of the campaign, throughout the important battles of Jitra, Kampar and Slim River, had shown the necessity to abandon the old conception of attacking by outflanking movements in favor of concentrated fire and penetration on a narrow front by sudden raids. If one catches fish slowly by throttling them in a big net, it is essential that they should not escape in all directions through the sides.

In Malaya the main roads ran lengthwise throughout the peninsula, with jungle on either side except where cultivated rubber plantations allowed the deployment of troops for a kilometer or so on either or both sides of the road. Because of this special characteristic of the country, large forces could not be used on a wide front. We had noticed that when the enemy's front was broken their troops took refuge in the jungle, but finding they could not escape through it, were driven by hunger to surrender after two or three days.

The Army Commander, General Yamashita, appeared still to prefer the tactics of large-scale outflanking movements from the west coast, but the staff was very impressed with the significance of the breakthrough by the 5th Division using concentrated power on a narrow front at Slim River, and urged that the same tactics be used by the Imperial Guards Division to break through the fortified position near Gemas, the barrier to Johore State. It was decided that the Imperial Guards Division should attack Gemas along the rear road running beside the mountain road on the north.

The coastal districts of Malaya are intersected by many rivers running into the sea, and these constitute serious obstacles. As there were practically no bridges in the area, our troops would have to cross the rivers by ferry boats. The Army Commander's plan required the allocation to the Imperial Guards Division of the greater part of the available bridge-building material, as well as most of the engineer units and tanks.

From the Army Commander's point of view, the move on Gemas was more than a simple tactical problem. It was complicated by the fact that the Konoe Imperial Guards divisional commander was of lower seniority than the commander of the 5th Division, and in this operation would command the larger force. The Konoe divisional commander was not happy with this position, about which there were long discussions.

The Takumi Detachment, which was in Kuantan on the east, was transferred to the trunk-road area of the west coast, and, as arranged, the Imperial Guards Division moved towards the rear of Gemas, inflicting a crushing defeat upon the enemy at Bakri. Depending largely on the small boats formerly used by the 5th Division with the Kunishi

Detachment, the Imperial Guards ceaselessly menaced the enemy's rear. Troops landing from boats in the neighborhood of Morib occupied Kajang, a strategic position on the main road. Naturally, the successes of the Imperial Guards facilitated the advance of the 5th Division, which, after the breakthrough at Slim River, was able to continue pursuing the enemy with undiminished momentum.

While the Imperial Guards continued their advance into Johore State, the 5th Division moved without pause towards Kuala Lumpur and reached the prepared position at Tanjong Malim—the last trench line before the federal capital—which had been prepared before the outbreak of hostilities. It appeared a very solidly built defense line, and severe fighting was expected before it fell. Owing to their heavy losses at Slim River, however, the enemy had sufficient strength to man only one line of firing trench, which was soon left behind like the cast-off skin of a snake.

On 11 January at 8 p.m. our troops entered Kuala Lumpur, capital of the Malay Federation, without serious enemy resistance. This metropolis presented a dignified and imposing modern appearance. There were Chinese merchants' shops on practically all the main streets, and from each of these hung the firm's name, written in *kanji* [Chinese ideographs]. We felt as though we had entered the crossroads of the central provinces of China.

The occupying troops had now been on continuous military operations for forty days since the departure from Samah Harbor, without a single day's rest. This must have been a rare occurrence in military operations, ancient or modern, domestic or foreign.

Kuala Lumpur had suffered no war damage and its recovery was swift. There were no breaches of military discipline, and the day after the Japanese troops entered the city the shop of the inhabitants were allowed to open. The severity of the punishment of thirty days' close arrest inflicted upon the commander of Okabe Regiment for the incident at Penang had impressed the whole Army—particularly the soldiers of the 5th Division.

Near Kuala Lumpur there were large airfields fully equipped by the enemy. The Endo Air Group took advantage of these at once, but fell into an unforeseen snare. Wire so fine that it could not be seen had been strung through the vegetation all round the aerodrome, which immediately it was caught by a man's leg, pulled a firing pin and exploded a land mine. These caused a number of casualties and we spent two or three days de-lousing them. We cleared the roads by rolling empty drums along. These booby traps seemed to betoken a loss of confidence on the part of the enemy, for they appeared to have been set out some time previously in preparation for retreat.

Anticipating an attack by enemy planes, our anti-aircraft guns were set up around the airfields and, as expected, the following night we were attacked by about twenty planes. There were not sufficient searchlights for our guns, but they reported that by direct open-sight firing they shot down five enemy planes. Everyone thought the gunners were telling lies, and while the Army was criticizing, the anti-aircraft gun commander, Colonel Ninomiya, was burning with indignation. Next day he brought in photographs of the remains of four planes his guns had shot down. Removing our helmets, we apologized for our discourtesy in doubting his first report. He was an authority on anti aircraft gunnery, on which he was for a long time employed as an instructor at the Military College.

The headquarters of the enemy was seized the following day. In the huge British barracks on the outskirts of Kuala Lumpur, fewer than one hundred officers and men of the Army command station established themselves for business. It was of course probable that the barracks would be an early objective for an enemy air attack, but I thought it would be possible to put several thousand men in safety in a corner of the barracks. It was an excellent place in which to work, and here, too, abundant Churchill supplies had been abandoned.

Are the Osaka Soldiers Weak?

IN TAIPING WAS THE 15TH Regiment of Independent Engineers, held there as Army reinforcements. The regiment formed the nucleus of second-reserve soldiers, natives of the Osaka neighborhood organized in Takatsuki, who had been mobilized as emergency troops.

Hitherto "Osaka soldiers" had been considered as synonymous with cowardly soldiers. In the heat of battle it was rumored that there were not a few of them saying, "Oh! We are tired," dropping out of the ranks and skulking behind the firing line, and in fact some of them did so behave. This was not unexpected, as the unit had been hurriedly mobilized temporarily as second-reserve troops, and it was hardly to be expected that they would act like first-line troops.

This unit, however, was one of the first to receive a citation for meritorious service in the Malayan campaign, which, to the whole Army, was an unexpected and undreamed-of happening.

The regimental commander, Lieutenant-Colonel Yosuke Yokoyama, was an old lieutenant-colonel of the 1915 period. His position can be appraised when it is realized that Lieutenant-General Suzuki, the Army

Chief of Staff, was of the same period, as was also Lieutenant-General Nobuichi Tanaka, Director of Headquarters Staff, Military Operations.

Elderly, short of stature, and dripping with sweat, Lieutenant-Colonel Yokoyama always rode a bicycle with the advance guard to survey bridges blown up by the enemy and to work put a plan for their repair.

About twenty trucks had been attached to the 15th Regiment, and these were always kept fully loaded with bridge beams and heavy planks. Nobody at Headquarters knew where such a large supply of these materials had been obtained. They were in fact obtained in the fighting zone. In nearly every town in Malaya there were one or more sawmills. On entering a captured town, most troops searched for provisions, but Lieutenant-Colonel Yokoyama had ordered the 15th Regiment of Engineers to search first of all for sawmills, and to get them working immediately sawing bridge timbers.

Following closely behind the advance guard with their fully loaded trucks, whenever they arrived at a blown-up bridge they would invariably find their experienced old commander with his plan of repair already worked out. The troops were so well trained, and worked so hard and so skillfully, that work which would have taken an ordinary engineer regiment a full day was completed in less than half a day, and sometimes in two or three hours, by the 15th Regiment, Independent Engineers, under Lieutenant-Colonel Yokoyama. Army Headquarters soon came to estimate their working capacity at more than three times that of other regiments.

The breakthrough at Slim River was very largely due to this regiment's miraculous speed in repairing roads and bridges destroyed by the enemy in their retreat from Kampar. Everyone in the 5th Division, to which the regiment was temporarily attached, was tremendously impressed by Lieutenant-Colonel Yokoyama, who invariably fulfilled without demur even the most unreasonable demands made upon him, and his men.

Lieutenant-Colonel Saeki, who showed outstanding courage and ability at the breakthrough of the Jitra line, and Lieutenant-Colonel Yokoyama were of the same period at the Military College and were also classmates, but there was a difference of one step in grade between them and other honors students. Because of a poor result at the Military Staff College, or perhaps because they had never entered it, neither of them had any hope of further promotion. In spite of this, however, they performed amazingly well on the battlefield and there were many others like them.

If all honors students leaving the Military College had led troops on the battlefield and fought as uncomplainingly and as courageously as did Lieutenant-Colonels Saeki and Yokoyama, there might perhaps have been a different end to the war. The fact is, however, that favoritism by the Personnel Section enabled many officers who graduated from the Military College with honors to play their cards well and enjoy long terms under peaceful conditions at home instead of being sent to lead troops on the battlefields of China and Manchuria. This caused many officers to hold their prospects of advancement above their obligation to risk their lives for their country. The Military Staff College was thus degraded to an academy for promotion and successful advancement in life instead of for imbuing officers with the belief that their first obligation was to their country.

The Bicyclists

THE MAIN REASONS FOR THE phenomenal speed of the onslaught in the Malayan campaign, were the special attention given to the equipping and training of infantry formations, and the great achievements of the Engineer Corps.

The horses of the 5th and 18th Divisions, which had been fighting on the mainland of China for a number of years, had become as well trained as their masters. When it was decided to use these troops in the south, however, motor vehicles and bicycles were substituted for the horses. Each regiment of infantry was allotted roughly fifty trucks for the transport of heavy machine-guns, battalion guns, regimental guns, heavy ordnance, quick-firing guns and the like, as well as ammunition. All officers and men who did not ride with the trucks were provided with bicycles. The divisional, army and transport units were reorganized so that their whole strength could be loaded on trucks. A division was equipped with roughly five hundred motor vehicles and six thousand bicycles. The time to accustom troops to these new conditions did not exceed one or two months immediately before the outbreak of hostilities. It was wholly the "doro nawa" model.

In Malaya, almost without exception, bridges were demolished in front of our advancing troops. When all motor transport was loaded with officers, men and equipment, it would have reduced their speed to a walking pace if they had had to wait for the advance of the infantry and the repair of bridges, and it would have taken over a year to fight our way down the peninsula.

With the infantry on bicycles, however, there was no traffic congestion or delay. Wherever bridges were destroyed, the infantry continued their advance, wading across the rivers carrying their bicycles on their shoulders, or crossing on log bridges held up on the shoulders of engineers standing in the stream. It was thus possible to maintain a hot pursuit of the enemy along the asphalt roads without giving them any time to rest or reorganize.

Mr. Churchill, in his memoirs, implies that the Japanese Army before the outbreak of hostilities made secret preparations in each Malay district for comprehensive aggression—even, he says, to the point of storing bicycles in the country. With regret, I have to say that these are not the facts of the case. The truth is that Japanese-manufactured bicycles, because of their cheapness, had become one of the chief exports from Japan to the whole of Southeast Asia, where they were widely purchased by the inhabitants. For this reason replacements and spare parts were easily available everywhere throughout Malaya.

The greatest difficulty encountered in the use of bicycles was the excessive heat, owing to which the tires punctured easily. A bicycle repair squad of at least two men was attached to every company, and each squad repaired an average of about twenty machines a day. But such repairs were only makeshift. When the enemy were being hotly pursued, and time was pressing, punctured tires were taken off and the bicycles ridden on the rims. Surprisingly enough, they ran smoothly on the paved roads, which were in perfect condition. Numbers of bicycles, some with tires and some without, when passing along the road, made a noise resembling that of tanks. At night when such bicycle units advanced, the enemy frequently retreated hurriedly, saying, "Here come the tanks!"

When in trouble, our troops would dive into the jungle carrying their bicycles on their shoulders. The difficulties of trying to break through jungle carrying their arms and with bicycles on their shoulders can well be imagined.

When engaged in battle, the troops left their bicycles in the rear with a few soldiers on guard. As soon as the enemy began to retreat, our troops had to follow in close pursuit. The men guarding the bicycles would obtain the cooperation of the Malay, Indian, and Chinese residents of the locality to carry the bicycles forward to our advancing troops. Such bicycle transport units would be commanded by a Japanese soldier, not even understanding the languages of the mixture of races following him as he went forward carrying the Japanese flag at the head of his bicycle column. The men who trotted along the well-paved roads, leading hundreds of silver wheels, were surely an army in the form of a cross for the emancipation of East Asia.

Attached to the seat of each bicycle was the individual equipment of the soldier, from eight to ten *kan* [65-80 pounds] in weight. Besides this, the soldier carried a light machine-gun and a small rifle over his shoulder. It was not easy work riding the bicycles, often for twenty hours a day.

The British Army formations were almost completely equipped with motor cars and trucks, and whenever we were able to steal a march on them and seize bridges in front of them, or destroy their vehicles by shellfire or airplane bombing, their soldiers had to abandon their cars and trucks and continue their retreat on foot.

Even the long-legged Englishmen could not escape our troops on bicycles. This was the reason why they were continually driven off the road into the jungle, where, with their retreat cut off, they were forced to surrender.

Thanks to Britain's dear money spent on the excellent paved roads, and to the cheap Japanese bicycles, the assault on Malaya was easy.

Part Five

Ammunition Supplies

THE OCCUPATION OF KUALA LUMPUR accomplished, the aim of the second phase of operations in Malaya began according to schedule. Frontline officers and men, during the temporary pause before the next advance, spent their time searching for empty oil drums in which to heat water for baths. Meanwhile, at the Army Command Post, the staff racked their brains over the plan to capture Singapore.

Forty days had passed since the beginning of operations, which fortunately had progressed according to plan from the outset. If conditions made possible the continuance of such headway, our troops should reach Johore Bahru by the end of January. Allowing roughly a week for siege preparations, we aimed to capture Singapore Fortress somehow or other not later than Kigensetsu (11 February).

In our opinion, based on interrogations of prisoners of war and reconnaissance by our Flying Corps, the defenses of the sea front of Singapore Island were, as anticipated, very strong, but those on the land in the rear of the fortress were nothing more than the sort of obstacles one would encounter in field operations.

According to the statements of officer prisoners, Lieutenant-General Percival was strongly of the opinion that it was necessary to strengthen the rear defenses of the fortress, but against the opposition of the Governor-General he could not carry out the necessary construction. The reason that had been given for this decision was that fortification of the rear "would make the civilian population of Malaya uneasy."

Whatever the period, whatever the country, there are always those who perpetrate such blunders!

An attack on Singapore offered unmistakable prospects of victory. The 5th and 18th Divisions would attack to the west of the Causeway, and the Konoe Imperial Guards Division would be withdrawn to the second line.

The plan for the attack on Singapore was prepared by General Staff Headquarters while at Saigon, but the whole plan was really the summing up of the investigations and experiments made during our Formosa days, modified in the light of experience on the battlefield. The men who invented the practical and realistic preparations for the capture of Singapore were those who had worked out the problems under the difficult conditions of the early period of investigation on Formosa.

The first problems dealt with covered preparations for the rear and for the accumulation of ammunition. The following four-point plan was worked out:

1. For the whole Army, 440 guns, with 1,000 rounds per field gun and 500 rounds per heavy gun up to the end of January. With the Army thrusting into the Province of Johore, these could be accumulated on the battlefront by 8 February.
2. Repairs to the railway as far as Gemas to be completed by the end of January, in order to facilitate the accumulation of ammunition on the battlefront.
3. About 50 motor boats and about 100 small motor-driven folding boats to be allotted to each division, for the crossing of rivers.
4. Rations and gasoline to be completely dependent upon Churchill supplies.

This plan was based on the assumption that our front line would advance as far as Johore by the end of January. Some thought that this was improbable of achievement and quite wild. It turned out in fact that all objectives were reached at the times planned.

Every member of the staff was zealous in examining all the problems for which he was responsible. When the quantity of ammunition demanded was mentioned, loud voices were raised:

"Isn't it rather a load?" (Lines of Communication)

"Isn't it too large an order?" (Intelligence)

"Say, this is rather absurd, isn't it?" (Railways)

Discussion in the military staff room quickly boiled over. The opposition, however, was not based on any authoritative foundation; it was merely emotional discussion and criticism. The difficulties were fully understood by everyone as by now we had all felt the weight of British firepower. It was eventually agreed from experience on the battlefield that there was absolute necessity for the full quantities of every type of ammunition to be provided.

Once more I realized that patience is a virtue in staff discussions. I pointed out that owing to the availability of Churchill supplies there was no necessity for us to transport even one bag of rice or one tin of gasoline. Success or failure in the attack on Singapore depended on the supplies of ammunition in the front line that were available for the attack. I implored the lines-of-communication people to use their utmost efforts.

Although the rear defenses of the fortress were weak, the railway was chopped to pieces, and motor vehicles were being worn out with hard use. It was not unreasonable for the lines-of-communication people to be surprised at the quantities of guns and ammunition which I required; my estimates were widely different from theirs. Further more, even Yamatsu, the head of the rear section, was astonished, as might have been expected, by my high-handed demand that this colossal quantity must be accumulated by 8 February. But, "That is all right if you say so," was his comment, and the subordinate staff officers apparently swallowed whole the unexpectedly large requirements. I talked things over with my old classmate, Staff Officer Hongo (Railways), saying, "Hello, cripple! Is your railway all right? Will you be able to haul trains to Gemas by the end of January?"

"I tell you," he replied, "you are breaking up the Railway Regiment and turning us into road coolies. Ha! But seeing that you are a classmate, if I can't do it, I'll take off my staff officer's epaulettes."

Watching and listening attentively, with an open mind free from bias, and shuffling about everywhere on his crutches, Hongo spurred his men to greater activity while himself avoiding medical treatment for the ankle he had injured at Singora. Superintending work on the spot, stimulating and guiding the whole Railway Regiment, finally he succeeded brilliantly in fulfilling the requirements which had at first seemed beyond all common sense. The reason was largely that officers and men alike recognized that the utmost exertion was required of everyone if Singapore was to be captured.

Other staff officers, without exception, helped by putting heart and soul into their work. One of the characteristics of the Malayan campaign was the wholehearted cooperation without any unpleasant opposition by the twelve men in the operations section. They all gave their whole attention and their utmost effort to the task. They were guided by the personality of General Yamashita, and the clear-headed, unselfish character of Suzuki, the Chief of Staff. An outstanding feature of the campaign was that General Yamashita, while paying close attention to every detail, never interfered with the work of his staff officers.

The Pursuit Sustained

OFFICERS AND MEN OF THE 5th and the Imperial Guards Divisions could be easily recognized. Their clothing was stained with sweat and dust, their faces were swarthy, their eyes hollow, and their noses sharpened. When Kuala Lumpur was seized according to schedule, the Army Commander, with a human touch, wished to give them some rest before again launching them on operations. But the overall strategy of the campaign made it imperative for us to advance rapidly to Johore Bahru, and even if possible to arrive there a day earlier than planned. This was incompatible with any notion of a rest period, however brief. The upshot of the matter was the formulation of the following three-point plan:

1. The Mukaide Detachment, which consisted of one tank regiment, one battalion of infantry, and engineers, was to attack opposite Gemas, the barrier to Johore, and hotly pursue the retreating enemy.
2. The main forces of the 5th Division in the meantime were to move to Kuala Lumpur to recover from their exhaustion, then without more ado to overtake the Mukaide Detachment and take over their attack on the enemy.
3. The Imperial Guards Division, carrying on day and night, was to pursue the enemy rapidly along the coast and menace the retreat of their main forces along the trunk road.

This plan was confirmed by the Army Commander without alteration. I then promptly telephoned to the Officer-in-Charge of Military Operations of the 5th Division, and asked him the number of days' rest he expected from his troops. "One day will be splendid," he replied. I told him the Army Commander intended his division to rest for two days. The voice at the other end of the telephone seemed surprised. "Thank the Army Commander for us," he said. "After two days' rest we will be able to advance twice as fast."

Since the landing at Singora, stimulated and urged by Army Headquarters to push on, until Army Headquarters were regarded as demons, the 5th Division had been so hard-pressed that it now expected it would receive at least several days' rest, which it badly needed. In saying "Give us one day's rest," while fully expecting several days, the officers of the division were laughing up their sleeves. When they were given two days their feelings were thoroughly stirred. Because of temper, the divisional commander could not speak; and also, because he was protective of the reputation of his division, he must not speak.

The tolerance of General Yamashita, who had a keen insight into human nature, created a level of morale which spurred men forward on scores of battlefields and in many campaigns; and in the front line it was possible to observe a subtle feeling that staff officers should put in an appearance there. When they did so, marked satisfaction was observed among the troops.

In other armies, when officers from Army Headquarters were dispatched to advanced headquarters during lulls in operations, it was customary for them to take with them a bottle of wine from the Army Commander. At the evening dinner, given by the divisional commander, it was usual for these visiting officers to listen to exaggerated tales of heroism or flattery related by the commanding officer or the resident staff, which buoyed up the faint-hearted ones.

The family tradition of the 25th Army was completely different. However desperate the fight, however dangerous the situation, a staff officer or someone from Headquarters showed up on the battlefield, not only because staff officers were numerous, but also because there was a tendency—characteristic of the Army since its formation—for young officers vying with each other to rush to the front line, and it was difficult to control them. In many cases they advanced to battalion headquarters, and it was by no means unusual to find that they had become fellow travellers with the advance guard. Personally watching the progress of a battle, issuing the next Army order, and again going to the front line to observe its application, on their return they would call at divisional headquarters in passing to report the state of affairs at the front. Such visits were frequent.

Location of headquarters in a position within sound of the guns is ideal, but it does not overcome the difficulty of rapidly interpreting information received from various sources. In the 25th Army, staff officers constantly visiting the front line were able to supplement all information received, and thus became the antennae of the Army Commander. The soldiers, encouraging these visits, expected in consequence that they would not be given orders to achieve the impossible, although at the same time they were quite prepared to be stretched to the limits of their capacity.

The Mukaide Detachment, which had been extended in this way, utilizing its high speed to break through enemy positions, advanced rapidly toward Gemas. The large number of bridges which had been blown up from their foundations were repaired at once by the Yokoyama Regiment of Engineers. When close to Gemas, the Mukaide Detachment met with obstinate resistance, and was unable to break through unaided. The 5th Division, however, restored to excellent spirits by its two days' rest, moved forward quickly over the repaired bridges and carried on the advance without delay. The advance guard was the 5th Division's second landing force, a regiment of infantry under command of the Sugiura Brigade Commander. These troops, who had landed at Singora on 27 December, had followed the division down the Malay Peninsula, and now led the pursuit of the retiring enemy.

Mr. Churchill in his memoirs states that "reinforcing the landing strength of the Japanese Army on the Malay Peninsula were five divisions," and he gives an account of these which is clearly a mistake.

Combining with the Mukaide Detachment, the rested troops of the 5th Division, recovered from their fatigue and stimulated by competition with the Imperial Guards Division, which kept abreast of it along the coast, rushed towards the north gate of Johore Strait, which was the enemy's last line of defense.

Breaking Through Gemas

WHEN THE MUKAIDE DETACHMENT REACHED the Tigabesar Bridge, roughly ten kilometers from western Gemas, which had been destroyed about 3 p.m. on 15 January, its leading infantry troops were suddenly subjected to heavy shellfire from inside the jungle. The terrain of the land was such that both sides of the road were covered with dense jungle which restricted the movement even of tanks. Thus the cooperation of other arms with the infantry was extremely difficult. The 8th Australian Division, which had newly arrived on the battlefield, relying on the advantage of its position, fought with a bravery we had not previously seen.* Furthermore, the enemy air force, with a strange combination of fighting and bombing, made a high-altitude daytime sortie over the battlefield and raided our unprotected motor transport, disconcerting both our front and rear areas.**

On 15 January the 5th Division took over command of the Mukaide Detachment. The commander of the 9th Infantry Brigade, Major-General Kawamura, who was also controlling the Mukaide Detachment in the attack on the enemy at Gemas on the 16th, immediately followed up the attack by pushing forward reinforcements from the rear, but it was not possible to capture Gemas easily. Then a detour through the jungle to the south was made, but because of the difficult terrain and obstinate resistance there was little progress. Finally, in a night attack we broke through

---

* The troops engaged were those of the 2/30th Battalion.
**This attack was made by Dutch bombers protected by Australian fighters.

the Australian front in the early dawn of the 19th, and by that evening were in possession of the whole line.

While fighting desperately in Gurun, my old classmate of the Kobayashi Battalion, as I have previously mentioned, was condemned to heavy punishment for the misconduct of subordinates in Penang. Now, as head of the Mukaide Detachment in Gemas, he also had his fill of hardship. I was sorry for this and felt that his position was unbearable. Thinking it would bring him some consolation, I visited him in the front line without saying a word to anyone. I found it a somewhat trying experience. I could offer no apology for having been the one to inform him of the heavy punishment ordered by the Army Commander. It would be natural for him to resent it.

In the battle zone, crouching under enemy fire, together we talked anxiously about the regrettable incident in Penang. It was ironic that because of the misdeeds of subordinates in Penang the severe punishment of thirty days' close arrest was imposed upon a friend predestined from a former life to gather up the ashes* of those with whom he had played together, suffered together, and trained together at Ichigaya Military College.** There was no alternative. I must bear his grudge against me for the sake of the whole Army even when sacrificing a friend who was crying, "Please forgive me." While apologizing for the way I had hurt him, I took from my plan bag a small piece of cake, which consoled our wounded hearts just a little.

Soon shellfire became concentrated on the rubber jungle. Before long, men were being blown about by the blast from the shells, and for some little time we were very concerned, but creeping under the barrage like squirrels we pushed ahead.

The strategy by which the Imperial Guards Division was pushing along the west coast with irresistible force would soon threaten the enemy front of Gemas. Finally, after holding us in check for about five days, the enemy began to retreat in the direction of Kluang. The Saeki Detachment, taking the lead, pushed rapidly ahead. Fretting from enforced idleness since Jitra, Lieutenant-Colonel Saeki marched at the head of his unit. Again, in order to observe things for myself and to help,

---

* When one's friend dies in battle, by a sworn pledge one must gather up his ashes.
** Ichigaya Daijo is the Hill of Ichigaya on which a military college was established that came to be known as the Ichigaya Military College. It was the only one in Japan, and from it all army officers graduated. At the end of the war a military court was held there by the Allies, at which General Tojo and Mr. Koki Hirota, both former Prime Ministers, were tried and condemned to death.

I went forward by car to the front. As the shellfire was heavy, the driver and I took cover in the jungle by the roadside, but immediately afterwards I went forward on foot to the front line. Bullets were hitting a car behind mine and its driver was wounded, but my car escaped damage.

With fresh reinforcements the enemy prepared a fortified position in several lines with a nucleus of artillery, and this appeared likely to hold up our advance; but the enemy's position at Gemas had in fact already become untenable. Forecasting that the battle would progress rapidly, I took possession of a high-class car which the enemy had abandoned, borrowed a driver from the Saeki Detachment, picked up a soldier who had been wounded in the front line, and started on a speedy return to Headquarters. Shortly afterwards, we ran over a land mine skillfully buried in the road. There was a terrific explosion which blew the car, with us in it, about a foot in the air and threw us off the road. Fragments of glass, dust, and the dense smoke of the bursting mine were blown in our faces. At the moment I was quite resigned to the idea that this time I was knocked out. The red flash of the explosion would, I thought, set fire to the gasoline in the car. Forcing open the door with difficulty, we jumped out. None of us felt any pain. From the interior of the burning car I took my map case and my sword. The driver had been wounded in the face by flying glass, and we all waited by the roadside for an empty car to come along when one did, we took aboard my previous driver, whose wound was serious. In this car we returned to Headquarters, feeling very sorry that two first-class cars had been destroyed in one day. But we consoled ourselves with the thought that there would be other captured cars.

I reported minutely to the Army Commander on the strategic position in the front line. When I apologized for the loss of the two destroyed vehicles, General Yamashita simply replied, "Look here, you must be a little more careful of yourself," and tears shone in the eyes of the generous-hearted general.

Soon the Sugiura Brigade caught up with Kawamura Brigade on the battlefront and took over the line. Repairing damaged bridges and continuing the rapid pursuit of the retreating enemy, the brigade occupied Labis on the evening of 21 January. In the interval we had advanced to Yong Peng, crushing the obstinate resistance of the enemy, who made use of every obstacle of the terrain. Our fresh troops showed great fighting spirit and pushed forward grimly. Staff Officer Sugita, who travelled with the unit, notwithstanding a broken collarbone caused by a motorcycle accident, would not go to hospital; encased in plaster, he still carried on his duties as intelligence officer and made a good pair with Staff Officer Hongo, who hobbled around on crutches.

Command of the Skies

THE ACHIEVEMENTS OF THE 3RD Air Group, which had acted in cooperation with the Army since the commencement of hostilities, must remain in memory eternally. In a short, rigorous offensive it took full advantage of enemy aerodromes and the fuel and ammunition supplies captured on them.

Staff Officer Kawashima, in charge of the Miyashi air-military cooperation squadron, and Sasao, Chief of Intelligence, were on close terms of mutual confidence, and maintained excellent personal relations with the staff officers of the 25th Army. These two officers concentrated their whole attention on the operations, and regarded land and air operations as inseparable.

In Singapore Fortress there were a hundred anti-aircraft guns, and these, together with enemy fighter planes, were very troublesome to our daylight bombing attacks. Every night, however, after our bombers returned, Staff Officer Kawashima used to carry out a bombing attack in a single-seater fighter plane. According to the account of a prisoner of war, these night bombing raids worried the enemy considerably.

When the Takumi Detachment seized the Kuantan airfield, the overland supplying of fuel and ammunition was seen to be impossible. The problem was overcome by loading several hundred small boats with these necessities and sending them across the Gulf of Siam. This expedition was led by Staff Officer Suzuki. Although obstructed by submarines and fighter planes, this boat transport, by sheer weight of numbers, managed to cross the gulf and accomplished its important role as the supply force of the Air Group.

British fighter planes at the outbreak of hostilities were Brewster Buffaloes; their bombers were Blenheims, Beauforts, Hudsons, and so on, and in efficiency our new, untried machines were inferior to these. Estimating that in point of numbers the ratio of strength was one enemy machine to two of ours, it became possible for us in time to grasp command of the air.

About the middle of January, however, as the battle for Johore approached its final stages, there was a temporary change in the air position. The British were reinforced by some Hurricane planes from England, which broke through our air blockade of the Malacca Straits and enabled the landing in Singapore of reinforcements for the Australian 8th Division, much to the joy of the enemy authorities there.

According to Mr. Churchill's memoirs, British planes flying in formation at high altitude often dropped bombs at the same time as they were sweeping the ground with machine-guns. This caused very little damage to our ground units. But the Hurricanes flying low over the rubber forest were a serious challenge. Their intrepid pilots continually machine-gunned our roads, shooting up our motor transport and blocking traffic—defects which could not be remedied by orders or scolding from our Army Headquarters. Until then, our mobile corps had been advancing on the paved roads in broad daylight, taking no precautions against enemy air raids. While the Hurricanes were flying, even single cars moved off the road into the cover of the jungle, and all convoys had to move off the road and get out of sight at the first alarm.

Is Jealousy the Monopoly of Women?

THE DIGNITY OF CHARACTER OF Field Marshal Count Terauchi, Commander-in-Chief of Southern Armies, inspired reverence, and he was certainly a worthy leader of every Army Commander under his orders. But his staff-officer service was self-righteous and map-tactical, and because of this it was not possible to inspire subordinate officers with the spirit of their Commander-in-Chief. The conferring of a letter of commendation on the Takumi Detachment without advising 25th Army caused some disagreement between 25th Army and General Headquarters. Unpleasant feelings between the two also arose over the use of the 18th Division.

At the time of the capture of Alor Star, the plan for the campaign had provided for the remainder of 18th Division to land in the face of the enemy near Mersing, in southeastern Malaya. But as the resistance in the northern part of Johore State became extremely tenacious, it was decided that the main strength of the enemy field army would have to be destroyed on the mainland, by cooperation between our forces operating on the east and west coasts of the peninsula.

At Mersing, the enemy had large forces in a strongly fortified position. Their air force, as I have said, had been reinforced by Hurricane planes from England, and it was obvious that if any landing was attempted at Mersing we would have to be prepared for losses not less than those we suffered in the landing at Kota Bharu.

After the breakthrough at Gemas it was natural to consider that the effectiveness of the enemy forces would diminish and that they would seek the earliest possible refuge in the fortress of Singapore. It was therefore better to change the existing Army plan and land the remainder of the 18th Division at Singora which was done without the loss of a single soldier, and arrange for them to move to the front line by land. They caught up with the rest of the Army in the Kluang district, providing a most useful reinforcement to maintain the momentum of the assault towards the island of Singapore.

This change in movement of the remainder of the 18th Division was made after full discussion with the Navy through their liaison staff officer, Nagai, who from start to finish of the campaign lived continuously at Army Headquarters. We had talked over every aspect of the change of plan, and the final decision was unanimous. Staff Officer Nagai was a bright, cheerful person who did not discriminate between Army and Navy, and he was friendly with all Army staff officers. Elsewhere there were bitter quarrels every day concerning the respective spheres of influence of Army and Navy, but at 25th Army, through out the Malayan campaign, we endeavored to secure unity with the Navy by making available to Navy staff officers without exception every bit of information great and small concerning the operations. Every thing was revealed to them and discussed with them. Consequently, the Commander-in-Chief of the Southward Squadron was in close touch with the 25th Army, and moreover had expressed an identical opinion in regard to landing the rest of the 18th Division at Singora.

Regardless of this, the staff officers at General Headquarters, Saigon, persisting in the previous plan, stubbornly advocated a landing at Mersing in the face of the enemy. They seemed to be jealous of the unanimity of opinion between 25th Army and the Navy in the field. The Chief of Staff at General Headquarters sent a very unpleasant telegram to the Chief of Staff, 25th Army. It read, "In future liaison, restrict information and be watchful that matters under negotiation between General Headquarters and 25th Army do not leak out in advance to the Navy."

At 25th Army Headquarters we had made an important decision concerning the landing at Kota Bharu—about which opinion had not been unanimous in Central Headquarters (Tokyo)—and this had been arrived at with confidence and in a spirit of compromise by the Army and Navy in the field. Since then, we had moved forward in an atmosphere of mutual respect which rose superior to the usual inter-service rivalry. Now, without any antagonism, working together towards the last phase of our common objective, we were about to achieve success. Cooperation on both sides left nothing to be desired. In all probability it was General Yamashita's influence and popularity with the Navy that had caused feminine jealousy to spring up among a section of the staff officers at General Headquarters in Saigon.

When we received the telegram from their Chief of Staff, our whole staff was speechless with astonishment. Immediately a reply telegram was drafted as follows: "In carrying out operations in this great war which must influence the destiny of the Nation, our policy is to cooperate harmoniously, forgetting differences between the Army and Navy, laying bare our hearts in matters great and small and keeping the closest possible touch. In this we will never change."

There was some anxiety that the frigid feeling between General Headquarters, Saigon, and the 25th Army might operate to delay the capture of Singapore.

The Assistant Chief of Staff at General Headquarters, Lieutenant-General Aoki, arrived by plane from Saigon to visit General Yamashita at Army Headquarters in Gemas. His personality did much to mollify the intense feeling. Could not the staff assisting the Commander-in-Chief have been chosen from similar men? Insistence on correct war principles based on facts, and backed up by the authority of senior headquarters, would have prevented perverse action by anybody.

Finally, according to the arrangement between 25th Army and the Southward Squadron, the remainder of the 18th Division embarked at Camranh Bay on 20 January, landed at Singora on the 23rd, and by overland transport concentrated at Kluang without the loss of one man.

But in this problem General Headquarters, which had lost face, retaliated by action through the Air Force. Without the slightest warning, the main strength of the Air Force was switched to the operations in the Dutch East Indies, regardless of the fact that the decisive battle for the Pacific theater of war was about to take place in Singapore. To deprive the Army of the cooperation of the Air Force at this juncture might well delay the capture of Singapore, which was near at hand. It was a case of "plowing the land but forgetting the seed."

As might have been expected, even General Yamashita did not suppress his annoyance. "All right," he commented, "in that case we shall not rely upon the cooperation of the Air Force. The Army will now capture Singapore single-handed." And all those concerned sprang to their feet with a grim resolve. Later, on the high ground of the Sultan's Palace and in Army Headquarters assembled under shellfire on the heights of Bukit Timah, there remained foremost in our minds the motive for which we fought at the risk of our lives under our Army Commander.

It is often thought that jealousy is a prerogative of women only, but among the male sex, particularly among military men, jealousy not inferior to that found among women is often experienced. When anyone accomplishes a commendable task, there is a tendency to unite efforts on all sides to crush the achievement rather than to help and develop it. I sometimes wonder if there was a similar tendency on the enemy side, or if perhaps this was characteristic only of us Japanese, nurtured as we were on a narrow island. While relationships at Advanced Headquarters of 25th Army were excellent, rivalry and friction were to be observed over questions of leadership in the field. Perhaps this was due to the fact that we were cursed by having a jealous General Staff.

Mopping Up Bakri

WHILE THE 5TH DIVISION WAS fighting the bitterly contested battle of Gemas, the Konoe Imperial Guards Division, which was advancing along the coast, moved through northeast Malacca, and with the Kunishi Pursuit Unit (4th Infantry Regiment) and the Iwaguro Pursuit Unit (5th Infantry Regiment) attacked at the Muar River.*

The Kunishi Unit, having one battalion engaged in the small-boat maneuvers, landed its boats in the enemy's rear, while the main body of the unit, moving by land, on 15 January seized the mouth of the river without any fighting.

The Iwaguro Unit, moving on Salang, encountered on 13 January roughly six hundred of the enemy in the neighborhood of Machap. Crushing them, it advanced to the line of the river and made preparations to cross it. Towards its mouth the river presented a very difficult obstacle, but fortunately enemy resistance was not very strong, and the troops of both pursuit units succeeded in crossing the river on the morning of 16 January.

Powerful enemy forces, newly reinforced, had moved north and taken up a strongly fortified position to the west of Bakri.** The commander of the Iwaguro Regiment attacked the enemy from the front with his main strength and a tank company assigned to the unit, while the Ogaki Battalion crept through the jungle from the seacoast to cut the enemy's path of retreat to Bakri.

---

* The 45th Indian Brigade had been given the task of preventing a Japanese crossing of the Muar River. The landing of the small-boat detachment behind its positions threatened the flank and rear of the main defenses of Johore Province, and to meet this threat the 2/29th Australian Battalion was withdrawn from Gemas to support the 45th Indian Brigade; the 2/19th Australian Battalion was withdrawn from Mersing to strengthen that support.
** This force was the 2/29th Australian Battalion (less one company and one platoon), with one troop of 4th Australian Anti-Tank Artillery. After the engagement described by the author in this and the following paragraphs, the battalion broke through the Ogaki Battalion lines and linked up with the 2/19th Australian battalion. The two battalions suffered heavy casualties, but with a few survivors of the 45th Indian Brigade they broke through the Japanese position at Pant Sulong and rejoined the 8th Australian Division at Yong Peng, having succeeded in preventing the Konoe Imperial Guards Division from cutting the Singapore road behind the main British force.

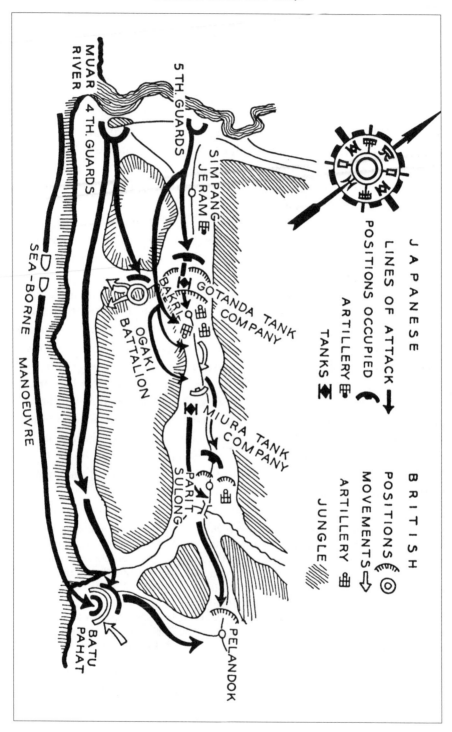

The battle of annihilation at Bakri and Parit Sulong.

The Gotanda Medium Tank Company came under heavy fire in a mined zone and lost its ten tanks one after the other—destroyed by a heavy concentration of shellfire and by mines.

Because the violence of the frontal attack completely absorbed the attention of the enemy, the Ogaki Battalion was able to penetrate through the jungle across their line of retreat. The confused enemy, upon realizing this, reversed their main effort against the Iwaguro Regiment attacking from their front, and counterattacked the Ogaki Battalion in their rear. This unit, while holding the enemy at bay, gradually withdrew, its casualties including the battalion commander.

Increasing the weight of its attack from the front, the Kunishi Unit also attacked from the direction of the coast and again intercepted the enemy's line of retreat at the easterly bridge of Pant Sulong, finally cutting them off and annihilating about one brigade. Thus we achieved a great success. It was a glorious exploit.

Between 16 and 23 January a desperate fight had occurred. When the Gotanda Medium Tank Company lost all its tanks, the surviving officers and men of the company had attacked on foot, reaching the enemy artillery position and the bridge at Pant Sulong, where the last of them met a heroic death after holding up the enemy for some time. Their sacrifice will live long in my memory. Captain Miura was a charming student in the days when I was a company commander at the Military College. Even after receiving his commission he remained an unassuming youth. As an officer he was thoroughly dependable and his sense of responsibility was strong. Stirred to action by the death of a colleague before his eyes, in imagination I can see him now, undaunted by a serious wound, going into action like a demon—and to a heroic death on the battlefield.

The enemy defeated and mopped up in Bakri were the 2/29th Battalion, 8th Australian Division, and the 45th British Indian Brigade. The force which made the flank attack through the jungle was the Ogaki Battalion, and it was a strategic situation such as held one in breathless suspense. For many of those thrown into such hazardous circumstances it was a war of extermination. After an investigation of achievements, a troop citation was awarded the Ogaki Battalion and the Gotanda Company, and these became the revered sacrifices of the whole Army.

The Arrival of the Assault Groups

THE TAKUMI DETACHMENT, AFTER taking possession of Kuantan, changed direction west and, groping its way along the mountain tracks and fording rivers without bridges, arrived at Kuala Lumpur on 25 January. On the 29th they concentrated at Kluang.

General Headquarters had arranged for the whole of the 18th Division to land on the eastern coast. The Koba Regiment disembarked at Kota Bharu and there joined the Takumi Detachment. The original plan called for the balance of the division to land at Mersing, but these troops were instead landed at Singora, while the Takumi Detachment and the Koba Regiment pushed on down the coast to capture Kuantan. Then the Takumi Detachment turned west while the Koba Regiment continued along the coast to take Endau and attack Mersing, a fortified position to which the enemy attached considerable importance, holding it with a brigade of the Australian 8th Division. The position consisted of numerous concrete pillboxes surrounded by two and three rows of barbed-wire entanglements. The guns could be trained over either the sea or the land.

The Koba Regiment crept skillfully through the jungle and pressed its attack entirely in the rear, while simulating an attack from the sea. The enemy, apparently becoming confused, finally abandoned the stronghold, which was completely destroyed. The strength of the Koba Regiment was barely two battalions, and we had grave misgivings about its attacking a force roughly three times its strength. Army, however, cooperated with the Koba Regiment by moving the Saeki Regiment of the 5th Division northward from Kluang, a diversion which drew off some of the enemy's troops from Mersing. This materially assisted the Koba Regiment.

Prisoners of war, after capture, asked the commander of the Koba Regiment, "Why did the Japanese Army only attack from the rear?" and, "Why was it that when putting up such an imposing appearance of attack from the sea not even one man was landed?" The prisoners appeared bewildered and confused by the course the battle had taken.

After the battle, Colonel Koba (who later had the lobe of his ear perforated by an enemy bullet) told Army Headquarters, "Frankly, if we had attacked that position from the sea we couldn't possibly have captured it. It made me shudder just to look at it."

The Mersing operation as finally decided upon was only undertaken after much acrimonious discussion, but the final decision on the method of attack undoubtedly saved several thousand casualties.

The original plan for the Malayan campaign had provided for the whole of the 18th Division to be employed on operations on the east coast, and two of its regiments, comprising the Takumi Detachment and the Koba Regiment, had landed at Kota Bharu. The divisional commander, General Mutaguchi, was thus left in control of the divisional artillery and barely a regiment of infantry, and these troops were eager for action and fretted from enforced idleness at Camranh Bay, anxious to play their part in the capture of Singapore.

Every day General Mutaguchi persecuted the Army Commander with telegrams. Finally, on 20 January, he was ordered to embark, and on the 23rd with his remaining troops he landed at Singora, where he was instructed to advance overland without loss of time to overtake the Army's main forces, a thousand kilometers away, in time for the attack on Singapore.

On the 18th Division's own resources this was an impossibility. It had barely 250 vehicles, and even without becoming involved in any fighting it would have taken two and a half return journeys for each vehicle to move the remainder of the division over the distance.

It was expected that desperate efforts would result in the opening of the railway as far as Gemas by the end of January. In the meantime it seemed there was not a truck or vehicle of any kind which could be spared to assist the division; all available transport was occupied moving ammunition to the front for the final assault on the fortress of Singapore. The only method by which assistance could be rendered was by reducing the vehicle strength of the Konoe Imperial Guards and 5th Divisions. Accordingly, the Army Commander planned, by negotiation, to squeeze as many cars and trucks as possible from each of these two divisions. We knew that by picking up the excellent British service vehicles after each battle the divisions had acquired nearly twice the number with which they had originally been equipped. I had frequently inquired about the actual numbers of vehicles they had, but the replies I received had not been quite honest. We estimated they had at least five hundred vehicles above their authorized number.

In reply to inquiries by telephone of those in charge of operations in both divisions, such as, "How many motor cars can you send us for welcoming the Mutaguchi Division at Singora?" the answer from both divisions was, as expected, "We have no reserve strength at all."

To this I could only say, "Very well. If you cannot dispatch any, we will not say anything against you, but His Excellency, General Mutaguchi, who is a graduate of the same years as the divisional commanders Matsui [5th] and Nishimura [Konoe] will be greatly embarrassed."

Pretending not to have understood, as I wished to make sure of their will to help, and then speaking in a harsh manner, I said, "I wish to receive your answer again," and cut off the telephone.

Before long a telephone message came from General Matsui saying coldly he would help in some way or other. "All right," said I, "please let me have one hundred and fifty first-rate trucks from your division, together with drivers, and dispatch them to arrive in Singora on the early morning of 24 January. Report to Army urgently the name of the officer in charge."

Shortly after, there came a telephone call from the Konoe Division, and an identical conversation ensued.

Although both divisions insisted stoutly, "Of nothing comes nothing," meaning to say, "One cannot wave a sleeve with no arm in it," the sum total of three hundred trucks was disgorged.

Lieutenant-General Mutaguchi and the troops who had landed in Singora, overwhelmed with exhaustion by their efforts to march south ward at top speed, were suddenly shocked by the unexpected arrival of these vehicles. With those belonging to their own division they now had over five hundred. Loading them to breaking point with officers and men, they were able to drive to Kluang Army Headquarters and on 28 January to join up with the Koba Regiment and the Takumi Detachment, which had arrived there earlier.

Excluding the Kawaguchi Detachment, which had been sent to Borneo, the full strength of the division was now concentrated.

When ruddy-faced Lieutenant-General Mutaguchi reported that day to the Army Commander, he said how deeply moved he was by the assistance given him by the other divisional commanders, which had enabled his troops to reach the combat zone fresh and without a casualty in time to participate in the assault on Singapore. Not only Lieutenant-General Mutaguchi but everybody else was pleased too.

During the attack on Singapore, Mutaguchi's 18th Division led the Army from start to finish, capturing Bukit Timah and occupying the Keppel military barracks. His conduct resulted in a deep friendship between himself and General Yamashita.

Deep Emotion in Johore Bahru

FOLLOWING THE SEIZURE OF LABIS by the Sugiura Brigade, the commander of the 5th Division instructed the Kawamura Brigade to press hard on the district running along the railway line. Taking possession of an aerodrome at Kahang at 7 p.m. on the 25th, General Matsui's main force detoured to the south from the east and seized Kluang at midnight the same day. The Sugiura Brigade hotly pursued the enemy from the main road sector and seized Ayer Hitam at the same time.

Repairing a bridge that had been thoroughly destroyed by the enemy, and acting in concert with the Kawamura Brigade in routing resistance from the road, they brought the front line to Rengam, within hailing distance of the pivotal point of Kluang.

Breaking through several fortified lines of enemy positions to the south of Rengam, the 5th Division took Layang Layang on the 28th and the Sedenak area on the morning of the 31st, capturing and disarming approximately fifteen hundred enemy troops froth the 22nd Brigade of the 9th Indian Division, who, after being defeated, escaped into the neighboring jungle.

At half-past three on the afternoon of the 31st the leading troops of the division charged into Johore Bahru.

At the outset, the Konoe Imperial Guards Division had considered making a raid on the 5th Division front to intercept the retreat of the main enemy force, but during the fighting in the vicinity of Bakri and Pant Sulong, the 5th Division single-handedly broke through the enemy lines around Kluang and continued its southward advance.

Altering our original schedule, while one section of our forces opposed the enemy in the Yong Peng area, our main strength attacked them at Batu Pahat.

The assault battalion, which had landed in the enemy rear from small boats [between Batu Pahat and Senggarang], was putting up a strenuous fight in an unsupported siege. By sending the Kunishi Pursuit Unit farther down the coast to Senggarang, and attacking there, we rescued the assault battalion and threw the enemy into a confusion which baffles description. Raking up all our forces in the area we repeated our attacks for roughly about a week, and finally the enemy, after they had nearly crushed our assault battalion, at last met their fate—the collapse of all their forces in the district.*

Making Mersing their right wing, and evacuating Kluang, the enemy retired to their last line of resistance across the Johore River, from which they were promptly driven out by the rapid pursuit of both the Konoe and the 5th Divisions. These troops, after landing at Singora, had broken through the Jitra line, captured Alor Star, and maintained the progress of operations according to schedule right to the day. They had indeed hit the nail right on the head splendidly.

---

* The British troops withdrew to the neighborhood of Rengit. Some managed to rejoin the main British force overland, but the majority—comprising about 2,000 men—were evacuated by sea by the Royal Navy on four successive nights.

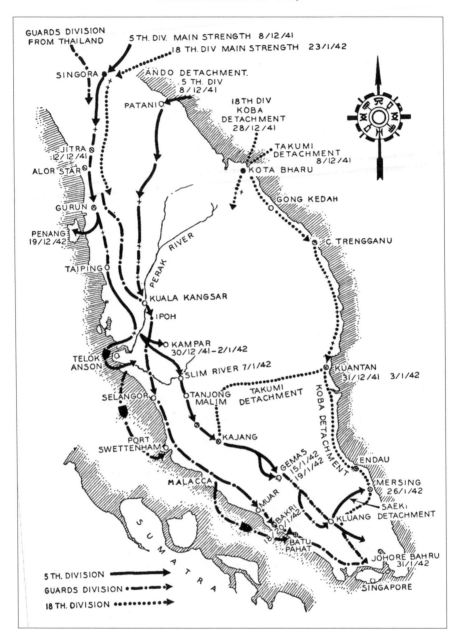

The Malayan campaign of the 25th Army.

The troops were not exhausted. The unit with the best cars rushed into Johore Bahru, where remnants of the enemy were still appearing and disappearing, and suddenly—look!—on the high ground of the Sultan's Palace the Japanese Flag was fluttering spiritedly in the sea breeze. And did it not command a bird's-eye view of Singapore?

Since landing in southern Thailand barely fifty-five days ago, we had made an overland dash of eleven hundred kilometers—exactly comparable with the distance from Tokyo to Shimonoseki [half the length of Honshu, the principal Island of Japan]. We had fought ninety-five large and small engagements, and repaired more than two hundred and fifty bridges. The speed of this assault was unparalleled in the history of war.

On an average our troops had fought two battles, repaired four or five bridges, and advanced twenty kilometers every day. Our small boats, without armaments, had maneuvered and carried out landings up to six hundred and fifty kilometers behind the enemy's lines on the western coast, and had even surpassed the achievements of troops on land.

Singapore, the British stronghold which for over a hundred years had dominated Asia, now lay before our eyes pawing the ground in its last moments.

Those who had braved the sea passage, landed in southern Thailand, crept through the almost impenetrable jungle, destroyed the stubborn enemy, and achieved the apparently impossible by bringing the Malayan campaign to a successful conclusion, were the frontline officers and men. Malaya was the gift resulting from their strenuous efforts.

The fight for Singapore was now on. This first-class modern fortress, flaunting its impregnability, appeared undaunted before our tired eyes. Johore Strait was over fifteen hundred meters wide at high tide. The Seletar Naval Base protected its left front, and enemy fighter planes were continuously patrolling over the straits. From various places in the rubber jungle rose columns of dense black smoke. The enemy had nearly a thousand guns large and small, and an unlimited ammunition supply—all awaiting our attack; their anti-aircraft guns held our airplanes in check with dense barrages. We knew, however, that in the rear of the fortress the defenses were weakest, and we had to exhaust every means in our power, whether by the plan of the gods or the plan of the devils, to reduce this great fortress by 11 February, the anniversary of the coronation of the Emperor Jimmu Tenno.

On the high ground of the Sultan's Palace a map was drawn up giving full details of the fortress as observed. After a thorough investigation of the deployment of our heavy siege guns, the preparations for attack by our divisions, and the enemy's defensive dispositions on the foreshores, a fresh plan for the final attack materialized. Everyone acknowledged the necessity for modifying the original plan.

Returning to Kluang Headquarters that evening, the staff worked all night on the final plans for our assault on the fortress. Staff Officers Asaeda and Kunitake assisted very ably. All staff officers in the rear were impressed with the necessity for accumulating the full quota of ammunition supplies laid down—namely 1,000 rounds for field guns, 500 rounds for heavy guns. Intelligence was asked for its appreciation of the strength of the enemy, who had recently received reinforcements from England and Australia. From Tokyo, Tominaga, Head of the Personnel Bureau, and Tanaka, the Chief of the Operations Section, visited Army Headquarters. Senior officers' discussions continued throughout the night.

The material results of the Malayan campaign from the landing at Singora to the time of arrival of our troops on Johore Strait were as follows:

1. Japanese forces numbering approximately 35,000 men, against the British 80,000, destroyed five brigades—roughly 25,000 men.
2. Booty captured comprised 13 airplanes, roughly 330 guns of various types, roughly 550 light and heavy machine-guns, about 50 tanks* and armored cars, about 3,600 motor vehicles, and about 800 locomotives and railway trucks.

The Japanese losses were 1,793 men killed in battle and 2,772 wounded—a total of 4,565 casualties.

Quite unexpectedly, the sickness rate was very low. In particular there were scarcely any sufferers from malaria. The spirit of the troops remained high throughout the campaign. Operations progressed normally without any excessive driving of the troops, and rigorous military discipline was maintained. The reason for all this was probably the brief periods for rest and recuperation given all troops after completion of their tours of duty in the front line.

Great victories are not expressed in figures. Two important factors in winning them are expressed in the phrases, "The troops labored for hours" and, "They were firmly confident of certain victory when in conflict."

Mr. Churchill in his memoirs criticizes our military operations thus: "Before the Great European War of 1914–18 there was a thorough inves-

---

* Evidently Bren-gun carriers. The British forces had no tanks.

tigation [by Japan] of conditions for warfare in Malaya, and a large-scale plan of invasion was exhaustively prepared."

If such had been the case, our task would have been much easier. In the Malayan campaign of 1941–42, there were in fact very few of our officers or men experienced in Malayan conditions. In the whole Army they could be counted on the fingers of one hand. I myself had spent barely an hour making an aerial reconnaissance over northern Malaya and southern Thailand.

If, as Mr. Churchill states, the preparations for the campaign had been carried out exhaustively over a long period, I firmly believe we could have shortened by at least one month the time taken for our assault.

General Yamashita, while travelling in Germany, had had discussions with Marshal Goering and officers of German military technical schools, and they had told him that in the event of war in the Far East the reduction of Singapore would probably take nearly a year and a half with five divisions.

Part Six

Singapore—the Pivot

SINGAPORE WAS BRITAIN'S PIVOTAL point in the domination of Asia. It was the eastern gate for the defense of India and the northern gate for the defense of Australia. It was the axis of the steamship route from Europe to the Orient, north to Hong Kong, through to Shanghai, and to the treasures of the Dutch East Indies to the south and east. Through these two arteries alone, during a period of many years, Britain controlled the Pacific Ocean with Singapore as the very heart of the area.

The young and spirited empire-builder, Sir Stamford Raffles, controlling a few troops, landed in the territory and hoisted the Union Jack on 29 January 1819. By 6 February, by skillful diplomatic measures, he pacified Lamon, the Mohammedan king of Johore, with barely 650,000 dollars, thus acquiring a perpetual lease. He then set to work to establish a commercial port. Singapore, at that time a village with barely a hundred and fifty or a hundred and sixty people, was a desolate, savage jungle with nothing more than barbarian villages scattered here and there. Then in 1824 the whole island was formally transferred to the British East India Company.

In 1923, two years after the Washington Conference had solved the problem of abolition of the Anglo-Japanese Alliance, Britain commenced strengthening the defenses of the island. The Washington Agreement restricted expansion of the Japanese Navy, but permitted Britain to proceed with a plan for the fortification of Singapore at an estimated cost of many millions of pounds sterling, the project to be completed over ten years, while at the same time the defense measures of other countries was selectively restricted. In 1938, with completion of the large floating dock and the King George VI graving dock, Singapore became a first-class modern fortress, one of the four great fortresses of the world, ranking with Gibraltar, Pearl Harbor, and Malta. It was ready for use and the British went so far as to boast of its magnificence and power.

With the outbreak of the China Incident in 1937, the policies of Britain and Japan became sharply against each other in eastern Asia. Britain established her East Asia army headquarters in Singapore under the supreme command of General Pownall, planned the unification of the local volunteer forces, and consolidated the defenses with Australian and Indian soldiers. Then, with the assistance of America, she reinforced her military position in epoch-making fashion just prior to the outbreak of hostilities, when the Japanese—American conference was at its peak and tension at its highest.

Britain's boast that Singapore was an impregnable fortress, and her attempted coercion of Japan by dispatching to Singapore the two great battleships *Repulse* and *Prince of Wales*, were things that remain fresh even now in the memory of the people of Japan.

Singapore was naturally easy to defend, and with consolidation of its equipment could be shaped into an impregnable fortress. Facing the seacoast, a battery of 15-inch guns was installed which dominated the eastern mouth of Johore Strait and protected the vast military barracks at Changi. The fortress was constructed out of steel and concrete, and the world's greatest guns directed their forbidding muzzles towards the sea front. The military airfields of Tengah, Kallang, Seletar and Sembawang were good bases of operation for a large air force, and in Seletar naval harbor the two aforementioned docks were installed which could easily take in fifty-thousand-ton battleships.

The British boasted about the huge graving dock, the King George VI, which was 1,000 feet long, 130 feet wide, and 35 feet deep. About 900,000 cubic yards of cement were used in its construction. The floating dock, little if any inferior in capacity, was constructed in England and towed out to Singapore in two separate pieces. It had an overall length of 1,000 feet, an overall width of 300 feet, and was anchored in a mooring place 70 feet in depth. About 1,500,000 tons of fuel oil, sufficient to maintain the whole of the British Fleet, and to provide for any emergency, was stored in a number of huge storage tanks. The fortress took nearly ten years to build, cost over ten million pounds sterling, and was completed in February 1938.

At the opening ceremony of this great naval port, a threatening attitude to Japan's southward advance was revealed by the attendance of battleships of every nation of the British—American allied camp. In the spring of 1937 a plan to equip completely and to consolidate the fleets of both hemispheres was introduced into the British Parliament. But, as this work was not yet completed, it was a case of having "the chicken house ready but no chickens."

In this great fortress, which Britain boasted could never be captured by attack from the sea, there was, however, an important weakness. As already stated, the rear defenses in the region of Johore Province were incomplete. This resulted from a defect in the organization of the fortress, or rather from a defect in the plan of military operations.

In other words, to land in southern Thailand, brave the intense heat and the long distance of eleven hundred kilometers, and advance through dense jungle, was probably deemed an impossibility by what seemed, to the British, common-sense judgment. A Japanese Army contemplating such operations in an emergency would, it appeared, in view of the long distance overland, have to labor for perhaps more than a year to reach Singapore from Thailand. In the meantime it was not difficult to imagine that the British would complete fortification of the landward front.

In barely fifty-five days, however Japanese Army overwhelmed Malaya, carrying everything before it, and during the campaign the British, not being gods, were never certain of our whereabouts.

According to Mr. Churchill's memoirs, Singapore's rear defenses (the Johore front) were believed to be in readiness. This was accepted by everyone as a matter of course.

On the morning of 19 January, in a telegram from General Wavell, Mr. Churchill for the first time heard not only that there were no permanent fortifications for the rear defense of Singapore, but also that since the outbreak of hostilities, especially since the Japanese had been building up strength in the southern part of Indochina, the lack of rear fortifications had not even been considered or discussed by any commanding officer in Singapore. The suggestion had not even been made that field-operations fortifications should *be* constructed.

It seems inconceivable that the British in Singapore should neglect to report the truth of the non-existence of rear defenses. In the circumstances, Mr. Churchill's rebuke was quite proper. Among the commanding officers in the Malayan theater there was not one who had a tithe of the enthusiasm and feeling of responsibility of Mr. Churchill. This, however, was to be considered the unexpected good fortune of the Japanese Army.

The Plan of Capture

OUR ESTIMATE OF THE BRITISH defenses and strength in Singapore was made on the basis of information that had been accumulated by all possible means. The five chief points were as follows:

1. Before the outbreak of hostilities it was estimated that the British forces in Malaya numbered from five to six brigades of regular troops, and two brigades of volunteers. Later, after examination of prisoners of war taken up to the end of January, this estimate was revised. Enemy troops in Singapore were then believed to comprise: (a) No. 3 Army Corps (9th and 11th divisions), reduced to about half strength by casualties in battle and losses of prisoners; (b) Australian 8th Division (two brigades and 2/4th Machine-Gun Battalion), reduced to about two-thirds strength by casualties and prisoners lost; (c) 53rd and 54th Anglo-Indian brigades, annihilated; (d) 18th British Division (54th and 55th brigades); (e) reinforcements of about one brigade of fresh troops from India; and (f) roughly two brigades of the Malay and Chinese (born in the country) Volunteer Army. This, we considered, gave a grand total effective strength of roughly two divisions, with an actual fighting strength of about 30,000 men (though the real fighting strength was about twice our estimate).
2. The enemy, relying on the strength of the fortress, would probably resist strongly, but owing to the fact that there was a tremendous number of non-combatants in Singapore, it was unlikely they would resist to the last man. With the addition of the refugees who had fled into the island during the hostilities on the mainland, the population of the island was considered to exceed one million. There were sufficient rations for the army for from one to two years, but there were not enough provisions to feed the entire population for any length of time. This was a very serious weakness from the point of view of defense.
3. The pivotal point of the defenses was the sea front only. After the commencement of hostilities, rear defenses were hurriedly constructed in about two months. They were well sited, and behind barbed-wire entanglements, but without permanent fortification they were little more formidable than ordinary field entrenchments. We considered that these positions would be relatively easy to neutralize with field-army guns lighter than 15 centimeters.
4. The key point of the defensive positions was the sector east of the Dyke road (the Causeway), because of the naval-port defenses. The

last line of resistance of the city would be the heights of Bukit Timah. Loss of the reservoir would be fatal.*

5. The rise and fall of tide in Johore Strait is roughly two meters and the current flows fairly fast, but there was a possibility we would be able to use collapsible motor boats. Because of the presence of enemy gunboats and their remaining air force, the crossing of the strait presented some difficulty, and it did not appear possible to exercise effective control of troops who survived the crossing. Fortunately, mechanical mines had not been laid in the strait, except at its mouth. The adoption by the enemy of "seafire" tactics (ignition of crude petroleum discharged on the surface of the water) was anticipated and counter-measures were taken.

The Singapore we had once seen in a dream we now saw with our own eyes from the heights of the Sultan's Palace. But the predetermined fundamental plan for its capture was not changed by observation. In the ordinary way, all Army, divisional, and heavy artillery units would be ordered to search out the enemy position, and then, after investigation and analysis of the results, the plan of capture would be based on the effects of the bombardment. The Army order for the assault would then be issued accordingly.

The enemy, exhausted and demoralized after their retreat from the mainland, had sought shelter in the fortress. We had to begin our attack without giving them even a day's respite to rest, reorganize and recover their morale. We knew accurately our own fighting power and the condition of the enemy, and had the whole island fortress under close observation. It was decided to issue the orders for assault without delay. I finished writing the final plan for the reduction of Singapore by sitting up all night. It was approved by the Army Commander at Kluang Headquarters the following morning. On 1 February at 10 a.m., divisional commanders and senior officers numbering about forty were assembled in the Skudai rubber jungle, and to the rumble of the guns General Yamashita impressively issued the Army orders to those present. Reading in a clear voice, his face was flushed, and on the cheeks of the men listening tears could be seen. The spirits of the seventeen

---

* The reservoirs on Singapore Island were storage reservoirs only, being fed by pipeline from Johore across the Causeway. When subsequently the Causeway was demolished and the reservoirs and distributing pipes were damaged by shellfire, there was not enough water to supply the island's population of one million people for more than a few days.

hundred men killed in action since the landing at Singora were believed by all to be present at this meeting.

Each of us received, in the lid of a canteen, a little of the Imperial gift of *Kikumasumune*,* and we drank a toast: "It is a good place to die. Certainly we shall conquer."

Before landing at Singora we had left our small trunks with our spare clothing and other possessions in the custody of Saigon Headquarters, which we left equipped with map cases only. As a result of two months' fighting, our underwear was infested with vermin, but on this day we changed into completely new garments from Army reserve stocks.

"Life is desired by all men, death disliked by all. But this day, standing on this earth, if we meet death, which we all must welcome once one day or another, will we not be happy that it comes while we are participating in this battle?"

The Battle Plan for the Assault

THE SALIENT POINTS OF THE plan for the assault were to crush the enemy to the north of Johore Strait; to block them in the sector east of the Dyke road (the Causeway); to assault from the Causeway to the west; to advance first of all to the strategic line on the heights of Bukit Timah; and after that to occupy the whole island.

The most important essentials may be summarized as follows:

First Period: Preparations

1. Having defeated the enemy in the neighborhood of Johore Bahru, a section of each division will mop up enemy stragglers and take possession of the north bank of the strait. To protect deployment of our artillery, all inhabitants within twenty kilometers of the strait will be evacuated. The area will be searched for enemy detachments and observation of terrain on Singapore Island established. The Konoe Imperial Guards Division will make active feints on a wide front to divert the enemy east of the Causeway.

2. The division will concentrate its main forces as follows: Imperial Guards Division—Tebrau and Senai district; 5th Division—east side of Skudai; 18th Division—east of the heights of the source of water supply.

---

* A type of wine used on special occasions. The fact that the wine drunk here was an Imperial gift indicates that the occasion was one of most unusual solemnity.

3. Army artillery with 48 15-centimeter howitzers, 16 other guns, and one company of balloons will occupy positions around Hill 572, and, together with divisional artillery, bombard the enemy airfields and destroy their most important entrenchments in the area east of Kranji River. At the proper time we will destroy the enemy artillery. The artillery of both the 5th and Konoe divisions will fire upon important objectives such as aerodromes and oil tanks while the Army artillery fires upon Tengah and Sembawang aerodromes and the Sungei Mandai Kechil oil tanks. The boundary between the targets of Army and divisional artillery units will be a line connecting the lower waters of the Serangoon River, the northern extremity of Seletar aerodrome, Mandai Station and Kranji River.

For the attack, the standard to be used is: (a) for ranging and registering on targets and attack preparations—100 rounds per field gun, 50 rounds per heavy gun; (b) period of preparation for crossing Johore Strait-400 rounds per field gun, 125 rounds per heavy gun, (c) crossing Johore Strait to the capture of Bukit Timah heights-250 rounds per field gun, 125 rounds per heavy gun; (d) future battles and reserves—250 rounds per field gun, 125 rounds per heavy gun. This gives a total of 1,000 rounds per field gun, 500 rounds per heavy gun.

After the advance to the shores of Johore Strait, the number of days to the beginning of the attack to be approximately five days. This will be subject to modification according to circumstances.

Second Period: The Attack on Singapore

1. Complete preparations for the assault on the city. In cooperation with a bombing attack by air force units, the whole of the artillery from X morning to carry out artillery preparation—i.e., fire on enemy positions prior to the infantry attack, to destroy coastal defense equipment, demolish entrenchments, and subdue or destroy enemy artillery. The allotment of duty for Army and divisional artillery is respectively as follows: Army artillery is to dominate enemy artillery and destroy their key positions in the front line; divisional artillery is responsible for cooperation with the front line and the domination of enemy artillery from 1600 to 1800 on X day, on the plan of the commander of Army artillery.

When putting these essentials into execution, according to conditions from time to time, especially in the enemy fortified positions, there will be a certain amount of change.

2. The main forces of the 5th and 18th divisions, during X day and night, pressing on to Johore Strait on the north-bank sector, will complete preparations for assault under protection of the artillery. The

advance of each division to the south of the line between the seaplane base and the Malayu River above its first bend will be limited to the minimum strength needed for preparation for attack.

3. The Konoe Division will, from X – 1 day, continue with a display of force until midnight on X day, and then, leaving behind a section of the division, and concealing its movement as well as possible, will concentrate in the sector between the Tebrau River and the seaplane base but concentrate roughly two battalions of infantry in the neighborhood of the north coast of the Malayu River.

4. Every unit on X day, commencing movement after sunset, will connect with the assault-supporting fire of the artillery units. At half an hour after midnight on X day, the first units of 5th and 18th divisions will disembark together on the enemy shore. One section of the 18th Division will check any attempt by enemy naval vessels to dominate the western extremity of the channel. When their disembarkation units have secured their landing, the main strength of 5th and 18th divisions will cross Johore Strait. On the second evening the Konoe Division, Army artillery, tanks, and the remainder of the 5th and 18th divisions will cross the strait, and on the third evening the remainder of the Army.

5. Troops landing on Singapore Island will endeavor to crush enemy positions and enlarge their footing up to the morning of X + 1 day, advancing to the line at the extremity of Tengah airfield without however interrupting the advance to the Jurong River and the line on the high ground of Bukit Mandai. When this line is established, preparation will commence for the assault on the Bukit Timah heights. In cooperation with the artillery, tanks, and the Air Force, the infantry will advance and break through the enemy fortifications to the reservoir on the heights. The Konoe Division will concentrate in the rear of the 5th Division, and at an opportune time advance to the eastern side of the source of the water supply from the direction of Mandai.

6. After advancing the line to the positions stated in the foregoing paragraph, if the enemy does not surrender, the 18th Division will occupy the half section of streets to the south, and the 5th Division the half section of streets to the north, and later the fortress of Changi. The Konoe Division will immediately occupy the fortresses of Seletar and Changi. A section of the 18th Division will remain on guard against enemy troops in the fortresses of Blakan Mati and Ulu Pandan, which will be captured as required.

In exactly one year from the time we commenced to prepare for military operations in the south we were now preparing for the assault on Singapore. Without doubt, the sword we had so hurriedly polished would fall upon the head of the fortress which had been prepared for a hundred years. On reflection, the Malayan campaign seemed undoubtedly the most daring military enterprise in Japanese history.

The face of a bosom friend, Take-no-Uchi, who died in Bangkok, that of a pupil, Captain Miura, who was badly wounded in the face, and of Lieutenant Ofuji, who was separated from me at Jitra, floated vividly before my eyes. "Unashamed I shall follow afterwards," I thought. Their memory was deeply engraved upon my heart.

Formerly, before an old-time siege, it was customary to advise the enemy general to surrender. In the Pacific war, however, such examples of advising before we attacked were not numerous. Hong Kong was one exception. In the Malayan campaign we did not adhere to our old custom, for we knew that tradition and pride prevent the British Army surrendering without fighting a battle for the fortress, and more over a preliminary summons to surrender would have been a serious blunder as it would have made known to the enemy our intention of forcing the difficult passage of Johore Strait. It would be time to urge surrender when we had seized the heights of Bukit Timah, pointed a dagger at the throat of Singapore and sealed the fate of the enemy. Our swift and sudden attack was one of the important reasons for our success.

To the Heights of the Imperial Palace

IN DETERMINING THE POSITION FROM which Army Headquarters would exercise supreme command of the battle to decide the destiny of Japan and the emancipation of Asia, there were many aspects to be considered. But, notwithstanding the risks involved, we chose the heights of the Imperial Palace [Istana Hijau, or the Green Palace]. It was an obvious target for enemy planes, but it possessed such outstanding advantages for observation and signals communication that we decided this was where Headquarters should be.

The Sultan of Johore, who had built the Imperial Palace regardless of expense, boasted of its beauty and majestic appearance. It stood on the heights on the north side of Johore Strait looking down on Singapore Island. It was within easy range of the enemy artillery, and at times even machine-gun bullets came flying past, for the enemy lines were not more than two kilometers distant. From the palace the naval port of Seletar lay beneath one's eyes, and Tengah aerodrome appeared as if it could be grasped in the hand. It was on our infantry front line and it was also our forward artillery observation post.

There was reasonable and genuine opposition to the occupation of the palace as Army Headquarters. Many believed that it was too exposed to enemy fire for use by Army, and divisional headquarters felt strongly that Army had stolen a march on them. It was, however, the only position from which the Army Commander could have a close view of the whole battle line from the crossing of Johore Strait to the capture of the heights of Bukit Timah. The spiritual effect alone of being able to see every detail of the battle was of sufficient importance to override all opposition, which was strong even among members of the staff.

The Army Commander's decision ended all discussions, and the minimum number of staff personnel necessary pushed forward to the palace while the rest remained in the rear in the rubber jungle.

Although the palace stood in an exposed position, the unanimous opinion was, "Anyhow, if we are to die, will not the heights of the Imperial Palace be a suitable place?"

Standing on an excellent lawn, the red-brick and green-tiled building, of whose splendid appearance the Sultan was so proud, was perfectly visible to the enemy. Shells sometimes fell on the lawns, turning up the earth and leaving craters like pitted pock scars. At the eastern end of the building there was a five-story observation tower, with a narrow spiral iron ladder leading to the top, where there was a four-and-a-half mat room, glassed in on all sides. It gave the impression of a small castle tower.

A warship has a steel conning-tower, but here we had a glass-covered battle command post. Struck by stray enemy bullets, several of the glass windows were smashed, but although not constructed for warfare, the building was strong and powerful. We decided to use the glass-enclosed room for the military operations room, and for about a week we were practically confined there making preparations for the attack. With field glasses, the movements of even individual men over on the enemy side of the strait could be clearly seen.

In this observation post was drafted the Army Commander's first telegram: "I, this whole day, pushing forward the command post to the heights of the Johore Imperial Palace, will observe directly the strenuous efforts of every divisional commander. (Signed) Lieutenant-General Yamashita." Thus under hostile shellfire, Army Headquarters gave silent encouragement to the officers and men of the whole Army.

Normally there are numerous arrivals at and departures from Army Headquarters, and many people disregard the regulations for preserving concealment and privacy. In this place, however, there was no traffic, for visitors to Headquarters came at the risk of their lives from enemy fire. The staff practically lived on dry bread and tinned food, and on no account was any cooking allowed. While we lived together at the Army Artillery Unit Observation Post, enemy shells sometimes flew over the heights, but the glass-covered observation room towering in the sky was practically a safety zone. When the enemy surrendered we inquired, "Why did you not shell the heights of the Imperial Palace?" The reply was, "It was not thought that under any circumstances such a distinct building would be used as Army Headquarters." Up to the last it was the most suitable military operations command post, and our use of it completely surprised the enemy.

Distressing Preparations

CONCEALMENT OF THE PLAN FOR invading Singapore Island was absolutely necessary. The main Army forces and vehicles of all descriptions, except the patrols, the guards, and the staff necessary for preparation for crossing the water barrier, were protected from enemy observation by the rubber jungle in a position suitably isolated from Johore Strait.

In accordance with the plan, all inhabitants within approximately twenty kilometers of the strait were evacuated; enemy patrols and spies who were disguised and used small radio transmitters and signal shots were difficult to distinguish from the civil population. We had to avoid killing innocent people by fire and sword. The columns of refugees, removed from the houses in which they had lived for so many years, irrespective of age or sex, with their personal possessions over their shoulders, moved out slowly. Five- and six-year-old girls, with quart bottles of drinking water hanging from their shoulders, pulled along by their mothers' hands, were jostled along in a long line. Seeing them trudging barefoot along the hot asphalt roads, thinking of one's own children left behind in the Fatherland, it was difficult to view this as a matter of military necessity, but there was no alternative but to avert our faces and steel our hearts against compassion. We knew that the hardships of the refugees would be over in a short time, and in the meantime we could help as many as possible by giving them transport in empty trucks that were returning northward.

In about a week, every detachment working almost to exhaustion had completed preparations. The principal task of carrying out an accurate artillery survey, amending existing defects on our maps and exactly plotting enemy positions on them was satisfactorily executed. Other things which had to be undertaken were calculating the necessary data for artillery ranges, the accumulation of ammunition to complete the full quantity required per gun, preparations by the engineers for crossing the strait, the overhaul of boat equipment (an important matter), and cutting down jungle and opening up roads from troop concentration points to the water's edge.

The crippled Staff Officer Hongo (railways), Staff Officer Kato (ammunition), Staff Officer Kera (boat preparations), Staff Officers Asaeda and Kunitake (attack preparations of each division) and Staff Officer Sugita (intelligence), all watching the enemy movements and giving full attention to their tasks, had not a moment's leisure. Especially diligent was the railway unit, which had repaired eleven hundred kilometers of rail that had been badly damaged by the retreating enemy up to the boundary of Johore State. This had been completed by the end of January, and within another week the full requirement of ammunition per gun had been accumulated. The work was completed as the result of a supreme effort, the spirit of which permeated all the troops on the lines of communication.

Motor traffic reached the limits of congestion, thrusting forward with supplies for each Army division and every artillery unit near the front line, at the northern extremity of Johore Strait. In all probability nearly three thousand motor vehicles were in use. The central and seacoast roads were restricted to outward and return journeys respectively, and in Skudai, in the south, movement was permitted only by night. Traffic was very strictly controlled since violation of the rules laid down could obstruct the preparations of the whole Army. Control, however, was not easy.

The commander of the Tank Brigade organized all movement of motor vehicles, which were kept in order by numerous traffic-control squads. A surprising amount of labor was saved by the engineers' preparations for crossing the strait. Selected officers, non-commissioned officers and men supervised by day and night the work carried on at the water's edge inside the jungle, warding off attacks by crocodiles, watching enemy movements on the opposite shore, hourly investigating the condition of the constantly changing tidal currents and measuring the depth of the water at as many points as possible. One party reconnoitered for the presence of obstacles on the opposite shore in order to indicate secretly the road to be followed by the main forces moving into position.

The fuel stored in Singapore was a quantity equivalent to six months' supply for the whole British Fleet. If, after we commenced the channel crossing, the enemy deliberately and without warning opened the oil-feed pipes onto the streams inside the island and onto the waters of the strait and then ignited it, the battlefield would be transformed into a sea of fire. From the commencement of the operation this possibility had greatly worried General Yamashita, who, during his visit to Germany, had been told of such an occurence by a German general. Staff officers repeatedly experimented with drums of oil thrown into the water of a small pond behind our lines, and on the smooth water it certainly appeared possible that the surface of the water could be set afire. On Johore Strait, however, with the rise and fall of tide and the strong current, it would not be easy to cover the whole surface with oil, so we did not consider seriously how to cope with the situation; nevertheless, to lessen the possibility of the enemy's attempting to set the waters of the strait afire, the oil tanks were immediately attacked and destroyed by heavy artillery bombardment. The whole island was hidden in black smoke, which hampered us to a great extent, for it prevented observation the fall of our shells either from the ground or from the air.

One problem was to protect our main forces crossing the strait from attack by enemy gunboats. This duty was given to the right wing of the 18th Division. One section of artillery was placed in concealed positions at the water's edge, and laid its guns to fire low across the surface so that they could secure direct hits on any small craft crossing their line of fire. Large rafts were also built with which to block the entrance to the strait and obstruct any vessels attempting to enter it. All preparations were completed in about a week. The hardships experienced by officers and men during this preparatory period were not less than those of the battlefield.

Army orders demanded that all preparations should be complete by noon of 7 February but, except for the artillery, no reports that preparations had been completed had been received by that time. In reply to urgent telephone calls the divisions answered, "We will finish without fail by the evening of the seventh."

The Army Commander, however, after mature consideration, decided to postpone the attack for one day. No division, of course, made any comment on this decision, but there is little doubt they were all very pleased at the extra time given them. The postponement was typical of General Yamashita consideration for those under his orders, which marked him as a commander of outstanding qualities.

All preparations having been completed, and reconnaissance reports synthesized without necessitating any alteration whatever in the Army plan, everything was now ready for the attack. The commander of the Konoe Imperial Guards Division, who had been directed to carry out a demonstration on X – 1 day and to cross Johore Strait in the rear of the

5th Division on X + 1 day and evening, was, however, not satisfied. He wanted his division to join in the first attack, and suggested to the Army Commander the desirability of amending one section of Army orders, which were on the point of being issued, to enable him to do so.

General Yamashita revised his orders accordingly, and this matter later gave rise to serious problems.

A Demonstration to Mislead the Enemy

THE KONOE DIVISION HAD BEEN ordered to contain the exhausted enemy at the eastern end of Singapore Island by a strong demonstration, and they carried out this task thoroughly, in a manner befitting the reputation of the division. The divisional staff planned that on X – 1 day and night (7 February) a section of the division would attack and occupy Ubin Island, an important strategic point two or three hundred meters high, closely overlooking Changi Fortress and Seletar Naval Base. The whole island is virtually a rocky mountain, and originally produced bauxite. Since 1940, the British had been making strenuous efforts to complete its fortifications and the Island had been a prohibited area to all except those working there. Owing to the deep mud surrounding it, landing on its shores could be expected to be difficult.

The Konoe Division staff officers were confident of the ability of their troops to capture the island, but for the attack they required twenty collapsible motor launches, all of which had been allocated for the main attack on Singapore Island.

Although the whole Army admired the Konoe Imperial Guards for the manner in which they had carried out the duties assigned them, they had a reputation for occasionally taking pride in defying Army orders.

Early in the evening of 7 February I drove to the Division Headquarters, then to the headquarters of the crossing detachment. They took twenty collapsible launches, and silently carried them on their shoulders through the jungle to the water, where they set them and started the engines—praying their high-pitched noise would not be heard by the enemy. Each boat carried eight men and all crossed three times to Ubin Island, taking over in all about four hundred officers and men. At the time my feeling about these men was that if they drew upon themselves a heavy enemy attack, it would considerably assist the main landings on Singapore Island. A few shells came over and a red signal flare was fired, but the resistance was unexpectedly light and Ubin Island was successfully occupied without any enemy reaction. During the evening, two mountain guns were landed on the island.

From the morning of 8 February all thirty-six field guns of the Konoe Division, twelve infantry guns, and four heavy guns concentrated heavy fire on Changi Fortress. They fired from an extended front. In general it is the practice to put a battery (four guns) fairly close together for purposes of command, but on this occasion our guns were scattered in ones and twos throughout the rubber jungle where they could not be observed by the enemy. In fact, they would probably be fooled into believing that each gun position was a separate battery. Effective air reconnaissance by the enemy of our positions in the rubber jungle was practically impossible. They could judge our gun positions only by the reports of the firing.

The enemy appeared surprised at our bombardment and reacted strongly with artillery several times our strength. At about noon, the enemy fire became intense, but it did extraordinarily little damage except to the innocent rubber trees, the trunks of which were torn to shreds and the branches thrown in all directions. In this war were they to be regarded as something without blood and life?

Notwithstanding the very heavy bombardment poured on the jungle, there were no casualties among the officers and men of the Konoe Division deployed there. At four o'clock in the afternoon I made my way back to the Imperial Palace with the welcome news of the successful beginning of the battle for Singapore.

On the evening of X day (8 February), the 5th and 18th divisions assembled on the secretly prepared jungle roads and advanced to the water's edge, where they began to prepare for crossing the strait. Right up to the last, this movement was concealed in the deep jungle of the rubber forest.

At the appointed time our artillery opened fire. The guns were spread over the elevated ground around Johore Bahru. The pivot of the battle for Singapore was the Causeway across the Johore Strait, which runs on through the heart of Singapore Island. As our guns had occupied positions which were almost perfectly concealed, from which they could shell both sides of the Causeway, they could not have been better placed for the battle.

As I have said, the heights of the Imperial Palace had been selected for Army Combat Command Post because of the view the position afforded over the whole battlefield, of course, the observation post was perfectly exposed to the enemy's fire, and as X day wore on this steadily became more violent. Shells fell heavily on the lawns around the palace, and splinters scarred the palace walls, but the building itself was not seriously damaged, although it seemed to be the calm eye of the enemy artillery storm. Buildings and trees around the palace were blown in all directions and the shelling became so heavy that it seemed as if it would change the contour of the ground.

After our shells had set fire to the oil tanks, black smoke covered Singapore Island and prevented observations of the fall of our shells. Our gunners therefore had to rely on firing by the map, basing their aim on the topographic surveys made days before.

Mr. Churchill's memoirs state that on the morning of 8 February, a patrol boat reported that the Japanese Army was concentrating in the rubber jungle to the northwest of Singapore Island and apparently intending to attack there. Of course it cannot be assumed that an accurate idea of military strength can be obtained from the sea looking through thick jungle. Occasionally however, enemy fighter planes flew very low above the rubber trees, and one of them was shot down. Some of these planes may have observed our troop concentrations. Strangely enough, throughout the British bombardment the pivotal assembly points of the 5th and 18th divisions remained quiet, with apparently only a very few guns firing in their direction.

In view of the general situation, our main forces were deployed on the front east of the Causeway—that is to say, on the front of the Imperial Guards Division. The disposition of Lieutenant-General Percival's forces was eloquent testimony to the importance he placed on this sector, which he defended with the full strength of his 3rd Army Corps (9th, 11th and 18th divisions). The sector west of the Causeway was defended by troops of the 8th Australian Division.

It seems, in fact, that our plans worked better than we had thought they would. The demonstration by the Konoe Division in their capture of Ubin Island obtained better results than we expected in attracting the enemy's attention to the eastern sector, and in this respect the distinguished service of the Konoe Division must be acknowledged.

The Blue Signal Flares

AFTER CONCEALMENT IN THE JUNGLE for about a week, the 5th and 18th divisions, without even paying their respects to the sun, began to move on the evening of 8 February. While they had been assembling in the jungle, fifty small motor boats and a hundred collapsible launches had been prepared for each division. These were now given their final inspection and were then carried on the shoulders of the troops for several kilometers along the jungle roads to the water's edge—a task which was by no means easy.

When our infantry and engineers arrived at their selected positions at the water's edge, at 11 o'clock at night, the whole of our artillery opened fire on the enemy pillboxes, trenches and wire entanglements defending the Singapore side of the strait. Our barrage covered the whole shore of the strait in order to make it difficult for the enemy to judge the points at which our main attack would be launched. This was the first time the enemy had experienced the full power of our artillery. Four hundred and forty guns were in action and the field guns fired two hundred rounds per gun during the night and the heavy guns one hundred rounds, every shot a wound to the fortress. Wire entanglements were everywhere cut, pillboxes destroyed, and trenches blown in; machine-guns at the water's edge were almost completely silenced.

The troops of both divisions who were in the first wave of the attack—roughly four thousand men—went aboard three hundred boats at 12 midnight of 8 February as arranged. The sound of the boats' engines was drowned by the noise of our bombardment. As our boats touched the opposite shore, our star shells shed a faint light over the scene. Silently the men jumped out of the boats, sinking up to their loins in the mud of the shore; but they forced their way through the mud, mangrove roots and broken wire entanglements protecting the enemy position, and rushed the British trenches and pillboxes. Our bombardment had forced the enemy troops to keep down in their shelters, and it enabled our men to get among them before they recovered from the effects of the shellfire.*

In the Army Command Post at the Imperial Palace there was an atmosphere of tension, but nobody was doubtful of victory. Everything which the staff had to do had been done to the limit of human ability, and there was nothing more to do now except await the result. The issue, victory or defeat, would soon be decided.

From the glass door of the palace tower, as one looked down on Johore Strait and at the blaze of fire on both sides, one gained but little idea of the progress of the battle. There was no difference in the sound of our own shells and the enemy's. The boom of artillery, the crash of explosives, the flash of the guns and the red lotus flames of fires enveloped the whole of Singapore Island.

At ten minutes past midnight on the morning of 9 February, first of all on the 5th Division front, and shortly after on that of the 18th Division, blue flares were fired high in the sky, signifying that the landing had

---

* The whole weight of the Japanese assault fell on just over two Australian battalions (2,500 men) in the front line.

been accomplished as planned. At the Army Command Post not one man, Army Commander or staff officers, could speak. The moonlight shone dimly on tears flowing down all our cheeks. The second line of units crossing the strait about half an hour after midnight arrived on the enemy shore and ran into heavy machine-gun fire, which we could hear from the Command Post through the din of battle, as our infantry gradually extended over the whole front.

Throughout the operations in Malaya the Yokoyama Regiment of Engineers, which served continuously with the 5th Division, had given distinguished service unsurpassed in the whole Army. They had fought with the infantry and repaired roads and bridges at unprecedented speed. At the crossing of Johore Strait they upheld their splendid record.

For the attack on Singapore they handled approximately one hundred collapsible motor launches in which they crossed Johore Strait under heavy enemy fire, carrying infantry to the assault again and again—three, four times—continuing throughout the night under the increasing enemy barrage.

One of the boat commanders, Troop Leader Lance-Corporal Yamamoto, standing at the bow of a raft made of three launches lashed together, was continually drenched with spray thrown up by enemy shells hitting the water around the boats. While fully loaded with men of the second line of assault troops, a shell burst on the gunwale of one of the launches composing the raft, killed the two other coxswains and severely damaged their boats. Yamamoto was the only man left capable of handling the launches, which had fifty men aboard. He landed them on the enemy shore and then collapsed like a falling tree. When the squad commander of the troops lifted him in his arms he saw his lungs protruding through his ribs. Yamamoto had said nothing about his wound until he landed the troops in his charge, and while the squad commander still held him in his arms he said, "Long live the Emperor! I am indebted to you for your kind assistance. Excuse me for going a step ahead of you." And so saying, he breathed his last.

When both Yamamoto's neighboring coxswains were killed, the fifty men on the launches felt they would be unable to land without their coxswains and that therefore they too must die, but Yamamoto's miraculous endurance despite his wound enabled them all to land safely. In consequence of his bravery the Yokoyama Engineer Regiment was awarded a letter of commendation as a unit and Troop Leader Lance-Corporal Yamamoto was posthumously awarded an individual letter of commendation; a proclamation was issued to the whole Army announcing that he had been promoted two grades in rank.

The achievements of the 18th Division were in no way inferior to those of the 5th. The section of artillery which had been placed to fire across the surface of the water was quickly in action, and sank one enemy gunboat which attempted to interfere with the passage of our troops across the strait.

The first crossing, at the same time as that of the 5th Division, was successful, but the men in the second line had to fight from the moment they landed on the enemy shore, and the enemy resisted stubbornly all night.

The Koike Engineer Regiment was responsible for transporting the troops of the 18th Division across the strait. In the soundness of their preparations and in their fighting capacity they were quite the equal of the Yokoyama Regiment. During the week of preparation prior to the crossing they had reconnoitered in the jungle at the water's edge in order to observe closely the British positions on the island side. In particular they had located machine-gun posts on the flank of our attack, and made important observations on the tides and the state of the enemy shore which were of great assistance when it came to landing our assault forces.

Sergeant Hisamitsu Fukui was leader of the squad who carried out this work, and when the movement across the strait began, he commanded the boats carrying the first group of troops, landing them at a weak spot in the enemy position which he had discovered on his previous reconnaissance.

Having crossed the strait twice, successfully landing all the troops he carried, Sergeant Fukui was severely wounded by machine-gun fire, but nevertheless continued to stand bravely at the bow of his boat. Waving the control flag, he brought his flotilla back to the Johore side, after which he collapsed and died. For his distinguished service Sergeant Hisamitsu Fukui also received an individual posthumous letter of commendation.

By dawn on 9 February, as the sun began to peep from behind the black smoke, the whole of the infantry of both divisions—the 5th and the 18th—and part of the artillery had already landed on the enemy shore. From the high ground of the Imperial Palace the troops could be seen threading their way through the low rubber trees, sweeping away the remnants of the enemy and attacking Tengah aerodrome. Although enemy planes had been flying the previous evening, there were none to be seen on this morning. As enemy positions were seized, the Rising Sun flag was hoisted over them and our artillery was asked to lengthen its range. Black smoke rose high and thick from the burning oil-storage tanks, but in some places it hung in low clouds. Here and there in the front line of our infantry, enemy armored cars were on fire.

At sunset on the 9th, after the Konoe Imperial Guards Division reported having forced a passage across the strait in their sector, the Army Commander and most of his staff, on a raft made of three boats lashed together, crossed the strait in the 5th Division sector. The enemy artillery, behaving as if it was trying to block the passage after our troops had crossed, continued to shell the channel heavily. But before dawn the shelling of the strait had subsided, and the peace and beauty of the moon on the water was in extraordinary contrast to the tumult of the shellfire and the gruesome casualties of a few hours earlier.

Watching the Konoe Division crossing near the Kranji River, one saw the water glowing redly; it was as bright as day. Immediately the question arose: had the enemy flooded the strait with petroleum and set fire to it? For an answer we had to wait for news from the Konoe Division.

As General Yamashita climbed the low cliff on the enemy side of the strait, a group of European prisoners of war watched him curiously. They were the first living sign of our success in the battle. At last we had set foot on a corner of Singapore.

The Only Mistake

IT IS DAWN ON THE 10th. The Army Command Post on Singapore Island has been established, and connected by telephone and submarine cable with the Imperial Palace. The main strength of the Army staff is still on the Johore side of the strait directing the crossing of the tanks, heavy guns and ammunition to Singapore Island. All reports indicate that on all fronts the forcing of the strait has proceeded without a hitch. The front lines of the 5th and 18th divisions have already taken possession of Tengah aerodrome, and are now consolidating on the western side to prepare for an attack against fortified positions on the heights of Bukit Timah.

In a tent in the rubber forest on the north side of Tengah aerodrome, the Army Commander, General Yamashita, was eating a breakfast of dry bread when suddenly Staff Officer Kera rushed in, steam rising from his bald head. Usually a jovial, smiling man, this officer now agitatedly reported that halfway through the previous evening the Konoe divisional commander, looking pale and angry, had come to Army Headquarters at the Imperial Palace with his chief of staff and shouted, "The Konoe Division, just as they commenced to cross the strait near the

Causeway, became caught in petroleum to which the enemy set fire. The frontline regiment was enveloped in fire while on the water and was almost annihilated. The leader of the Kobayashi Infantry Regiment was seen swimming in a sea of fire and his fate is unknown. This disaster is Army's responsibility! Reckless forcing of a passage without adequate preparation causes unnecessary casualties. For what reason have the Konoe Division been allowed to make such a crossing? Such an occurrence is most surprising and regrettable."

Originally, Army orders for the assault on Singapore assigned the Konoe Division as the second line, but the commander of that division emphatically demanded to attack shoulder to shoulder with the other two divisions, and the Army Commander acceded to his request. Rightly or wrongly, all action by Army is the responsibility of Army. But the responsibility for such changes must rest upon those demanding them.

General Yamashita, who was not easily perturbed, inquired about the annihilation of the regiment, and his face changed color.

Presently a Konoe Division staff officer dejectedly put in an appearance. Turning and facing him, I asked, "When one regiment was annihilated by the enemy's flooding the water with burning petroleum, how did it become known?" The staff officer replied, "One of the engineers who made the crossing with the Kobayashi Regiment survived and returned to report."

"You great fool!" I thundered out in my rage. "When your front line crossed the strait was there not even one staff officer with them? One man from the engineers brings back a report without verification and you swallow it whole and become frenzied. Return to your troops, have another look at the battle, and come back and report the facts. Remember, your division asked for Army orders to be amended. Can't you carry them out when they are altered in the way that you requested?"

Did not this episode show the true nature of the Konoe Division, which boasted of its long tradition? When asked how the division was to be used subsequently in the battle, I coldly replied, "There is no reason for any further change in Army orders. We can take Singapore with the 5th and 18th divisions." Then General Yamashita remarked in a very loud voice to the Konoe Division staff officer, "Return at once to your divisional commander and tell him the Konoe Division can do as it pleases in this battle." The weak-willed Konoe divisional commander who had demanded a change of Army orders so that he might thrust his division into the first line of the attack could scarcely have dreamed he would receive such scathing criticism in the middle of a decisive battle.

During the afternoon of that day there came a telephone call from Headquarters at the Imperial Palace: "The Konoe Division's report this morning was a mistake. At the time we verified the situation, the division's front line, after trifling losses, was in the midst of an attack on the enemy's position on the southern side of the Causeway. The division commander reports to the Army Commander that he will this evening carry out a further advance on the Causeway sector."

This incident was the only regrettable mistake throughout the Malayan campaign.

Slaughter on Bukit Timah

BUKIT TIMAH IS A STRATEGIC point on Singapore Island, situated about seven and a half English miles northwest of the city, with an altitude of 177 meters. It is the highest point in the island. Its name is composed of two Malay words—*Bukit*, mountain, *Timah*, tin—and its meaning is therefore "Tin Mountain." At its base there were roughly three hundred dwellings, and also rubber factories, race courses, golf clubs and so on, together with large army storage warehouses established by the British. On its northeastern slope was situated a reservoir, the source of water supply for Singapore's one million citizens. According to our intelligence reports, this strategic point appeared to be strongly fortified with concrete positions.

Considering the situation seriously, it appeared we would have to wait for the advance of our heavy guns before we could take this position by storm. It was, however, of the utmost importance that no opportunity for reorganization be given the enemy, and the idea of capturing the heights of Bukit Timah in the initial attack on the fortress had been constantly in our minds, in view of the manner in which the battle had developed, it was decided to make an immediate assault.

We were disgusted with the unseemly behavior of the Konoe Division, so now, without even making a rough estimate of the position, we decided to capture the heights with the 5th and 18th divisions only.

Observing the progress in the battle of both divisions, we advanced on foot to the south. The small number of enemy planes which had failed to escape had been abandoned by their owners, and they looked lonely standing on the runway of Tengah aerodrome.

I entered the British barracks. Fresh bread and soup were still on the dining tables and clothing and suitcases belonging to the troops were lying around. "Good heavens!" I thought. "There is no doubt they were considerably agitated when they escaped." From this we knew that our successful forcing of the strait by our whole Army had not been expected by the enemy and had come as a complete surprise.

Astonished by the state of affairs revealed by our inspection of the barracks, we then came to our senses and realized we still had to capture Bukit Timah heights and the reservoir. We instinctively felt now that to launch an immediate attack might be stupid and that it would be wiser to wait for the arrival of our heavy artillery.

Suddenly a violent rain squall swept over the battlefield, soaking us with rain and washing us clean of sweat. Happily, together with soldiers of the 18th Division, we hurried through the rubber jungle to the front line. After a while we noticed one another's faces. We all looked like negroes. "I say, look at your faces, they are black as ink," called the troops. "Yours too, Mr. Staff Officer. Ha, ha, ha!" laughed the soldiers. None of us had noticed the blackening of our faces. Soot from the burning oil tanks had been falling on the leaves of the rubber trees for several days, and the heavy rain washed it off onto the troops as they passed beneath, turning their skins and their uniforms as jet black as an Army service coat. Queer as we were in color, we continued to grope our way to the 18th Division while trying to shelter from the rain in the rubber trees.

The divisional commander, his chief of staff, and Staff Officer Hashimoto were listening silently to the reports of the guns. They greeted us with: "Congratulations! Many thanks for your trouble." Looking closely at Lieutenant-General Mutaguchi I saw bloodstains on the left shoulder of his coat surrounding a small hole where evidently a bullet had penetrated. "Ah, sir, you are wounded," I said. "Be silent," he replied. "The truth is that while our boats were crossing Johore Strait the third time I was hit by one of the enemy machine-guns which still remained in action. While we suffered no damage during the first landing, during the second and third landings the enemy kept on firing even as they were retreating."

Staff Officer Hashimoto, who was close by, supplemented his divisional commander's story. "During the first landing," he said, "it appears that our bombardment kept the enemy troops well down in the bottom of their trenches, but during the second and third landings, manning their parapets they resisted splendidly. At Headquarters they broke through and attacked a pillbox we had occupied, and Staff Officer Ino lost both legs in a hand-grenade explosion. Wasn't he unlucky? The divisional commander was wounded and another staff officer received a bomb wound. It was a desperate fight while it lasted. . . . The divisional commander says what about the Army plan? We're still under shellfire

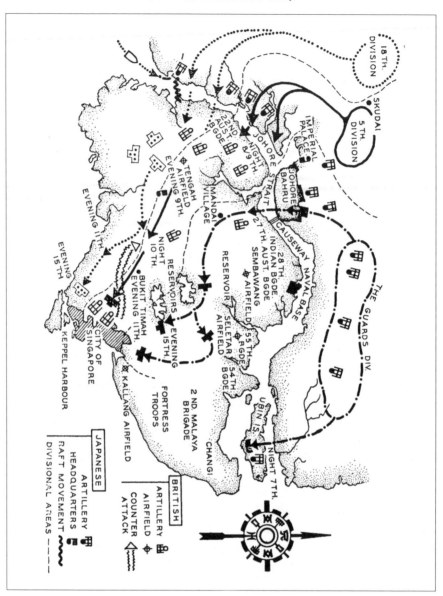

The capture of Singapore.

and our artillery has not yet crossed the strait. We're in a quandary, I tell you!"

The divisional commander's expression was full of anxiety, and I understood the difficult position quite well, but when one remembered the obvious confusion of the enemy at Tengah airfield it gave one confidence that our sudden surprise attack had been perfectly carried out.

The Army Commander wished to attack Bukit Timah heights almost immediately, before the enemy came to life again and reorganized. As there were no guns to support the attack, it would have to be made that night with the bayonet. The only comment by the 18th Division commander and his staff officers was, "If the Army Commander thinks it should be done, we will make a full-strength surprise attack tonight with our divisional commander in the lead. The attack should be made this evening before the enemy has had time to rally." It was a comment that expressed the high morale of the division.

Going to the 5th Division, we asked for their opinion. After Lieutenant-General Matsui had been told the views of the Army Commander and of Lieutenant-General Mutaguchi, he replied, "If Mutaguchi can do it, so can I. My division will make the attack with out artillery support."

Both divisions thus agreed to make the night attack. As the results proved, the decision was thoroughly sound. The attack was perfectly successful. When I left Army Headquarters I was ordered by General Yamashita to coordinate each division's action in accordance with the conditions on the ground.

At that time I had no data on which to decide whether we should make a night attack, or resume the attack after our heavy guns had crossed the strait. Whether because of the Konoe Division's feint attack, or for other reasons, the enemy's main forces still faced the Konoe Division on the Seletar Harbor—Changi Fortress sector, and the 8th Australian Division was defending a broad front. The key Bukit Timah position was almost vacant. In the barracks of Tengah aerodrome I got the idea of surprising this vacant nest.

The plan provided for the 5th Division to attack with its full strength on the north side of the Chua Chu Kang road and the 18th Division with its full strength on the south side, with the crest of Bukit Timah heights as the objective. The advance commenced at dark, and throughout the night of 10–11 February the battle zone was in an extreme state of tumult.

Army Headquarters, consisting of about forty persons, including the Army Commander, moved to a position in a fortified enemy anti-air-craft-gun position at the edge of the jungle to the south of Tengah airfield. Apparently the enemy had hastily constructed the position at the outbreak of hostilities. It consisted of a single barrack building around which was a trench surrounded by barbed-wire entanglements. It was a key position discharging two functions simultaneously: protecting the airfield against both ground and air attack.

On the evening of 10 February, and throughout night, enemy gunfire raged at its most extreme intensity over the whole island. We believed that Ulu Pandan Fortress was being defended with roughly one brigade, but the 18th Division bypassed the enemy there and pressed forward in its attack on Bukit Timah heights, which the 5th Division, having moved slightly to one side, was assaulting from the direction of the Causeway.

At midnight, while I was half dozing and half listening to the artillery fire, my reverie was suddenly destroyed by indications of a strong force crawling around the perimeter of Headquarters. We knew there were remnants of the enemy still straggling in each sector, but we had not one reserve soldier at Headquarters. The Army Commander had insisted that every available man was required by the divisions engaged in the assault.

Suddenly there was a violent explosion and the barrack building shook. The smashing of windows set up a frightful din. It appeared that a number of enemy troops making an outflanking movement had fired a trench mortar into our Headquarters. As I have said, the Headquarters staff, including the Army Commander, numbered no more than forty men. A certain senior staff officer said to me, "Can't you get some reserves quickly? Even one company from both divisions?" Silently, and not appearing to listen, I pretended to snore. Shaking my bed, he said a second time, "I say, do something quickly. We will be all right with one company." Of necessity I then got up, but I rejected his proposal out of hand, telling him that both divisional commanders were leading their men in the night attack, and were too busy to be bothered with such a request. Again this staff officer asked, "Can't we get some troops from one of the divisions? Isn't it unreasonable and rash to risk damage to Headquarters? Do you want to get us all killed?"

I replied, "We are behind trenches and wire entanglements and have twenty sentries on guard. They are enough. I don't mind if the enemy do retreat past us." Shortly afterwards we heard the senior adjutant giving orders to the sentries.

Since the beginning of the assault, Headquarters had been enveloped in an atmosphere of tension, aggravated by the possibility of enemy trench mortars dropping bombs on the barracks building. I exchanged glances with Staff Officer Asaeda and we both broke into a smile; in a calm state of mind we waited for the confusion to die down.

With the approach of dawn on the 11th, the threat to Headquarters passed away. To begin with, a reassuring message, "Have seized Bukit Timah," arrived from the 18th Division, and there was soon a similar report from the 5th Division; both reports were brought by dispatch officers on foot. The morning sun rose peacefully over the island battlefield on Kigensetsu, the anniversary of the coronation of the Emperor Jimmu.

Welcoming the Kigen Festival

AS I HAVE MENTIONED, THE capture of the Bukit Timah heights was prearranged to the day. So also was the period which we had determined for the surrender of the enemy general. Up to Kigensetsu we had dreamed of the surrender of Singapore, and now the dream promised to become reality. Pinned down by the throat, the enemy perhaps would accept our advice to surrender, but we did not know. With such a hopeful observation, our note advising capitulation, drafted by Staff Officer Sugita, was dropped from the air behind the enemy lines. It read as follows:

The Japanese Commander to the British Commander:
    In a spirit of chivalry we have the honor of advising your surrender. Your Army, founded on the traditional spirit of Great Britain, is defending Singapore, which is completely isolated, and raising the fame of Great Britain by the utmost exertions and heroic fighting. I disclose my respect from my innermost feelings. Nevertheless, the war situation is already determined and in the meantime the surrender of Singapore is imminent. From now on, resistance is futile and merely increases the danger to the million civilian inhabitants without good reason, exposing them to infliction of pain by fire and sword. Furthermore, we do not feel you will increase the fame of the British Army by further resistance. From first to last our counsel is that Your Excellency will cease to think of meaningless resistance, and from now on, yielding to our advice; promptly and immediately will suspend the action extending over the whole British battlefront. It is expected that you will take measures to dispatch an Army messenger as stated below. If on the contrary you continue resistance as previously, it will be difficult to bear with patience from a humanitarian point of view, and inevitably

we must continue an intense attack against Singapore. Ending this advice, we show respect towards Your Excellency.

1. The Army messenger's route of advance shall be by the Bukit Timah road.

2. The Army messenger, hoisting a white flag as well as the British flag, will be escorted by a number of soldiers as a protection.

(Signed) Japan's Army Commander,
Lieutenant-General Tomoyuki Yamashita

Enemy anti-aircraft guns greeted our airplanes with a fierce barrage. Managing to avoid the fire, a reconnaissance plane, clearly showing the Japanese markings, dropped a signaling communication tube containing the surrender advice on the outskirts of Singapore city. The long streamers of red and white fluttered in the wind as the tube descended. A signal was then sent to Imperial General Headquarters and General Headquarters by Army Headquarters. "The Japanese Army, having stormed and captured Bukit Timah heights, has advised the surrender of Singapore city upon which we look down."

After passing the night within sound of the enemy guns, which prevented sleep, the next morning, accompanied by an orderly, I examined the progress of the battle on the Bukit Timah sector. We hurried along the main road in a small enemy car which had been captured. When we reached the southeastern extremity of Tengah aerodrome, we found that bombs or heavy-caliber shells were blowing large holes in the roadway. As the firing was intense, our engineers had not yet begun repairs. Abandoning the car, the orderly and I continued on foot. Just at that moment there came a shellburst which shocked our eardrums, while the blast jarred our spines. The flash seared my eyes, and I was thrown into the roadside ditch. In my agitation I thrust myself into an earthenware drainage pipe. The heavy shelling continued—one discharge—two discharges. Up to this moment I had had no experience of such heavy projectiles, which tore holes in the ground fifteen or sixteen meters in diameter and four or five meters deep. They were probably fifteen- or sixteen-inch fortress guns which had been swung round 180 degrees to fire over the land instead of over the water out to sea, and they were apparently attempting a demolition bombardment of Tengah airfield and the road.

Crouching like a crab inside the earthen pipe, I imagined what would happen if a shell fell on me. It did not appear as if anything of myself would be left. I had landed on the island with the intention of dying, but unconsciously I drew myself further into the pipe. The shells were frightful. However, after getting to know the firing interval of the heavy guns, I raised my body, which was covered with mud and dust, and unseen by anyone began to crawl out of the pipe.

After the debris of one explosion had fallen there was an interval of several minutes until the next shell landed. I escaped the first—the second—but still felt no guarantee of security; but at last I scrambled out of the danger zone. I rose to my feet, at the same time clearing away spiders' webs from my head. "It was fine, nobody was looking," I said to myself, and felt ashamed.

We arrived at a three-forked road. It being almost immediately after the assault, our own and enemy wounded were lying where they had fallen, mingled with each other, unattended to and groaning. Enemy motor cars and trucks which had been destroyed blocked the road in all directions and it was difficult to pass through them.

Reaching General Matsui's Headquarters in an enemy air-raid shelter, I congratulated him and together we rushed up hurriedly to the crest of Bukit Timah. The soldiers of the 18th and 5th divisions were mixed together, as reorganization had not yet commenced. From the atmosphere of the battlefield it did not appear as if the enemy were likely to surrender immediately. I peeped out over the front from our advanced line. The villages of Bukit Timah were being completely wiped out by shellfire; a soldier showed his face from inside a drainpipe where he was chewing a piece of dry bread. Recalling my own position but a short time ago, I smiled wryly.

As noon approached, the enemy bombardment increased and a large force of enemy soldiers surged up the heights like a tidal wave under cover of the barrage. They were supported by armored cars. It appeared as if the British were staking everything on a counterattack. "This is gallantry, is it not?" I said to myself, and involuntarily I was lost in admiration.

According to our bearings it was believed the 18th Division was separated from the 5th Division by a deep valley. A hand-to-hand struggle could be seen proceeding on the 18th Division front. I said to myself, "We cannot keep on in this way. Before long we will have to move out of Army Headquarters. We must get the heavy guns and tanks across the strait to support our troops."

Hurriedly I returned to Headquarters.

Owing to the clumsy work of the Konoe Division, the Causeway had not yet been reopened to traffic, and the Engineer Regiment was now ordered to set every available man to work to complete repairs, notwithstanding enemy action. While waiting for the work to be completed, all the boats were assembled and some tanks, ammunition, and artillery were ferried across the strait during the day, but it was not until evening that Army Headquarters moved up the mountain halfway between Tengah aerodrome and Bukit Timah heights. There they were directly behind the frontline troops, where the observation was good and they were well protected. We had to be prepared for heavy shelling by the enemy as soon as their presence became known.

From the divisional staff officers in charge of operations we obtained by telephone frequent and detailed reports of the progress of both divisions in the battle. The 5th and 18th divisions, competing with each other for supremacy, appeared somewhat exhausted after the day's fighting. The Konoe Division was now the only chessman we still had to play. When told, "The Konoe Division can do as it pleases," they kept good countenance, and the whole division had passed the evening of 10 February with the enemy still on the heights of Mandai in front of them. The Konoe Division had scarcely appeared to be moving. They were now ordered to advance without a moment's loss of time on the eastern side of the reservoir and strike at the enemy's flank in the midst of their counterattack on Bukit Timah. This was the key to the solution of the difficult strategical position of the other two divisions.

The assistant commandant staff officer at Army Headquarters jumped into a car and personally attempted to hasten the movement of the Konoe Division, but without effect. The Army Chief of Staff repeatedly visited them, but I regret to say the petulant Konoe Division Headquarters showed no disposition to help the other divisions in their emergency. Those divisions maintained the battle on their own, grasping the opportunity to further distinguish themselves despite their difficulties, while the Konoe Division, who had been told to do as they pleased, were having to be coaxed and cajoled like cross children. Unable to do anything about it; our affable Chief of Staff and the strategic specialist assistant commandant appeared angry and embarrassed, and we spent the evening of Kigensetsu, the anniversary on which we wished to secure the surrender of Singapore, in an uncomfortable atmosphere. I accompanied these two officers on another visit to Konoe Division Headquarters. On arrival there I said to Staff Officer Asaeda, "Hello, Asaeda! Will you please bring me the seniority list?" "What?" said he. "The seniority list?" He was a quick-witted man, but on this occasion appeared completely taken aback. "Oh, it's a trivial matter," I said. "Matsui, Mutaguchi, and Nishimura, our three lieutenant-generals, are Army graduates of the same year; if by any chance someone has to take command of the Army, let us investigate the position." Listening by my side, our Army Chief of Staff and the assistant commandant assumed expressions of profound thoughtfulness.

During the night enemy heavy shells fell through the roof of the Army operations section and two or three of the signals staff were wounded by fragments of tiles. A certain staff officer, rudely awakened from a nap, agitatedly ran out clasping his pillow in his hands, calling, "Hey! This place is getting too dangerous. How about moving Headquarters a little to the rear for safety's sake?"

"By heavens, no!" I replied. "If we have to die, let us die together in the front line. We'll never get another such opportunity."

Throughout the fighting there was a youth at Headquarters who all the time went calmly on with his work. His name was Morita, and he was eighteen years old. He was an excellent and pleasant-mannered mess steward. He boiled water under the eaves and did his other jobs, looking out in the intervals between shells. Without any chance of glory or promotion he went on with his work, a genuinely unspoiled youth. It seems to me that as human beings grow older they hold life more precious, and avarice emerges in conformity with class advancement. Even though one's remaining days are short, there is always a lingering desire for the insignificant life that remains.

The 5th Division attack on the reservoir sector at dawn on 12 February was driven home by sheer weight of numbers and the cooperation of the flight groups. The enemy had ceased to think of Bukit Timah heights, and it was natural that they should defend desperately the heights around the circumference of the reservoir—their last lifeline. All their serviceable guns were concentrated on the area and they seemed to be using up all the ammunition in their magazines. The fire on the position was of great intensity.

Also cooperating with the 5th Division was the full-strength of the Tank Brigade and all our heavy guns as they came across the strait.

Realizing that this was a battle to finish the British army defending Singapore, we poured all our fighting strength into the battle line. It was a battle in which the fame and honor of both armies—no, more: of both countries—were at stake. For five days the life-and-death struggle had continued.

The 18th Division, which had to act in concert with the 5th in this action, moved along the seacoast and drove a strong wedge into the enemy's left wing. The Konoe Division at last began to move, and by a detour from the north of the reservoir penetrated the flank of the enemy's main force. Thus was the general trend of the battle determined.

The flight group heavily attacked an enemy convoy attempting to escape by sea. Together with the Navy, it had in the last fifteen days attacked and sunk in the waters around Singapore about eighty large and small British ships. Some of these events are recorded in Mr. Churchill's memoirs.

Our Army was not deployed over the whole front, and the strategic position seemed to reach a climax when we received a signal from General Headquarters. "On 15 February an officer attached to the Court of the Emperor will be dispatched to the battlefield. We can postpone the visit if the progress of your Army's operations makes it desirable to do so. We wish to hear your opinion."

There were some who said, "Let us welcome him," and others who argued, "We must postpone the visit of the Emperor's envoy for a little while"; and so opinions were divided into two camps.

Once previously, during the China Incident, I had been in a similar position when conducting military operations in Shansi together with the Itagaki group. During a bitterly contested battle for the reduction of Taiyuan Sheng, on 7 November, Shidei, the aide-de-camp to the Emperor, arrived on the battlefield. I immediately began to think of the reduction of the mountain stronghold Yen Hsi Shan.

After a general discussion we unanimously resolved: "On the 15th day of February the enemy will positively surrender to the power of the august Emperor." We drafted these words as a telegram of welcome to the Emperor's envoy.

On the evening of 14 February the Konoe Division completed repairs to the Causeway and pushed forward. Our heavy guns moved in rapid succession to positions on the heights to the east of the reservoir. For the first time, our whole Army was across Johore Strait and concentrated on Singapore Island.

The True Spirit

ON THE MORNING OF 15 February I was called to the telephone by Staff Officer Hashimoto, the Officer-in-Charge of Operations of the 18th Division. "Today," he said happily, "the division will attack with its full strength towards Keppel Barracks. Will you be good enough to look in at our position?"

"I will start immediately," I answered. I had been out to the 5th Division so often as to have almost become a nuisance, but I had not yet been to the 18th Division.

All my work at Headquarters had been completed. Today without fail we must take Singapore in order to welcome the officer attached to the Emperor's Court. I made preparations to set out, and, accompanied by an orderly, and moving in the intervals between enemy shellfire, drove out towards the coast road by car, intending to call in person at 18th Division Headquarters.

Changing the plan, however, we drove straight through to the front-line headquarters of the Koba Regiment, which overlooked the enemy position but was also under enemy observation so that the movement of even one Japanese soldier brought down concentrated shellfire on the position.

The regimental commander, with the regimental colors beside him, was crouching for shelter in what I thought was a narrow firing trench, but which I subsequently found out was an octopus trap. He was watching the enemy position and, raising his bald head only, directing his subordinates.

Every time a shell exploded they pulled their heads like snails down into the octopus trap. They were in the midst of preparations for an attack at 2 p.m., which had been ordered by their division. The frontline battalion commander was Major Kojiro Ito, an officer of the same period as myself. The artillery with which he was to cooperate in the attack was a battalion of mountain artillery under command of Lieutenant-Colonel Kusido and eight heavy mortars under command of Lieutenant-Colonel Tanaka. These officers were my seniors by one year. On the right-hand side of the Koba Regiment was the Oku Regiment, in the same stage of preparation for the attack. Both headquarters were about two or three hundred yards from the enemy front line, and under the intense bombardment we were powerless to do anything.

After roughly a week of fighting since we crossed Johore Strait, the ammunition accumulated for the assault on Singapore Island was nearly exhausted. We had barely a hundred rounds per gun left for our field guns, and less for our heavy guns. With this small ammunition supply it was impossible to keep down enemy fire by counter-battery operations.

Our only standby was Colonel Tanaka's 40-centimeter (16-inch) mortars. For mobility these were taken apart and loaded on handcarts, and at night placed in position in the front line firing trench. Their shells, brought forward by the same means, thoroughly inspected and overhauled, were loaded and fired upon the enemy in Keppel Barracks at the rate of about one round every ten minutes.

The enemy were apparently resting while waiting for our attack. The Ito Battalion decided to launch one, and like men rising from their graves the men began to emerge from their trenches. Immediately a large number of British guns directed an intense barrage on the position. It seemed as if everyone on the battlefield would be suffocated by the dust and smoke from the bursting shells.

Takeda, the divisional chief of staff, who had come forward to direct the attack, concluded reluctantly that it was a sheer impossibility to proceed with it, owing to the fact that the troops were exhausted by previous attacks and the violent bombardment by the enemy. Arms and legs were flying through the air and heads scattered everywhere. Twisting my body like a crab and hiding my head behind an old tree, I wished to myself that I had a steel helmet. A soldier, edging close to me, took off his own and put it on my head. We were complete strangers to each other. "Mr. Staff Officer," he said, "it is dangerous to be without a steel helmet. Please wear this one." I thanked him and returned it to him, but he did not put it on his head again. I was deeply moved by the spirit of self-sacrifice of this soldier with whom I had not even a nodding acquaintance.

The regimental headquarters trench became shallower every time a shell exploded close to it. Frequently we were half buried. At last, carrying the regimental colors, we moved out of the trench and sought shelter behind the brick wall of a wrecked house, to which we clung like geckos. A soldier beside me had his head blown off, and blood was scattered everywhere. Two of his comrades stood up holding a blanket. "How will this do for a coffin?" asked one. They wrapped the corpse in the blanket and carried it on their shoulders to an abandoned trench about twenty yards in the rear. The regimental adjutant called to them, "It's too dangerous to bury him now. You'll be wiped out by a shell. Do it later." Undeterred, the two men carried on with their self-appointed task. Several times they were enveloped in the smoke and dust of bursting shells and we thought they had been killed, but after the smoke of each explosion cleared away they were to be seen still digging. It was an act of madness. Finally they finished digging the grave, laid the corpse in it and filled it again. Taking two or three pieces of bread from a haversack, they laid them on the head of the grave and sprinkled water on it from a water bottle. Then, taking off their helmets, they made a profound bow to the comrade in arms they had just buried, and calmly walked back to the front line.

It had been decided to carry on with the attack and the troops had just commenced to move out of the trenches. There was no time to inquire the names of the men who had shown such reverence for their dead comrade. In all probability they were soldiers of the Ito Battalion. I was so impressed by their sense of duty to a fallen comrade that I felt as though I had worshipped in the presence of the Revered Gods. The regimental commander who saw the incident was similarly affected. The furious bombardment eased off about four o'clock in the afternoon and moved away from the Ito Battalion. I started homeward thinking, "If the enemy resists in this manner he probably contemplates fighting from house to house and it will take more time to capture the fortress. Our artillery ammunition is almost exhausted. We will have to concentrate on a new plan." Tired and heavy-footed, my orderly and I moved back along the road by which we had come that morning.

Just prior to the assault, Major Matoba, who had been attached to the operations section at Army Headquarters, was transferred as battalion commander to the Oku Regiment. During the day's fighting he had been shot through the chest. I met him as he was being carried, bloodstained, on a stretcher to the rear. Putting my mouth to his ear to rouse him, I said, "Hello, Major Matoba! Here is a gift of wine bestowed by the Emperor," and poured the water from my flask into his mouth. I knew that giving a wounded man a drink was prohibited, but thought the major was near his end and that the water would be a drink in the hour of death. He had been completely unconscious, but he opened his eyes and said faintly, "The Imperial gift cup," and with an effort swallowed the last few drops of water in the flask. He did not die, and subsequently made a miraculous recovery.

We had left our car concealed under the shade of a tree. Returning to the spot, we found that it had been blown up and only a few fragments were left. It was the third car I had had destroyed by shellfire. Proceeding on foot, we arrived at 18th Division Headquarters, where I explained the strategic position minutely to the divisional commander, Lieutenant-General Mutaguchi. As I was leaving, Staff Officer Hashimoto pulled my sleeve and whispered, "Just a moment, sir, just a moment." When out of earshot of the divisional commander he said in a low voice, "The Old Man says he wants to go up to the front line again and will not listen to us. Will you do something to stop him?" I said to the general, "I think at the present time Your Excellency should remain in the background. The shellfire is very heavy and the way to the front line dangerous, and moreover your subordinate commanders in the front line who are doing their utmost will think you have come there to spur them to further effort when really they can do no more. Your presence there will only increase their difficulties. Please wait until night." And with these words I sought to prevent him from taking an unnecessary risk.

"Mr. Tsuji," he said, "I do not wish to go to the front line to supervise the actions of my regimental commanders. But it is possible that in tonight's attack they will both be killed and I wish to shake hands with them before they die. I would not think of going to the front line with the cold-hearted intention of supervising my subordinates. That is not the action to be expected of a divisional commander." He then firmly shook hands with me, and his staff officers sighed with relief. There were strong bonds of affection throughout the 18th Division. Not only were the rough Kyushu coal miners physically strong, but they showed an extraordinarily strong sense of loyalty to their comrades and officers, irrespective of rank. The sympathetic general who wished to shake hands with his battalion commanders, and the two soldiers burying a dead friend under a hail of shells typified the spirit of the division. The men who put forth their utmost energy in action, and, forgetting home and self, charged willingly into the jaws of death, showed the high morale of the Japanese Army which fought in Malaya. As my pen comes thus far in narrating these records of the Malayan campaign, I close my eyes and look back upon that time. The years have passed quickly since those days, which I cannot now think of without deep emotion when I consider the changes which have occurred. Ah! Indeed, in Malaya one saw and shared the true spirit of the Army.

During my interval of penance*, which involved denial of all connection with the defeated Army of the Fatherland and the shame of travelling incognito for several years, I could not forget, even though I tried, the spirit of the comrades with whom I had fought in the Malayan campaign.

The numerous and disgusting later breaches of military discipline must be considered in comparison with the far more numerous fine and noble actions on the battlefield. Beside them any discreditable actions will in time be swept into oblivion. On the battlefields of Malaya where we conquered, courage and comradeship were the spirit of the Army. As regards the opposite side, could it not be that in their defeat some shamelessness and corruption were also concealed?

Conscious of the nation's eternal life, and of the large number of departed spirits who have fallen like heroes—the deceased of the family, the husband, the father, the child—who were offered as sacrifices, and who are now neglected because of defeat and ruthlessly abandoned, one must believe there will come into existence a new Japan yearning for enlightenment.

Every morning and evening, as we bow before the *ihai*** of our deceased blood relations, the tears that cannot be kept back will be a denial of the trust and sincerity of human beings and a weak resistance to a cold-hearted society unless we have faith in the love

---

* The author spent the immediate postwar years wandering through Southeast Asia.
** A small wooden tablet bearing the name and date of death of a deceased family member. It is set upon a stand within the *butsudan*—the family Buddhist shrine.

of country and patriotism which still exists in spite of defeat.

Hoisting the White Flag

AS THE DAY WAS GRADUALLY drawing to a close, I sorrowfully said farewell to Staff Officer Hashimoto, who was leaving Headquarters. I began to walk down the hill when I was called to answer an excited call on the telephone. Putting the receiver to my ear, I said, "What is the matter? Is it urgent at this time of day?" Trembling with excitement, the voice of my dear friend Staff Officer Hayashi answered, "The enemy has surrendered! Has surrendered!"

Unconsciously dropping the receiver, I thought, "Ah! Seventy days of fighting. . . Keppel Barracks and the death struggle. . . Jitra's bloody battle." Like a magic lantern it all flashed before my mind. How would the heart of the nation be when this news came over the radio? It seemed a dream. Only a few moments ago we were engaged in a life-and-death struggle. "Perhaps I am dreaming," I thought. I pinched the flesh of my thigh hard through my trousers. I was certainly awake and in my right senses. It was no dream. From several places in the firing line cheering voices rose in the air. Then, originating in some corner, the Japanese National Anthem, "Kimi Ga Yo," spread in a wave over the battlefields.

During the day on the 5th Division front, the battle had raged as violently as in the Keppel Barracks area. Our front line had only been able to advance to the southern end of the reservoir. The troops had never before been under such heavy shellfire, from which the trenches afforded very little shelter. The division had attacked from the main road sector supported by the full strength of the "Tiger's Cub" Tank Brigade, but the troops were finally brought to a standstill at half-past three in the afternoon. Then suddenly, ahead of the most forward troops, who were renewing their assault along the central highway, there appeared a large white flag.

Major Wylde, an English staff officer, came bearing the flag of truce. Like lightning this was reported to Bukit Timah headquarters. Immediately on receiving the news, Staff Officer Sugita, in charge of intelligence, who was in a plaster cast because of a broken collarbone, was taken by car to the front line, where he personally delivered to the bearer of the flag truce documents which had been prepared at our Army Headquarters. The British staff officer at once returned to Singapore with them to enable the British commander of the fortress to consider our proposals, which were as follows:

1. At eighteen hours on 15 February, both Army Commanders to meet at Bukit Timah.

2. The British Army to promptly suspend resistance all along the line and disarm.

3. Normal administration of the economic structure to continue, maintaining every existing business, obeying our demands in succession, then handing over to the Japanese Army.

4. Ships, aircraft, vehicles, weapons, ammunition, provisions, fuel reserves and so forth, the whole of the buildings and land belonging to or used by the Army, communication facilities, harbor equipment, airfield equipment, maps and documents—all are to be handed over to the Japanese Army without damage, demolition or destruction. There must be absolutely no conduct whatever that will cause injury to the Japanese Army.

5. Those involved in termination of conflict with the Japanese Army must make assurance doubly sure and suppress at once any local conflicts which may arise.

6. All prominent persons on the side of America, the Dutch East Indies, and Chungking* are to be immediately held as prisoners of war and placed under protection of the Japanese Army.

7. All Japanese men held as prisoners of war are to be handed over forthwith to the Japanese Army.

8. Committees are to be appointed for Army, Navy, Air, Finance, Administration, Sanitation, Prisoners of War, etc., the presidents of which are to be responsible for meeting the requirements indicated by the Japanese authorities.

The streamlined motor car with the Union Jack and the white flag crossing each other stopped in front of the Ford Car factory north of the three-pronged Bukit Timah road. The British Commander, Lieutenant-General Percival, accompanied by Brigadier Torrens, Brigadier Newbigging (Deputy Adjutant-General) and Major Wylde, were led to the place of interview by Staff Officer Sugita. General Yamashita, who was roughly five minutes behind time, entered, followed by his staff officers, exchanged handshakes, and took his seat. How did the English general feel surrendering to his enemy after defeat? The faces of the four English officers were pale and their eyes bloodshot. General Yamashita indicated to General Percival a document written in English, saying, "I wish you to answer these questions very briefly."

The questions and answers were:

"Does the British Army surrender unconditionally?"—"Yes."

---

* Chiang K'ai-shek's wartime Chinese capital.

"Are there any Japanese prisoners of war?"—"Not even one man."

"Are there any Japanese men held prisoner?"—"All Japanese civilian prisoners have been sent to India. The guarantee of their position is being entrusted to the government of that country."

"Do you agree to this document unconditionally?"—"Please wait until tomorrow morning for the answer."

"Then, in that case, up till tomorrow morning we will continue the attack. Is that all right, or do you consent immediately to unconditional surrender?"—"Yes."

"Well, then, there will be a cessation of hostilities from 10 p.m. Japanese time [8:30 p.m. Singapore time]. The British Army, using a thousand men as a police force, will please maintain order. In case of any violation of these terms, a full-scale attack on Singapore will immediately commence."

General Percival then said, "I wish to receive a guarantee of the safety of the lives of the English and Australians who remain in the city."

"You may be sure of that. Please rest assured. I shall positively guarantee it."

In this way the curtain dropped on the campaign for the occupation of Singapore. Even more dramatic was the arrival at that time of the Emperor's military aide-de-camp at Bukit Timah. In 1819, one hundred and twenty-three years earlier, Stamford Raffles had landed on this island. Everything that Great Britain had since built up here in the Far East had now been beaten to a standstill.

After General Percival had gone, escorted by the beaming General Mutaguchi and others, we returned to Army Headquarters, where the customary rites and ceremonies were performed. When we had left Headquarters on this same morning, maps and documents had been spread all over the operations room. Now they were neatly stacked in order. On a table covered with white woven material were set out dried cuttlefish, excellent chestnuts, and wine, the gifts of the Emperor. Someone without our knowledge had made the preparations.

By both the Army Commander and the Army Chief of Staff we were hospitably entertained. General Yamashita said, "You have done a good job. Thank you very much. From now on you can drink sake whenever you like."

Remembering the fighting of nearly a hundred days, all present raised their full wine cups and, worshipping from a distance and facing the northeast,* they drank a silent toast. The cheerful voice of the Army

---

* That is, facing Tokyo, in the direction of the Emperor's palace.

Commander at that moment became charged with feeling, and hot tears flowed into his wine cup.

Since my appointment to the 25th Army as Staff Officer in Charge of Operations, I had vowed to the Gods to abstain from wine and tobacco until my cherished wish was accomplished. We had expected that on this day we would drink until our glasses were "bottoms up." But what actually happened was that we could not enjoy our wine or eat our delicacies. They tasted bitter and seemed to choke one's throat because of the three thousand several hundred seniors, colleagues, and soldiers with whom we could not share this day's joy. Thinking of the feelings of the families of the dead men caused the wine to be bitter wine indeed.

Major Take-no-Uchi, a great swordsman, who had fallen in Bangkok on the first day of fighting, had been a heavy drinker. I quietly raised my glass of sake to his memory. "Forgive me, Take-no-Uchi, why did you not wait until Bukit Timah? I am the only one left."

That night, after finishing drafting the telegram planned to be sent to Imperial Headquarters and to the whole Army, I fell into the sleep of the dead. A year of fatigue, it seems, had set everybody dozing off at the same time. The following morning, all concerned, having taken a bath, escorted the Emperor's aide-de-camp to deliver to the troops the Imperial Rescript which had been received by telegram from Imperial Headquarters.

The Imperial Rescript

Throughout the campaign in Malaya the Army and Navy, in close and appropriate association, have carried out difficult and dangerous sea convoys, transport duties, and military landing operations. Officers and men, risking malaria, and enduring intense heat, have struck violently at the enemy, engaged in unremitting pursuit at lightning speed, destroyed his powerful army, and captured Singapore. As a consequence, Britain's base of operations in the Far East is overthrown and annihilated.

I deeply approve of this.

Thus, for Japan the curtain fell brilliantly on the struggle for the capture of Singapore, the great undertaking of the century.

Now let us calculate the results.

1. The military strength of the Japanese and British armies was respectively about one to two.
2. The principal gains were:
>   (a) Roughly 100,000 prisoners of war, of whom about 50,000 were white soldiers.

(b) Roughly 740 guns.

(c) More than 2,500 machine-guns.

(d) About 65,000 rifles and other small arms.

(e) About 1,000 locomotives and railway trucks.

(f) About 200 armored cars.

(g) Ten light airplanes.

(h) Several thousand motor cars and trucks.

3. In the final battle for Singapore, from the crossing of Johore Strait until the enemy surrender, our Army casualties were:

(a) Killed in action, 1,714 officers and men.

(b) Wounded, 3,378 officers and men.

(c) Total casualties in the final battle, 5,092.

4. Total casualties in the Malayan campaign from the landing at Singora to the surrender of Singapore were:

(a) Killed in action, 3,507 officers and men.

(b) Wounded, 6,150 officers and men.

5. The number of enemy casualties is not clear, but at least they were nearly three times our losses.

Part Seven

Rushing the Camera

ON THE OCCASION OF THE meeting of Generals Yamashita and Percival, the enemy general said, "This evening, as there will be great confusion in the city, if by any chance the Japanese Army should make a triumphal entry into the fortress, it will be impossible to guarantee that unforeseen happenings will not occur. Please wait until tomorrow morning."

"Yes. That will be so," agreed General Yamashita, acceding to General Percival's request.

On the morning of 16 February it had to be confirmed whether the order of their commander would be acceptable to the hundred thousand British troops in the fortress.

With Staff Officers Okamura and Kawajima, who came from Imperial Headquarters as liaison officers for the whole Army, I hurried into the city in a car from which a large Japanese flag, stained and disheveled, was flying.

Passing shell craters, burnt-out cars and trucks, and other traces of the recent severe fighting, we entered Singapore city, which was a whirlpool of chaos.

For the whole Japanese Army we conducted the first triumphal entry into the fortress. The first thing in the city to strike the eye was the waves of men in khaki uniforms. Many of them still carried their rifles, walking about and nibbling bread. Groups of them were squatting on the road smoking, talking, and shouting in rather loud voices. Strangely enough, however, there was no sign whatever of hostility in their faces. Rather was there an expression of resignation such as is shown by the losers in fierce sporting contests.

Taking out a well-worn camera for the first time, I photographed the surging crowd. Suddenly from all quarters, white and black soldiers rushed up around the car, shouting, according to the interpreter, "Please take a photo of everyone!" When I inquired why they all wanted their photographs taken, the nonchalant answer was, "Your photographs will be sent to Japan, and from there to world newspapers immediately. Our wives and families will see the photographs and know their husbands and sons have survived."

The British soldiers looked like men who had finished their work by contract at a suitable salary, and were now taking a rest free from the anxiety of the battlefield. They even bowed courteously to us Japanese, whom they hated.

The English storehouses and dwellings were swallowed in waves of looting Chinese and Malays. Even the women and children were all mobilized like thieves at a fire. The inhabitants, who were to be pitied, were today giving vent to the feelings of hostility that more than a hundred years of coercion had aroused, and each was struggling to get to the front and take by force an indemnity several times the value of his losses during the war. The wretched nations without an Imperial Rescript on which to base their conduct!

At Far Eastern British Headquarters, which were firmly closed, two sentries stood, still holding rifles. Their faces showed resentment. With due solemnity they opened the gate. Only a few British subordinate officers remained behind, and there was no agitation or confusion anywhere. Inside and outside, the Headquarters building had been neatly cleaned and swept. I climbed onto the roof of the four-story building. On Bukit Timah heights the Japanese flag fluttered in the breeze as if ruling the whole island. Black smoke with occasional bursts of flame from the burning oil tanks covered half the island.

We patrolled the changing city. Groups of plundering people, guarding their loot, were everywhere beginning bloody quarrels, and it was obvious that if we did not take action quickly our administration of the city would become extremely difficult.

A part of one of our units, under the command of Major-General Kawamura, was chosen with care to perform guard duties at the danger points. It immediately set about maintaining order in the city. The rest of the Army remained firmly on the outskirts. Even officers were strictly prohibited from entering the fortress without an Army order. This was the basis of the maintenance of military discipline after the cessation of hostilities.

Warning Against Celebration

ON 17 FEBRUARY BUKIT TIMAH headquarters was transferred to Raffles Institution. During the fighting it appears this had been used as a hospital. On the walls, pierced by shells, recent bloodstains still remained, but sick and wounded soldiers had already been moved elsewhere. Cleaning up immediately, we got down to business. The whole Japanese Army, worn, battle-stained and ragged after the campaign, had to be cleaned up and smartened again, and Army Headquarters had set the example.

All the staff below the rank of Army Commander were accommodated in a small building on the grounds of Raffles Institution. Several beds were arranged in a narrow room under a roof damaged by shellfire. Water for baths was heated in oil drums over fires out in the open, and we washed off the dirt of many days. Three meals a day were served on a table in the staff officers' room by the youth Morita. From Imperial Headquarters a telegram came informing us of the day prearranged for the triumphal entry into the fortress. It appeared that there had been paper-lantern processions of congratulation and rejoicing throughout the length and breadth of Japan. Hearing of this, General Yamashita sent a telegram: "The battle is no more than a prelude. The Army will not hold a celebration. Instead of a triumphal-entry ceremony, a ceremonial commemoration service for the dead will be solemnized on 20 February, and immediately after, we will begin operations in Sumatra."

Accordingly, on 20 February at ten o'clock in the morning, officers, non-commissioned officers, and soldiers selected to represent every division and every unit assembled on the Raffles Institution grounds. First of all, we erected with appropriate solemnity an altar for our three thousand five hundred dead, who included Major-General Okamura (18th Division Ordnance Chief), killed in action on Bukit Timah, whose memory we revered. Incense was kept burning all the time, and while its smoke rose, the voice of General Yamashita, reading the address of sympathy, often ceased entirely because of his strong emotion. The Army standard in eleven colors, resplendent of military service, today drooped low and did not move. Tears streamed from the faces of the officers and men standing in line. We who had survived must fight so as not to shame the spirits of the departed.

At the conclusion of the memorial service, the ceremony of handing over the citations was carried out before the tablets of the dead. The breakthrough at Jitra and the battles of annihilation at Bakri and Slim River had been actions of great value, but here warm attention was given to the dead and scant attention to the living. The thankless tasks performed by the signalers, engineers, and the cooperative flight units, for which there was no recognition, had also been of great value. It was General Yamashita who, of his own accord, suggested the handing of the citations to the dead rather than to the living.

Throughout the Malayan campaign the men of the Konoe Division, under their divisional commander, had fought bravely, but they had suffered little by comparison with the 5th and 18th divisions. In the maritime operations off the west coast, in the crushing enemy defeat at Bakri, and in the demonstrations on Ubin Island, there were never at any time any weaknesses such as would cause anxiety. This might have been expected as the men of the division were picked troops, singled out from the whole country, who moreover had a proud tradition. But it is regrettable that they did not have suitable men as leaders to command them. This affected not only the officers and men of the Konoe Division, but reflected upon the whole Army.

Sharing the Joy

THE NAVY, ESPECIALLY THE SHIPS of the Southward Squadron, had cooperated well in the brilliantly successful campaign. Several days before Singapore was captured, it was publicly announced over the radio by a section of Imperial General Headquarters, through Captain Hirade (Navy), that a naval landing party had penetrated and taken possession of the port of Seletar. "Oh?" was the surprised comment everywhere. The truth was that the Army Commander, General Yamashita, wished to allow the Navy somehow or other to receive the credit for this action, and, through the Naval Liaison Officer, Nagai, raked up all available men wearing naval uniforms, and arranged for them to enter Seletar Naval Base together with the Army. Needless to say, neither Naval Staff Officer Nagai nor anybody else believed the Navy captured Seletar single-handed. When the Navy heard the unexpected announcement from Imperial Naval Headquarters they were so humiliated they wished to creep into a hole.

Some officers in one section of Army staff were indignant at this self-righteous announcement, but the Army Commander said, "That's alright. Don't worry about it," and left it at that.

This matter being disposed of for the time being, General Yamashita sent thanks to Admiral Ozawa for his cooperation throughout the campaign, and cordially invited him to visit Army Headquarters. The admiral and his officers were taken to the heights of the Imperial Palace, and from there to the heights of Bukit Timah, and had the whole progress of the battle explained to them. Finally, to show our gratitude to the Navy, we of the Army asked, "Is there anything the Navy wishes? Anything you wish we will do."

In due course the Navy let us know what they wanted in Singapore. They asked for all the equipment at Seletar Harbor, one aerodrome, a number of houses, and roughly 500 motor cars.

The liaison officer who submitted the demands was urged to ask for more. "Are so few cars enough, especially when we have so many?" With humility he replied, "What I have already asked for will be sufficient." They selected very excellent cars and houses, which were required for use by their rear sections.

In Manila and the Dutch East Indies the respective services resisted the establishment of such harmonious relationships, especially in the struggle for the spoils of war; but in Malaya, neither prior to the start of operations nor throughout their continuation, was there any clash between the two services. A perfect relationship was maintained. On the suggestion of Admiral Ozawa, the Shonan [Singapore] Society was organized by the senior officers of the 25th Army and the Southward Squadron. This society, until after the end of the war, gathered every year to commemorate 15 February, and to promote friendship between the squadron and the 25th Army. If the whole Army and Navy had lived up to the principles of the Shonan Society, perhaps the outcome of the whole war might have been different.

There are invariably problems of man towards man. Both Admiral Ozawa and General Yamashita were men of strong personality, bound together by an attitude of mutual respect, which could result in nothing but good.

The victory ceremony of triumphal entry was carried out in lively fashion in Hong Kong and Manila, but here in Singapore only representatives of Army units, carrying boxes containing ashes of the dead, would pass through the city in solemn silence as a warning to the stubborn people who were defeated. The ceremony was the first step of the Army plan for administration of the occupied area.

The small detachment of the 5th Division, under command of Major-General Kawamura, maintained order in the city. By the enforcement of military discipline we planned to protect law-abiding citizens. All officers and men other than those of the guard detachment were forbidden to enter the city of Singapore except on official business, on which they were required to carry Army passes. Sightseeing parties under the leadership of unit commanders were taken on scheduled tours through the city, the men comprising such parties having been previously severely cautioned against any breach of regulations. It was, however, not easy to prevent unlawful trading transactions.

One day, alone, I was making a tour of inspection of the streets when a certain Malayan brought a complaint. He was a clerk at a large watch-maker's shop. On being led there, as the front door was closed to business, I was taken to the back entrance and up to the second story.

A second lieutenant and roughly ten men under a warrant officer were in the midst of repeatedly lowering the price of the watches which were displayed. The clerk was trying to prevent this, but the high-class Swiss watches were being knocked down to five and ten yen. This was essentially plunder. Certainly it was an indication that death by shooting would have to be enforced as a penalty for looting or plundering.

For me, in this instance questions and answers were unnecessary. "Fools!" I cried as I instantly smacked the faces of the officers and men concerned. On investigation, they turned out to be connected with the Flight Group. I made an entry of their full names in my notebook.

Making a further tour of the principal streets of the business center, I found more of the same petty thieving. It was as though I was conducting a crusade. On my way back to Headquarters a sergeant-major was walking along ahead of me carrying a large parcel wrapped in a *furoshiki*. He was wearing an official-business armband, but seemed to be nervous and excited. I ordered him to open his parcel. Two large crocodile-skin handbags and other high-class luxury goods fell out. It seemed that in all probability at least half of these would be plunder. It turned out that a subordinate of a major-general of a certain division was given an order to buy presents for the wife and daughters of the major-general. To the extent that there were in this campaign weak persons who were robust in the path of theft, so to that extent there would be weak units in the war, and the transgressions of military discipline would be more numerous.

Having smacked the faces of the men concerned in the illegalities which came under my notice, I submitted a full report to Army Headquarters. General Yamashita ordered a parade of all officers and, standing in the scorching sun, gave a scathing address on the enforcement of military discipline. The unlawful conduct of the previous day, as recorded in my notebook, was read aloud to the officers of the whole Army. A certain major-general, stricken with fear greater than that of enemy bullets, stood pale-faced without even wiping away the beads of perspiration on his face.

Those who changed the name of Singapore to Shonan, with hearts like the sun, in contrast to the people of today, considered the responsibilities involved and took steps to carry them out. Those who were conquered, those who assumed control, and those liberated from other governments—they all held their own ideas of right and wrong. We, the conquerors, without showing pride, had to practice moral principles as a starting point for the new history.

Immediately after the capture of Singapore, the establishment of the Shonan Shinto Shrine was discussed. A site was chosen in the virgin forest on the reservoir heights which had been the center of the battle for the conquest of the fortress.

Officers and men of the Japanese Army and a group of prisoners of war set to work with picks and shovels, and in a spirit transcending both gratitude and revenge they rendered service to the gods.

When we commenced building the memorial to our war dead on Bukit Timah heights, a tower was also erected for the purpose of holding requiem masses for the British officers and men who had fallen in the fighting. Although small, it was built by the hands of the Japanese Army which had conquered. It was a new symbol—a substitute for the bronze statue in Singapore of Raffles, which had been removed.

When we entered Singapore we were surprised to see that the airfields, harbor, and city had not been destroyed by the enemy. Seizing a junior enemy officer, we questioned him. "Why did you not destroy Singapore?" we asked. "Because we will return again," he replied. Again, we asked, "Don't you believe Britain is beaten in this war?" He replied, "We may be defeated ninety-nine times, but in the final round we will be all right—we will win that." This one junior officer prisoner of war spoke with the voice and the belief of the whole Anglo-Saxon nation.

A little more than three and a half years later, the curtain fell on the Japanese Army's government of Malaya–the seventh in the country's history. Smeared with the blood of young officers and men who gave their lives for their country on Bukit Tirnah heights, the Shonan Shinto Shrine changed to smoke in the blast of an explosive charge. The bronze statue of Raffles appeared on its pedestal for the second time; but without anyone knowing the reason, its color seemed to have faded. Judging from its expression, it may be that it had lost confidence in the principle of government by force.

In military operations we conquered splendidly, but in the war we were severely defeated. But, as if by magic, India, Pakistan, Ceylon, Burma, the Dutch East Indies and the Philippine Islands one after another gained independence overnight. Our reduction of Singapore was indeed the hinge of fate for the peoples of Asia.

Citations

[Citations are a very high distinction in the Japanese Army, and are usually awarded to formations and units; they are conferred on individuals only for exceptional gallantry. The following citations were awarded by 25th Army Commander Tomoyuki Yamashita on 15 February 1942.]

Citation
FIFTH DIVISION

The 5th Division, under the leadership of Group Commander Lieutenant-General Matsui, carried out the landing in southern Thailand at the commencement of our operations against Singapore.

Notwithstanding heavy rain and intense heat, marshes, swamps and dense jungle, in fifty-five days the division repaired more than two hundred bridges destroyed by the enemy, broke through enemy strongholds and overcame the resistance encountered at every juncture. After an advance of eleven hundred kilometers, it took possession of Johore Bahru, thus determining the fate of the enemy.

Next, the division commenced the attack on Singapore Island, effecting the landing thereon in the face of obstinate enemy resistance. Continuing the assault night and day and capturing fortified positions to the north of Singapore, it broke the enemy's plan of resistance.

During the whole campaign the division was under the command of Lieutenant-General Matsui, who fully manifested the tradition of exerting himself to the utmost in heroic fighting to fulfill an important mission.

Above all others the Ando Regiment, under the command of Colonel Ando, greatly facilitated the operations of the main body of the division by breaking deep into the flank of the enemy in the Patani district and destroying by a sudden attack a powerful enemy group in the Slim River area.

The Saeki Detachment, after landing at Singora, advanced rapidly, broke through active resistance on the frontier and in darkness and torrential rain drove a deep wedge in the Jitra line, throwing the enemy into confusion, which in the opening battle of the campaign started the collapse of a strong position.

Throughout the rest of the campaign, the unit under command of Colonel Tamura, under heavy fire, crossed hundreds of large and small bridges destroyed by the enemy, repaired them rapidly by working day and night, and thus greatly facilitated the operations of the rest of the Army.

The conduct of the division and of the units composing it has been in full accordance with the highest traditions of the Japanese Army, and in recognition of its great achievements this citation is hereby bestowed.

Citation
EIGHTEENTH DIVISION

The 18th Division, under command of Group Commander Lieutenant-General Mutaguchi, participated in the Malayan campaign from its commencement.

Its Takumi Detachment carried out the difficult landing at Kota Bharu in the face of the enemy, destroyed an enemy operational air base, and then by a rapid overland advance struck against Kuantan, thus ensuring the seizure of other aerodromes and crushing the obstinate enemy resistance in the area.

Again, with the Koba Unit, which had also landed at Kota Bharu, it advanced rapidly to seize the key enemy strongpoints of Endau and Mersing.

During the final attack on Singapore Island, this division, on the right wing of the Army, forced a landing against strong enemy resistance, pressed on to the rear of Tengah aerodrome, and in a night attack broke through a strongly fortified position, seizing the high ground to the south of Bukit Timah, thus sealing the fate of the enemy. Then attacking along the southwest coast of the island, in the face of heavy artillery fire, it broke through the enemy line and captured the high land in the vicinity of Keppel Barracks, the key position of Singapore.

Under the leadership of its distinguished and resolute group commander, the division demonstrated the traditional intrepid spirit of the Japanese Army, and in recognition of its great achievements I hereby bestow this citation.

Citation
KONOE IMPERIAL GUARDS: OGAKI BATTALION

This battalion, under command of Major Ogaki, participated with the Konoe Division in the drive along the western seacoast of Malaya, maintaining rapid pursuit of the enemy. Taking the lead from the Iwaguro Pursuit Unit Corps, on 15 January, it confronted a superior enemy force and checked its advance in the vicinity of the mouth of the Muar River, and, after crossing that river with great difficulty in the face of strong enemy resistance, made a surprise attack from the rear of the enemy position, which it destroyed.

Next, to undertake a surprise attack on the enemy around Bakri, the battalion made a detour from the coast road, and in the early dawn of 19 January, intercepted the line of retreat of the main enemy forces. Attacking and being counterattacked from all sides by superior enemy forces accompanied by armored cars, the battalion lost more than half its officers and non-commissioned officers and suffered very heavy casualties among the rank and file in the most violent battle of the campaign to that date.

Captain Seno, who then commanded the battalion, bravely sustained the attack on the enemy rear, cooperating closely with our forces attacking their front, and notwithstanding its own heavy losses the battalion wiped out an entire enemy brigade.

I recognize these actions as surpassing achievements which satisfactorily demonstrate the glorious spirit of the unit association which formed a nucleus with the battle commander.

Citation
GOTANDA TANK COMPANY

The Gotanda Tank Company, under command of Captain Gotanda, following operations in Malaya with Troop Leader Iwaguro in control, on 18 January participated in the battle of Bakri.

The infantry attack, supported by the tank company, penetrated the enemy line with great difficulty, and suffered very heavy casualties. When all the company's tanks were put out of action by enemy fire, the whole personnel, including the company commander, joined the infantry in the attack, and met a heroic death in battle.

In this action the Gotanda Tank Company, exhibiting a sublime spirit of sacrifice, materially influenced the progress of the battle and inspired their fellow soldiers in their difficult task of attacking an enemy superior in strength.

As a result, the Ogaki Battalion, intercepting the enemy line of retreat, was able to destroy a brigade of enemy troops.

The self-sacrifice of the Gotanda Tank Company is to be taken as a model for the whole Army, and its great achievement is acknowledged as unparalleled.

Therefore I bestow this citation.

Citation
ELEVENTH INFANTRY REGIMENT: ITABANA PLATOON
While the Watanabe Regiment was engaged in an attack on a fortified position in the neighborhood of Mengki Bahru on 26 January the Itabana Platoon arrived in the battle zone as a second-line company, and found a way around the strongpoint which was holding fast while our main forces and those of the enemy were engaged in a general action.

Penetrating to the rear of the enemy main line, the platoon, on its own initiative, attacked the enemy rear, causing much confusion. The platoon leader and the twenty-three men under his command fought desperately, and when their ammunition was exhausted, charged with sword and bayonet, inflicting tremendous damage on the enemy. Finally the whole platoon met a heroic death in battle.

Their valiant attack was responsible for the destruction of a large number of the enemy, and, it must be said, serves as an example for the future conduct of troops in battle. It is acknowledged as a permanently great achievement.

Citation
SHIMADA TANK COMPANY
The Shimada Tank Company, under the command of Major Shimada, operated with the 5th Division in Malaya, attached to the Ando Regiment. At Trolak in the Kampar district, working in close cooperation with infantry, artillery and engineers, at five o'clock in the morning the company attacked a strong enemy position, broke through a zone of land mines which were deployed in depth, and then drove right through the whole enemy fortified position and dealt a fatal blow to the enemy on both sides of the road.

Again at Slim River the tanks, singly, charged into the enemy lines, and Second Lieutenant Watanabe several times went out in his tank under very heavy enemy fire and destroyed demolition gear on enemy bridges, wiped out a fortified artillery position and destroyed the enemy headquarters. Up to about noon on 7 January they ranged over a front of about twenty kilometers, causing confusion among the enemy and enabling the extermination of two enemy brigades.

Later, in an isolated action they penetrated the enemy lines and secured several important bridges. I recognize these as distinguished achievements of considerable importance for the future operations of the division.

Citation

TANK DETACHMENT ATTACHED TO SAEKI UNIT

The tank detachment attached to the Saeki Unit under command of Troop Leader Saeki, on 11 December, during the operations in Malaya, under cover of heavy rain, attacked and penetrated deeply into the enemy position near Jitra. Then, concentrating in the rubber jungle, it attacked powerful enemy mechanized troops preparing to occupy a fortified position, pursued them and drove a wedge through the enemy fortified line and later cooperated with our main forces in a night assault.

Fighting continuously and heroically under intense enemy artillery fire, the next day (the 12th) the tank detachment enabled the Saeki Unit to dominate the enemy defense, thus starting the collapse of the strong Jitra line, and in the opening battle striking terror into the heart of the enemy.

I recognize these as surpassing achievements which were advantageous to our future military operations. Therefore, I bestow this citation.

Citation

FIFTEENTH INDEPENDENT ENGINEER REGIMENT

The 15th Independent Engineer Regiment, under command of Colonel Yokoyama, during the Malayan operations, invariably under heavy enemy fire, swiftly repaired more than fifty large and small bridges which had been destroyed by the enemy.

In the course of these extremely difficult operations they advanced eleven hundred kilometers with the 5th Division.

Furthermore, during the attack on Singapore, in the most difficult landing across Johore Strait, under heavy enemy fire, the troops worked on intelligent and exhaustive preparations which enabled the full strength of the 5th Division to complete the crossing of the strait in a very short time in the face of strong enemy opposition.

These great deeds; which were advantageous to our military operations, I recognize as distinguished achievements.

Citation

ELEVENTH INFANTRY REGIMENT: ASAI PURSUIT TROOPS, FIRST LIEUTENANT HAJIME ASAI AND THE TEN MEN UNDER HIM

After the breakthrough of the fortified position of Jitra by the 5th Division, the Asai pursuit troop received orders to seize the bridges on the southern edge of Alor Star. During an attack by our main forces they charged through the defeated enemy and arrived at the first bridge at ten minutes past ten on the morning of 13 December.

Under heavy fire from the enemy at the southern end of the bridge, Platoon Commander Asai, in a motor vehicle, immediately rushed across to the southern end, leaving his two corporals, Kaneko and Nakayama, to seize the northern bridge foundations and disconnect the enemy demolition charges.

Just as Lieutenant Asai was about to disconnect the charges at the southern end, they blew up, killing him. Corporals Kaneko and Nakayama fought with their bayonets against great odds, and killed several of the enemy. Corporal Nakayama was the first to fall and Corporal Kaneko was wounded.

The rapid, intrepid charge by those under the section commander caused panic and confusion in the enemy ranks and it was easy to seize possession of the railway bridge at the eastern side of the above-mentioned bridge, which thenceforth was of considerable value for the further operations of the 5th Division.

The heroic action and sublime sense of responsibility of Lieutenant Asai and his men must be a model for the whole Army, and I acknowledge such distinguished military service as unparalleled.

Citation

ODA ENGINEER COMPANY

The Oda Engineer Company, under command of Major Oda, landed in face of the enemy at Singora at the commencement of the Malayan campaign. Attached to the Konoe Division, they moved to the west coast of Malaya and operated by sea in small boats. Maneuvering skillfully along six hundred and fifty kilometers of coastline, they were frequently attacked by enemy aircraft and small surface vessels, suffering heavy casualties among their personnel and considerable damage to their boats.

With indomitable tenacity of purpose they carried out their duties heroically, and, landing at Port Swettenham, Morib, Muar, Batu Pahat and many other places, they attacked the enemy in the rear, invariably throwing his forces into confusion, becoming a serious menace to his operations and thus creating conditions which were advantageous for our whole Army.

At the crossing of Johore Strait they cooperated with the 5th Division, and although more than half their boats were damaged or sunk by enemy fire, and very heavy casualties were suffered, they completed the task assigned them, conveying their quota of 5th Division troops across Johore Strait to land on Singapore Island against strong enemy opposition.

I acknowledge these as preeminent achievements. Therefore, I bestow this citation.

Citation
NITAWARA FLIGHT UNIT

Throughout the operations in Malaya, the Nitawara Flight Unit cooperated closely with the ground units of the Army. Often under heavy enemy fire, the planes of the unit continuously searched over the jungle, obtaining information of ground conditions and enemy dispositions ahead of the Army. These served as data for attacks by our ground troops, including for the attack on Singapore.

At all times the unit showed an aggressive spirit and invariably provided intelligent reports for the guidance of the ground forces at the right times. For every group of units this was valuable and for Army Operations Branch this was indispensable for the conduct of the campaign. I acknowledge these as preeminently great achievements.

Citation
IIBUCHI TELEGRAPH COMPANY

The Iibuchi Telegraph Company, following the operations on 8 January, operated along the railway line from Sungkai to Kuala Lumpur. Driving off remnants of enemy forces and removing landmines along the track, they effected swift repairs to the telegraph line along the railway which had almost been destroyed by the enemy. Thenceforth, almost continuously under enemy fire, they constantly maintained the telegraph line, repairing it as our troops advanced and enabling continuous connection between Army Headquarters and 5th Division Headquarters. This greatly facilitated our military operations in the area.

Next, they received orders for the construction of a line of communication between Army Headquarters campaign post and 5th Division Headquarters, which was planned as the future main line for the reduction of Singapore. They carried out this task in time for the assault on Singapore to be launched on the date planned.

On 8 February, during the first landing on Singapore Island, they carried out the extremely difficult operation of laying a submarine cable across Johore Strait under intense enemy fire. This was secured firmly at both ends and kept connected with our forward troops throughout the battles on the island. They also carried out lines-of-communication work for the transport of our men through the jungle, often interrupted by enemy fire. Nevertheless, the work was carried out according to plan and completed in time for commencement of the crossing of Johore Strait. The maintenance of continuous communication with the assault troops was of the utmost importance to Army Headquarters during the fighting for Singapore. I recognize these as surpassingly great achievements. Therefore, I here bestow a citation.

Citation
FIRST LIEUTENANT TAKAHASHI, KONOE DIVISION
Army First Lieutenant Takahashi, Konoe Division, from start to finish of the Malayan campaign remained at the head of the advance guard of the division, invariably showing initiative advantageous to the other units of the division. At Bakri he led a detour to the rear of the enemy to intercept their line of retreat, and, at Senggarang, with barely one squad under his command, he carried out a reconnaissance which enabled suitable allotment of tasks for the units engaged in the battle.

In a brilliant night attack he led the movement which resulted in the capture of Senggarang Bridge, thus opening the way for the further advance of our main forces.

At the crossing of Johore Strait on 9 February he directed the crossing of the first unit of his division. On 10 February, during the attack on the Mandai heights, he detected a weak point in the enemy line, and, quickly seizing the opportunity, led his troops to take possession of Hill 185, which proved an important observation point for future attacks.

After capture of the high ground on the west side of Mandai, during the subsequent heavy fighting Lieutenant Takahashi met a heroic death in battle.

Because of his vigor and resolution in grappling with difficult situations, and his achievement of great success in every battle, his division will become a model for the whole Army and I here bestow a citation.

Citation

SERGEANT HISAMITSU FUKUI, KOIKE ENGINEER REGIMENT

Sergeant Hisamitsu Fukui, Koike Engineer Regiment, was appointed squad leader for constant surveillance and reconnaissance of Johore Strait during the ten days of preparation prior to the attack on Singapore Island. His duties were to obtain details of enemy positions on the enemy shore, and to observe the effects of the ebb and flow of the tides. He was to thoroughly observe all things and to collect all data likely to be useful for the crossing of the strait.

On the evening of 8 February, as boat leader during the crossing of the 18th Division, under intense enemy fire he stimulated and encouraged his subordinates.

Arriving on the enemy shore, he jumped into the water and held in position the lashed-together boats. On his return crossing he was shot through the body by an enemy machine-gun and severely wounded, but maintained his advance across the channel according to the command hand-flag signals. As he arrived on the shore he collapsed and died. His bravery and sublime sense of responsibility are a model for the whole Army.

Citation

LANCE-CORPORAL KIYOICHI YAMAMOTO, YOKOYAMA ENGINEER REGIMENT

Lance-Corporal Kiyoichi Yamamoto, Yokoyama Engineer Regiment, during the hazardous crossing of Johore Strait on 8 February, was maneuvering boats lashed together when enemy shells destroyed the right- and left-hand boats and seriously wounded him and his steersman. Lance-Corporal Yamamoto's chest was torn open, exposing his right lung through his ribs. He continued, however, to direct the boat forward and single-handedly brought it to the disembarkation point, without a hitch landing the troops aboard. Then saying, "Long live His Majesty the Emperor," and praying for the certain victory of the Imperial Army, he closed his eyes with composure and died. His vigorous sense of responsibility and indomitable courage I recognize as a model for the whole Army.

Appendix 1

Read This Alone—And the War Can Be Won*

Preface

1. In preparing this book, the aim has been to give officers and other ranks a thorough grounding in the purpose and special characteristics of the campaign in South Asia, and attention has been devoted in particular to the following features:

(i) Military, ideological, and economic aspects of the campaign have been treated together.

(ii) Regulations contained in General Operation Orders have been summarized, and only those relevant to the special conditions of tropical warfare have been here included.

(iii) From "Notes on Tropical Warfare" a selection has been made of those articles of direct importance to the soldier.

(iv) The book is designed to be read quickly, without strain, in the cramped conditions of a transport vessel.

(v) The style is simple, that the sense may be readily understood by all ranks, including N.C.O.s and private soldiers.

---

* This pamphlet, referred to by the author on p. 9, has been translated by G. W. Sargent, Department of Oriental Studies, University of Sydney, Australia.

2. The book is a synthesis of a variety of already existing materials, is indebted to opinions solicited from many quarters, and incorporates the fruits of training exercises carried out for research under similar conditions. It is intended for distribution to all officers and all other ranks immediately upon embarkation.

Imperial Army Headquarters

Chapter I
The Campaign Area in South Asia—What Is It Like?

1. A treasure-house of the Far East, seized by the British, the Americans, the French, and the Dutch

The remarkable exploits of Yamada Nagamasa in Siam (the present Thailand) took place more than three hundred years ago) but in the years between then and the 1868 Restoration all overseas expansion by the Japanese was brought to a stop by the rigidly enforced seclusion policy of the Tokugawa shoguns, and in that intervening period the English, the French, the Americans, the Dutch, the Portuguese and others sailed into the Far East as if it were theirs by natural right, terrorized and subjugated the culturally backward natives, and colonized every country in the area, India and the Malay Peninsula were seized by the British, Annam by the French, Java and Sumatra by the Dutch, the Philippines by the Americans. These territories, the richest in natural resources in the Far East, were taken by a handful of white men, and their tens of millions of Asian inhabitants have for centuries, down to our own day, suffered constant exploitation and persecution at their hands.

We Japanese have been born in a country of no mean blessings, and thanks to the august power and influence of His Majesty the Emperor our land has never once, to this day, experienced invasion and occupation by a foreign power. The other peoples of the Far East look with envy upon Japan; they trust and honor the Japanese; and deep in their hearts they are hoping that, with the help of the Japanese people, they may themselves achieve national independence and happiness.

2. A hundred million Asians tyrannized by three hundred thousand whites

Three hundred and fifty million Indians are ruled by five hundred thousand British, sixty million Southeast Asians by two hundred thousand Dutch, twenty-three million Indochinese by twenty thousand Frenchmen, six million Malayans by a few ten thousand British, and thirteen million Filipinos by a few ten thousand Americans. In short, four hundred and fifty million natives of the Far East live under the domination of less than eight hundred thousand whites. If we exclude India, one hundred million are oppressed by less than three hundred thousand. Once you set foot on the enemy's territories you will see for yourselves, only too clearly, just what this oppression by the white man means. Imposing, splendid buildings look down from the summits of mountains or hills onto the tiny thatched huts of natives. Money squeezed from the blood of Asians maintains these small white minorities in their luxurious mode of life—or disappears to the respective home-countries.

These white people may expect, from the moment they issue from their mothers' wombs, to be allotted a score or so of natives as their personal slaves. Is this really God's will?

The reason why so many peoples of the Far East have been so completely crushed by so few white men is, fundamentally, that they have exhausted their strength in private quarrels, and that they are lacking in any awareness of themselves as a group, as peoples of Asia.

3. A world source of oil, rubber, and tin

Without oil neither planes, warships, nor cars can move. Britain and America, controlling the greater part of the world's oil and having far more than they can use for their own purposes, have nevertheless forbidden the export of oil to Japan, which is desperately short of it. More than that, they even obstruct Japan from buying oil in South Asia.

Rubber and tin are likewise indispensable for military operations, and the countries of South Asia are the richest sources in the whole of the Far East for these valuable commodities too. Although our country has sought to purchase them by fair methods, the Anglo-Americans have interfered even in this. And in the unscrupulous behavior of these two countries in these matters lies one of the reasons why the present campaign has been forced upon us. The Dutch East Indies and French Indochina are clearly in no position by themselves to oppose Japan, but they too, with Anglo-American bolstering, and under intimidation, are maintaining a hostile attitude. If shortage of oil and steel is Japan's weak point, the greatest weakness in America's economy is shortage of rubber, tin, and tungsten, and these are supplied to America from South Asia and southern China. If Japan can master these areas, not only will she gain control of the oil and steel which she needs for herself, but she will strike at America where it hurts most. And herein lies the reason for America's extreme dislike of Japan's southward advance, and the malicious manner in which she has striven to obstruct it.

4. A world of everlasting summer

This theater of war knows no seasons. It is subject throughout the year to a heat comparable to that of midsummer in Japan. Hence we call it a world of everlasting summer. The heat commences soon after sunrise, reaches its peak around about noon, and continues until sundown. The monsoons vary in different localities, but in general southwest winds prevail from May to September, and northwest winds from November to March. At this time thunder and heavy rain is common after midday. These extremely violent cloudbursts, known as "squalls," are in quite a different class from the summer downpours we know in Japan. They are welcome in so far as they clear the oppressive atmosphere, but they also crumble roads, wash away bridges, and thus considerably hamper troop movements.

Again, because of the high humidity, gunpowder becomes affected by damp; rifles, artillery, and ammunition rust; spectacles mist over; and electric batteries run down quickly.

There are fruits available throughout the year, like bananas and pineapples, but the troublesome malarial mosquito is everywhere, harboring its grudge. In Java and the Singapore region, where the country has been opened up, motor roads run in all directions, but there are many undeveloped areas of forest or marshland where neither man nor horse can pass.

The temperature is high, as has been stated, but it is by no means an uncomfortable climate in which to live. The sea is near, and there is always a breeze. Indeed, it is for reasons of this sort that so many white people have chosen these lands as their homes.

Chapter II
Why Must We Fight? How Should We Fight?

1. Obeying the Emperor's august will for peace in the Far East

The 1868 Restoration, by the abolition of feudal clans and the establishment of prefectures, returned Japan to its ancient system of beneficent government by His Majesty the Emperor, and thereby rescued the country from grave peril—for the black ships of the foreigners which had come to Nagasaki and Uraga were ready to annex Japan on the slightest pretext. The New Restoration of the 1930s has come about in response to the Imperial desire for peace in the Far East. Its task is the rescue of Asia from white aggression, the restoration of Asia to the Asians, and—when peace in Asia has been won—the firm establishment of peace throughout the whole world.

The wire-pullers giving aid to Chiang K'ai-shek and moving him to make war on Japan are the British and the Americans. The rise of Japan being to these people like a sore spot on the eye, they have tried by every means in their power to obstruct our development, and they are inciting the regime at Chungking, the French Indochinese, and the Dutch East Indians to regard Japan as their enemy. Their great hope is for the destruction of the Asian peoples by mutual strife, and their greatest fear is that, with the help of a powerful Japan, the peoples of Asia will work together for independence. If the peoples of Asia, representing more than half of the world's population, were to make a united stand it would indeed be a sore blow to British, Americans, French, and Dutch alike, who for centuries have battened and waxed fat on the blood of Asians.

Already Japan, the pioneer in this movement in the Far East, has rescued Manchuria from the ambitions of the Soviets, and set China free from the extortions of the Anglo-Americans. Her next great mission is to assist towards the independence of the Thais, the Annamese, and the Filipinos, and to bring the blessing of freedom to the natives of South Asia and the Indian people. In this we shall be fulfilling the essential spirit of "one world to the eight corners of the earth."

The aim of the present war is the realization, first in the Far East, of His Majesty's august will and ideal that the peoples of the world should each be granted possession of their rightful homelands. To this end the countries of the Far East must plan a great coalition of East Asia, uniting their military resources, administering economically to each other's wants on the principle of co-existence to the common good, and mutually respecting each other's political independence. Through the combined strength of such a coalition we shall liberate East Asia from white invasion and oppression.

The significance of the present struggle, as we have shown, is immense, and the peril which Japan has drawn upon herself as the central and leading force in this movement is greater than anything she has ever faced since the foundation of the country. The peoples of South Asia deeply respect the Japanese and place high hopes upon our success. It is vital, above all, that we should not betray this respect and these hopes.

For this reason close attention should be paid to the points in the following section.

2. Treat the natives with kindness—but do not expect too much of them

These hundred million natives, treated as slaves by three hundred thousand white men, are physically—in the color of their eyes and skin—not unlike ourselves. They should, by rights, have received from the gods at birth the inheritance of homelands which are treasure-houses of the world. And if you stop to wonder for what past sins they now groan beneath the white man's oppressive rule, you may well pity them.

To the natives—whether you look at the matter from a geographical or from an historical viewpoint—the British, the Americans, the French, and the Dutch are mere armed robbers, while we Japanese are brothers. At least, we are indubitably relatives. But there are, even among the natives themselves, many who have become the tools of the white men, who spy for them, sell their blood-brothers, and betray Asia. Such peoples are particularly numerous in the higher ranks of the civil service and in the army, and these we should eliminate as persons who do us mischief; but if they come to offer submission, we must have the magnanimity to welcome and pardon them.

But countries of great natural blessings, where it is possible for men to live in nakedness and to eat without working, breed large populations of idlers.

What is more, after centuries of subjection to Europe and exploitation by the Chinese, these natives have reached a point of almost complete emasculation.

We may wish to make men of them again quickly, but we should not expect too much.

3. Respect native customs

The majority of the natives are Mohammedans. Just as the Buddist faithful revere their Buddhas and Christians revere images of Christ, so Mohammedans, by ancient custom, prostrate themselves reverentially in the direction of Mecca, the ancient city of Central Asia in which Mohammed was born. Again, Mohammedans never in any circumstances eat the flesh of pigs, which are despised as unclean animals. You will see men with white brimless hats on their heads—these are Mohammedans who have made the pilgrimage to Mecca, and they are greatly respected among the natives. In all the villages and towns there are places of worship called mosques, and even people of the most exalted station must remove their shoes before entering here. To enter wearing muddy boots would be a great affront to the natives. The weekly religious holiday is not Sunday but Friday. Even on normal days it is the custom to cease work for several minutes at certain times in order to bow towards Mecca in worship, and at the end of the year a month-long fast is observed. (No food is taken during the day, and only a light meal at night.)

In our society it is polite to remove one's hat on entering a house, but the native custom is to keep the hat on. Again, the left hand is regarded as unclean. No paper is used in the toilet, but the anus is washed with water by the left hand—hence you must never use this hand in offering things to people, nor must you touch the body of another person with it. The natives rejoice greatly at small profits which they can see with their own eyes, and have no understanding of greater profits in the future. When making purchases, be careful to pay at once and to make no unreasonable deals.

In general the natives think of their own special customs and habits as things of the greatest importance and value. If you interfere in those customs, no matter how kindly your intention, you will not be thanked. On the contrary, you will incur resentment. It is essential to refrain from well-meant expressions of your own opinions, to respect the native traditions and customs, and to avoid unnecessary friction.

4. *Destroy the genuine enemy—but show compassion to those who have no guilt*

In the Japan of recent years, where no one who cannot read English can proceed to higher education, and where English is widely used in all first-class hotels, trains, and steamships, we have unthinkingly come to accept Europeans as superior and to despise the Chinese and the peoples of the South.

This is like spitting into our own eyes. Bearing in mind that we Japanese, as an Eastern people, have ourselves for long been classed alongside the Chinese and the Indians as an inferior race, and treated as such, we must at the very least, here in Asia, beat these Westerners to submission, that they may change their arrogant and ill-mannered attitude.

The present war is a struggle between races, and we must achieve the satisfaction of our just demands with no thought of leniency to Europeans, unless they be the Germans and Italians. But pillaging, molesting women, and the heedless slaughter or maiming of people who offer no resistance, or any action which may sully the reputation of Japan as a country of moral rectitude, should be condemned by all in the strongest terms. You must do nothing to impair your dignity as soldiers of His Majesty the Emperor in His Majesty's Army. You must in particular show compassion towards the old and towards women and children.

5. *Who are the "Overseas Chinese"?*

Six hundred and fifty years ago the Mongol Emperor Kublai Khan came to attack Japan, and his invading army suffered almost complete annihilation when smitten by a divine storm [*kamikaze*] in Hakata Bay. Soon after this, Kublai Khan sent an expeditionary force against what is now known as Java. Three hundred thousand troops, borne in a fleet of a thousand ships, landed on the northeast coast of Java with the object of seizing the rare treasures of South Asia, but withdrew again—thanks to the cunning of their enemies—with little or no booty. From about that time the Chinese began to emigrate in large numbers to South Asia, and gradually, rising from humble positions as clerks, errand boys, or coolies, they became men of wealth, and by deceiving the naturally lazy natives and colluding with the British, Americans, French, and Dutch they increased their economic power, and today there are in this whole area some five million Chinese colonists. They contribute military funds to Chungking, but most of them are either led astray by Chungking propaganda or are forced by terrorists, whether they wish it or not, to make those contributions. We must offer to these people an opportunity for self-examination and guide them over to our own side. Two points, however, should be noted: first, that these people, by a variety of clever schemes concerted with the European administrators, are steadily extorting money from the native population, and that the greater part of the natives, resentment is directed against them rather than against the Europeans; and, second, that for the most part they have no racial or national consciousness, and no enthusiasms outside the making of money. Consequently you must realize in advance that it will be difficult, by merely urging them to an intellectual awareness of themselves as members of an Asian brotherhood, to enlist their cooperation in any scheme which does not promise personal profit.

6. *Be strong, correctly behaved, and self-controlled*

If you look at the history of past campaigns you will see that troops who are really efficient in battle do not plunder and rob, chase after women, or drink and quarrel. Those who flee and hide in the midst of bullets are the great braggarts and the great tormentors of the weak. Bear in mind that the misbehavior of one soldier reflects upon the good name of the whole Army, and discipline yourself. When a hero of many campaigns is court-martialed for plunder or rape, and finds himself sentenced to several years of penal servitude, there is no excuse. To go back home, remembering the banzais and the stirring emotions of the day you set out for the war, back to the parents, brothers, and sisters who have been daily visiting the shrine on your behalf, daily setting a tray for you in your absence, and praying for your safety, and to know that you have been punished for misconduct on the field of battle—what sort of a triumphal return can this be? What manner of apology can you offer to those brave comrades of yours who have died? This is a warning which should be particularly heeded by those who are in camp after the battle has finished, or are assigned to duties in the rear, far from the sound of bullets. Not to heed it is to invite a failure which can never be lived down.

You must discipline yourselves to correct behavior, that your meritorious deeds and feats of endurance may not be turned to nothing by a moment of dissipation; and when living in uncomfortable conditions and performing disagreeable tasks you must be patient and self-controlled, in the spirit of your dead comrades.

7. Preserve and protect natural resources

Thanks to the malignity of the Anglo-Americans, Japan is not able to buy anywhere in the world the oil which is vital to her. It is essential for our national survival to gain possession of the oil in South Asia, but it is unlikely that the enemy will surrender it to us easily. We must expect them to try by every means in their power to destroy it first. They will try demolition by bombing or by dynamite, but we must anticipate them, seize all oil dumps and installations, and keep a strict watch to prevent them from suffering damage.

With all other supplies, too, we should capture as many as possible and either utilize them on the spot or transmit them back to the homeland. We must bear in mind that once oil installations, factories, railways, or communications are damaged it is no easy task to restore them to their original state. Again, captured vehicles and arms are often rendered useless by being meddled with by people who do not understand the correct procedures. In past wars it has been common practice to destroy or burn all captured enemy supplies on the excuse that they would be an encumbrance. h this war not only must we consider it imperative to seize the enemy's supplies intact and utilize them to the utmost, but it is vital to bear constantly in mind that, on our own side, economy in the use of ammunition, foodstuffs, and fuel—be it only a single round saved, a scrap of bread, or a drop of petrol—lessens the drain on our national resources.

8. Is our present enemy stronger than the Chinese Army?

If we compare the present enemy with the Chinese Army, we see that while the officers are Europeans, the N.C.O.s and other ranks are almost overwhelmingly native, and that consequently the sense of solidarity in each unit between officers and men is practically nil. Although it must be admitted that they are infinitely more copiously supplied than the planes, tanks, motorized vehicles, and heavy artillery, much of this equipment is nevertheless outdated, and, what is more, the fact that the soldiers who operate it are ill-trained and without enthusiasm renders it worse than useless. Night attacks are what these people most dread.

9. You may be killed in battle—but don't die of disease

There will be, naturally, planes above you, tanks before you, warships blazing away at sea, and submarines operating beneath the surface; but there are yet other dangers, peculiar to the present campaign which you must heed. A great variety of deadly diseases, and the Great Enemy, the malarial mosquito, are lying in wait for you. It is an historical fact that in all tropical campaigns since ancient times far more have died through disease than have been killed in battle. In tropical areas, as in Japan, the majority of diseases enter through the mouth, but in South Asia you must take precautions also against mosquitoes and snakes. To fall in a hail of bullets is to meet a hero's death, but there is no glory in dying of disease or accident through inattention to hygiene or carelessness. And a further point you would do well to consider is that native women are almost all infected with venereal disease, and that if you tamper with them you will also make the whole native population your enemy.

Chapter III
By What Stages Will the War Progress?

1. From the long voyage to the landing assault

The battlefields are all in South Asia, separated by many hundreds of sea miles horn Formosa. To reach some of them takes a ship a week or ten days.

Several hundred warships and transports are now crossing this expanse of seal but, when you think of it, our ancestors conquered these same turbulent waters in wooden sailing vessels—the so-called Red Seal Ships—some three hundred years ago for purposes of trade, or sailed their length and breadth in "Hachiman" ships on military ventures. When the long and cramped voyage is over you must force a landing in the face of enemy resistance. Landing assaults have always, since ancient times, been held to be perilous undertakings, but our superbly trained, peerless Japanese Army has never yet registered a failure in any operation of this kind. Be confident, be well prepared, and perform feats which will bring upon you the wonder and admiration of the world.

2. *The attack on main positions and fortifications*

The enemy forces in South Asia consist of forcibly recruited, hastily organized armies of natives with a hard core of white troops, and are not in the same class as the Chinese Army, but they have considerable equipment in the way of artillery, tanks, and planes, and, inferior soldiers though they may be, you should not altogether despise them, Since it seems probable that, as a general rule, they will occupy positions at strategic points and resist from behind fortifications, you must not rest after crushing the enemy at the landing points but must make a forced march, or a rapid motorized swoop, through the sweltering tropical terrain and launch an attack at once upon the main positions.

In order to avoid prepared concentration of fire, and to achieve surprise, it may frequently happen that you will traverse jungle regions or wade through swamps and paddy fields.

3. *Securing enemy supplies and guarding strategic points*

After disposing of all enemy resistance, you must secure oil resources, keep guard on important factories, harbors, railways, etc., and take every precaution to ensure that the enemy forces—land, sea, or air—are given no opportunity to strike back. At such a juncture it is normal for a small force to garrison a wide area, and to this end a great many schemes must be devised, from the construction of obstacles and military positions to the conciliation and employment of the native population.

4. *A long occupation and the enforcement of order*

Realizing that the war may well be a protracted affair, you must carry forward preparations for a lengthy campaign, and as well as making the fullest use of the resources of the country, it will be important to take special care in the preservation of arms and clothing supplies. Since it is no small matter to transport supplies by sea all the way from Japan, you should fight and live on a bare minimum, and you should also—perhaps above all else—take good care to avoid sickness, that you may not succumb to the heat.

Chapter IV
What Are You to Do on the Ship?

1. *Keep your secrets*

The success of the landing assault depends above all upon surprise. If the enemy knows too soon where we intend to effect a landing, things can be made very difficult for us. An innocent remark in a letter can bring about the defeat of a whole army, and the loose talk of soldiers drinking in bars just before embarkation has often acquainted enemy spies with our secrets.

Think of the trials endured by the forty-seven Loyal Retainers in keeping their plans secret until the day of final revenge upon their lord's enemy, and mutually admonish yourselves to follow their example.

During the current China campaign a soldier who landed in South China wrote a letter and placed it inside an empty beer bottle, which he then sealed and tossed into the sea; and the bottle, carried by the tide, was later washed ashore on the coast of Korea. What if it had been carried to Vladivostok? Aircraft and submarines, seeking to discover the movements of our transport ships, not infrequently gain their first clues from scraps of paper found floating on the sea.

In disposing of soiled articles or other rubbish you must carefully observe the ship's regulations.

2. *Settle your personal affairs in case of emergency*

Since much of the action in this war will take place at sea, or since, after landing, small units may frequently be sent on ahead deep into enemy territory, you must resign yourself in advance to the possibility that the bodies of the dead may never be recovered.

> Corpses drifting swollen in the sea-depths,
> Corpses rotting in the mountain grass—
> We shall die, by the side of our lord we shall die.
> We shall not look back.

Such, from ancient times, has been the proud boast and the firm resolve of the men of Japan. Before going into the battle area—in the ship at the very latest—you should write your will, enclosing with it a lock of hair and a piece of fingernail, so that you are prepared for death at any time or place; and these wills should be gathered together by units and sent back to the base by some secure means of transmission. It is only prudent that a soldier should settle his personal affairs in advance.

Again, should the ship sink or catch fire it will be necessary for you to take to the boats or the water with only the minimum of equipment, and you should prepare yourself for this eventuality, so that at the time of emergency you may come in good order onto the decks, with lifejacket attached and carrying only your rifle, your water can, and some bread.

3. *Do not fall ill*

Not only will conditions on the ship be exceedingly cramped and uncomfortable, but the heat will be extreme. In these circumstances troops may easily suffer from seasickness or similar stomach disorders and thus lessen their resistance to disease. If only one of those men sleeping side by side on the mess decks, like sardines in a tin, should be carrying an infectious disease, the consequence may be catastrophic. If you wish to avoid distressing others and possibly inflicting losses far greater than a submarine or air attack might cause, take good care what you eat and drink in the period just before embarkation, and do not drink any unboiled water on the ship. If you feel out of sorts, go to the M.O. at once for examination and treatment. If you foolishly conceal the fact that you have an infectious disease, you will cause distress to the whole ship and kill many of your comrades.

4. *To prevent seasickness*

To avoid seasickness you will do well to attend to the following points:
(i) Keep your morale high and be always aware of the importance of the duty you have to perform.
(ii) If the ship is tossing, sleep with your head and feet pointing to port and starboard; if the ship is rolling, sleep with your head and feet pointing fore and aft.
(iii) Look only at distant objects, if possible, and do not concentrate on the motion of the ship.
(iv) Distract yourself as far as you can by playing checkers and similar games.
(v) For bad sailors, tightly binding the stomach and practicing the Respiration Method can be effective, both on the ship and in the small boats. (The Respiration Method is as follows: When the ship rises breathe in deeply; when the ship falls breathe out deeply. On the ship it is best carried out lying on your side. In a small boat it will be found even more effective if, at the same time, you straighten your legs as the boat rises and bend them as it falls.)
(vi) Over-eating and under-eating are both to be avoided. Always keep your stomach just sufficiently full. If you eat absolutely nothing

when seasick, you will get worse; food may repel you, but you should eat a little.

(vii) Get sufficient sleep.

(viii) For those of you who are fond of sake, a little does no harm; but do not drink to excess.

(ix) Constipation is to be avoided at all costs. Those who are constipated should take medicine to restore regular motions.

(x) Avoid heartburn. Do not eat oranges or other fruits of strong sugar content and acidity.

(xi) Walk about on deck and do physical exercises.

(xii) Useful as preventatives are bicarbonate of soda pills, stomach tablets, sedatives, "Bisu," and Jintan pills. Care should be taken in all these matters, but most important of all is that you should firmly believe, "I shall not be seasick." People who weakly tell themselves, "I may be sick." or "I hope I shan't be sick." are invariably sick. The fact that children who are too young to worry are the strongest of all on sea voyages should serve as a good example to you.

5. *Be kind to the horses*

Never forget that in the dark and steaming lowest decks of the ship, with no murmur of complaint at the unfairness of their treatment, the Army horses are suffering in patience. On a voyage through the tropics it is essential for horses to have good ventilation, fresh drinking water, and clean stalls. As the voyage stretches on, horses and men alike suffer from fatigue, but remember that however exhausted you yourselves may feel, the horses will have reached a stage of exhaustion even more distressing. Treat them with kindness and sympathy.

Fresh air and cold water are no less essential to horses than to men on a tropical voyage. Moreover, men can walk about on the open decks, but horses grow weak because they cannot be given proper exercise. It is helpful, therefore, to make them move backward and forward in their stalls.

6. *Grow attached to your weapons, care for them*

Salt breezes and damp are the enemies of your weapons. On a ship the air is always damp, and sea breezes blow in ceaselessly from everywhere. If you are not careful, your weapons will grow red with rust and be unserviceable when the moment comes to use them. Weapons are living things. The more kindly you treat them, the more you accustom yourself to handling them, the harder they will work for you on the battlefield. Pay good heed, however, not to set them off accidentally and kill your comrades.

7. Do not waste water

Water is your savior. The supply of water carried in the limited water tanks of a transport ship is small, and if you use the water as you would use it on land it will soon be exhausted. In tropical campaigns, when the water is gone it is the end of everything. To imagine that because the water in the sea is limitless the water in the ship is likewise is the height of stupidity. Everyone, from staff officers downward, must practice the most careful economy.

8. Precautions against fire

Nothing is more terrifying than a fire at sea. As the ship carries large quantities of petrol, do not smoke except in those places where regulations permit it. Your life jackets are stuffed with a material called kapok, similar to cotton wool, which is highly inflammable. Do not hold a naked flame in its vicinity.

9. What to do in an aerial or submarine attack

To avoid attack by aircraft or submarine, abide strictly by the regulations for the closing of all portholes and hatchways at night, regardless of the heat.

You must expect, in a long voyage such as this, to be subjected at least once or twice to aerial or submarine attack. At such times the most vital thing of all is that you should not panic.

The shells are not likely to hit their target. Even if the ship is struck and sinks, each vessel is equipped with boats sufficient to hold the whole ship's complement, and each individual has a life jacket. Proceed calmly, with light equipment, to your allotted emergency stations and there await the orders of your officers. Unnecessary chatter and pointless rushing about are strictly forbidden. Ships never proceed alone, so bear in mind that in an emergency you will certainly receive assistance from other vessels, and that since you are under observation by the soldiers in the nearest vessel, it is imperative that you do nothing foolish or cowardly which will make you a laughingstock for others afterwards. Since aircraft and submarines attack mostly by daylight, this last point is doubly important to remember.

10. A little carelessness can cause a great injury

The ship is crammed full within its severely confined space, with landing craft, motor vehicles, luggage, horses, and much else. Amid it all derricks are working, and soldiers on detail or the ship's crew are running about on their several duties. In stormy weather the waves may be washing across the decks. At night it is pitch-dark. Men sitting on the ship's rails to cool themselves have not infrequently been lost overboard, and any number of people have been known to slip at the mouth of the hold and fall down to the ship's bottom, or have had their heads crushed by luggage being loaded onto the deck. These are no tales of glory. Watch your step, watch your head, and do not enter into areas of danger or among the lifeboats and landing craft on the ship's deck.

11. *Ammunition, food, and water*
One special feature of a landing assault is that no supplies from the rear may reach the fighting troops for anything from five to ten days after the landing, the time varying with the circumstances. In a campaign like the present one, in which we shall be separated from our main base by many hundreds of miles of sea, the problem of supply will be particularly difficult, and, with this in mind, you must carry with you everywhere as much ammunition, food, and water as you can possibly manage without hampering your freedom of movement. The limit will doubtless be indicated to you by your officers, and you must not throw any of this into the sea on the excuse that it makes you too hot, or carelessly forget it.

12. *Particular care in the preparations for the landing assault*
When it is time for the landing, your ship will anchor some distance from the shore and you will transfer to smaller craft. Each soldier must not only have his weapons and other equipment well arranged that he may retain unhampered freedom of movement in the narrow space of the landing craft, but also he must take good care to check the efficiency of those weapons which he will use immediately upon landing and to forget no attachments or accessories.

The machine-guns, infantry guns, etc., of the units forming the first wave of the landing assault will be issued to these troops in the ship, and they must be loaded in advance into the landing craft and firmly secured with rope. The equipment of the second and subsequent waves of assault troops will have to be lowered by rope or in straw bags from the ship's deck to the landing craft in the water, and for this it will be essential to have ropes prepared in advance—that is to say, binding ropes for the artillery (or rifles), for the gun covers (serving also as portable shelters), and for the tripods (or base plates); binding rope for the accessory boxes and ammunition boxes; and ropes for lowering.

Clothing will vary according to the type of soldier, but, as an example, that for foot soldiers should be as follows:

(i) Footwear-reinforced socks. No pack, but water can and holdall slung across shoulders.

(ii) All ammunition, food, or mess tins in excess of the regulations should be stuffed into the folded tent, which is carried on the back like a knapsack. Alternatively they should be bound around the waist.

(iii) Small spoons and such-like should be tucked into your belt at the rear, or hung from the shoulders on string.

(iv) Respirators should be carried at the ready.

(v) Wire cutters should be thrust into your belt at the side.

(vi) Fit the life jacket with its release section on your right shoulder that it may not hinder your shooting.

(vii) Hand-grenades should be carried in the holdall.

12. *Fit makeshift floats to heavy armaments and ammunition boxes*

A convenient way to ensure that machine-guns, infantry guns, other heavy weapons, and ammunition boxes do not sink even if they fall into the water is to fit them with makeshift floats.

At times, too, it may be necessary to haul heavy armaments ashore through the sea, in which case two or three men can manage by means of ropes attached to the floats.

Chapter V
The Landing Assault

1. *Transferring to small craft from the mother ship*

When the small boats loaded on the mother ship have been lowered to the water, you will climb down to them by rope ladder. For this you must form single file and descend in good order without interruption. Rifles and light automatic weapons should be slung across one shoulder or the back, or it may be found convenient in some cases to place the sling about your neck and rest the gun sideways across the top of the life jacket or pack. Swords are best thrust into the belt, after the manner of the samurai of old. Ammunition boxes, motor vehicles, etc., should be lowered over the ship's rails to the boats below. In rough seas, when transferring to the boats is a difficult operation, it may be advisable to pack all light automatic weapons and rifles together in a tent and lower them to the boats by straw basket or on ropes. When you descend the rope ladder, grasp the central rope firmly, hold the upper part of your body close to the ladder, so that the weight of your body is taken on the shoulders, and move down quickly from rung to rung; and when you are down sit cross-legged in your allotted place at once that you may not obstruct the soldier following you. The landing craft will roll violently when the sea is rough, but it is constructed so as not to capsize. It is safe, no matter how the waves batter it. So do not move your position, but sit calmly where you are, and take care not to obstruct the activities of those who are managing the boat. Officers should post helpers at the top and bottom of the rope ladders.

2. *Directing fire from the landing craft*

Heavy machine-guns and light machine-guns should be mounted near the bow of the boat, and as the shore is approached and enemy fire is encountered, fire should be returned under the orders of the officer in charge. But the motion of the boat will make accurate aiming difficult. It will therefore be necessary to settle on auxiliary targets in the target area, such as hilltops, houses, and woods, and to sight them and fire in the brief moment when the boat rises to the crest of each wave. In firing light machine-guns one should bend and straighten one's body with the motion of the boat, and when using grenade-throwers it is best to rest the base plate on the gunwale and to fire when the boat is level. A sand-bag should be used beneath the base plate. When firing with machine-guns, the elevation arch and screw lever should be removed, and the operator should bend and straighten his body with the movement of the boat.

Infantry guns should be immovably fixed in the boat, and set at a suitably standard elevation. The boat's captain should direct the boat on a course coinciding with the required line of fire, and the gunner should fire when the boat reaches the highest point of a wave.

3. *Plunge boldly into the water*

When you are nearing the shore under concentrated enemy fire and at last your platoon commander gives the order "Jump in!", it is of the greatest importance that you should plunge into the water courageously and without hesitation. Even if the waves are rough or the water deep, with your life jackets you will be quite safe. Should you be out of your depth the waves will wash you in towards the shore. So don't worry. Jump in boldly as if you are determined to be behind no one. On coasts where there are sharp hidden rocks you must proceed calmly and cautiously, testing the ground at your feet with a bamboo pole. If you jump in from the right (left) of the boat you should hold your rifle in your right (left) hand, grip the gunwale with your left (right) hand, place your left (right) foot on the foothold, step over the gunwale right (left) leg first, and—bending your knees to keep your center of gravity low, and holding your rifle high—jump with legs apart so that both feet hit the ground at the same time.

In landing a light machine-gun, one of the gun crew should jump in first to receive the gun and then take over its firing, following behind the section leader.

When landing a machine-gun, two of the gun crew should jump in on one side, while two more in the boat should lower the gun backward from its firing position, attach the forward and rear levers, and hand the gun to the two in the water. These two should then carry it ashore between them. The section leader, after supervising the above operation, should jump in at once and proceed ashore with the gun. At times, if the sea is rough, it is best for four people to carry the gun, or for it to be dismantled and carried in parts.

4. *To reach the land is victory*

When a turtle gets onto dry land he is helpless, but when we reach the shore we have everything in the bag. The battle is won. Our opponents are even more feeble than the Chinese Army, and their tanks and aircraft are a collection of rattling relics. Victory is certain, and the only problem is how to win in the cleverest way. Conditions will vary according to the place of landing, but there are some regions where asphalt motor roads have been laid out in all directions, and it might be possible, after quickly commandeering all motor vehicles in the enemy territory, to fight entirely on enemy petrol and enemy food supplies; or perhaps small and intrepid units could penetrate deep into enemy positions under cover of night. Some such spirit of bold contempt for the enemy is necessary.

5. *Do not throw away life jackets*

Life jackets, which were precious friends aboard ship, are apt to be discarded as nuisances on shore. This is mere thoughtlessness. Under the direction of commanding officers all life belts must be gathered together and stacked in easily discoverable spots along the shore, where they are safe from the tide, for use by other units later. There have been, unfortunately, many cases when landing troops have shamelessly torn the straps from their life jackets and caused considerable trouble to later units.

6. *Make sure damp weapons do not rust*

Weapons which have been in sea water should be attended to at the very earliest opportunity. If you leave it till later, rifles and swords will rust and gunpowder will fail to ignite.

Chapter VI
Marching Through the Tropics

1. *Water is your savior*

To say that particular attention should be paid to water in a tropical campaign is perhaps to state the obvious and invite ridicule, but those without experience cannot conceive just how valuable water is, nor how difficult to obtain. It will be to your advantage sometimes to carry water with you not only in your water can, but in beer bottles or any other containers you may have at hand. The amount of water necessary for one day varies according to the heat, but you must reckon that, at the very least, one man will consume ten liters, and one horse sixty liters. However, water is not obtainable everywhere, and it is important to use it economically, and to replenish your supplies whenever good water is found. And, no matter how thirsty you are, do not drink in large quantities—it is always better to drink a little at a time. Pineapples and coconuts (the latter contain up to half a pint of fluid) are good for quenching the thirst, and in mountainous areas you will find that lopping a branch of wisteria and sucking at the open end, where the cut has been made, will prove helpful. In tropical areas some wisteria vines grow to a very large size, and these contain water in plenty. To obtain this water you should make an incision at the base of the trunk, and place a container at the cut; then chop through the tree at a point two or three feet higher up, and in this way you can collect the water from the lower portion. Since the water contained in all varieties of wisteria is harmless, you may drink without fear.

For the horses, it is necessary from time to time to place salt in their water.

2. *Sleep well, eat well*

As far as the battle situation permits, it is best to make marches in the cool period between nightfall and morning, and to rest at the hottest time of the day; but if such marches are carried out continuously night after night there is a danger that the troops will weaken through sheer lack of sleep. It is necessary, therefore, somehow or other to get sleep on as many occasions as possible. The principal causes of sunstroke are lack of sleep and an empty stomach. Normally your appetite dwindles to nothing in heat, but it is nevertheless absolutely essential to keep your stomach from becoming empty. You should therefore take your meals in small quantities at a number of times, or chew red peppers, salted plums, etc., all the while, taking as many with you as you can manage.

The following is an example of how meals might be taken on the march:

(i) Breakfast—eat half before departure, the remaining half about two hours later.

(ii) Lunch—divide into two portions, to be taken at roughly 10 a.m. and 1 p.m.

(iii) Supper—as usual; but in the case of a night march it is best to divide it into two or more parts.

3. *Clothing on the march*

When marching through the day, with the sun beating strongly down, it is a mistake to wear clothing which is too light and allows the sun's rays to penetrate to your skin. Protection for the head being vital, you must, of course, wear your cap, and you will find it helpful to cover or line the cap with green grass and twigs, or to fix these into the pack on your back so that they hang forward over your head. Clothing should be as loose as possible to enable the air to circulate, and it is a good idea to carry a fan.

For the horses, too, it is no less necessary to take such precautions as fitting sprigs of green leaves into their saddles and covering their heads with sun hoods (or some substitute).

4. *When you rest*

Short breaks in the march should be ordered at regular intervals, every thirty or forty minutes, and it is necessary to have a long two- or three-hour rest during the hottest period of the day. On falling out you should, of course, immediately unsling equipment and remove coat and shoes, but you should also beware of poisonous snakes. These lurk in thick grass or lie along the branches of trees, and if you do not watch where you put your feet or hands you may well be bitten. Particular care is necessary at night, and at such times too you must without fail, troublesome though it may be—by using the kit supplied and making smoke with smoldering grass and tree branches—take all possible precautions against the deadly malarial mosquito.

5. *Tires on motor vehicles and bicycles swell in the heat, engines become over-heated*

Since heat causes the air inside motor-vehicle or bicycle tires to expand, it is important before starting on any journey of more than half a day to examine tires closely and to see that the air pressure is 10 percent below normal. Again, because the high external and internal temperature results in the overheating of engines and loss of oil, thorough checks must be made, particularly of the cooling system. Bearing in mind that there may be no source of water en route, it is advisable to take reserves of cooling water with you from the time of departure.

Chapter VII
Camp in the Tropics

1. *Do not freeze in bed in the early mornings*

Even in the tropics there is a sudden drop of temperature in the latter half of the night. If you sleep in the clothes you have been wearing during the day, which may be damp with sweat or rain, it is likely that you will catch a chill or suffer from diarrhea. Always remember, whenever it is possible, to change into dry clothes before settling down to a night's sleep.

2. *Native settlements are nests of fleas, bedbugs, and infectious disease*

Native settlements—since the natives' standard of living is extremely low, and their ideas on hygiene are nonexistent—are nests of fleas, lice, bedbugs, and infectious disease. If at any time you make use of a native settlement it is advisable, whenever possible, to occupy only the local government offices or the public halls and to avoid the ordinary houses. When you have no choice but to use ordinary dwellings you should make sure that there is no direct contact between troops and natives. Strictly demarcate an area to be used only by troops, remove all natives from that area, clean it thoroughly, and disinfect it. On most occasions-rather than involve yourself in this troublesome procedure—you will find it far more convenient and agreeable to camp in neighboring plantations or coconut groves.

3. *When using temples and mosques*

You must do nothing to offend the religious susceptibilities of the deeply superstitious native population. As mentioned before, even the most distinguished local personalities are not permitted to enter a mosque without first removing their shoes. You should bear this in mind, and it is best, if possible, to avoid using places of worship altogether.

4. *Precautions against mosquitoes, dangerous animals, and poisonous snakes*

Against mosquitoes you must use the equipment with which you are provided. You should be most meticulous in the burning of anti-mosquito incense sticks or powder, the drinking of anti-malarial medicine, and the

application of anti-mosquito ointment. The best way to ward off dangerous beasts, provided there is no danger of your being spotted by the
enemy, is to light lamps and burn fires. If you discover a dangerous snake,
you must of course kill it. You should also swallow its liver raw, and cook
the meat. There is no better medicine for strengthening the body.

5. *Fuel for fires*
The wood of mangrove trees burns well in its natural state. The husks
of coconuts, sugarcane, and rice are also useful as fuel.

6. *Do not let your weapons be stolen*
When you go to sleep, exhausted, you are liable to leave your weapons in places where they may be forgotten by yourself or stolen by the
natives. For your own sake, and for the honor of the Army, you should
take the greatest care in such matters.

Chapter VIII
Scouting and Sentry Duty

1. *Carelessness is the great enemy*
Broiling in the heat, dog-tired, dizzy through over-exposure to the sun,
you reach the place where you are to camp for the night, and no sooner have
you heaved your sigh of relief at the prospect of a well-earned rest than you
are detailed to the further—and most important—tasks of sentry duty, visiting rounds, or patrol. The enemy is lying ready for us on land with which
he is thoroughly familiar, and, given the slightest opening, he can engineer
a counterattack or an ambush. That the whole Army may be given the
opportunity to rest, you must whip your tired bodies into renewed strength,
keep your eyes and ears even more alert than usual, and accept in full your
responsibility to make proper search and give warning of danger.

2. *When you stand sentry*
Choose your position carefully, where there is a cool breeze and protection from the direct rays of the sun. Remove your pack and other encum-
brances, and, in return for the weight removed from your shoulders, accept
the full weight of your responsibility as guardian of the Army's safety.

3. *Sending out patrols*
Use motor vehicles whenever possible, and see that the men carry only
light equipment. There are advantages in employing natives as guides or

intelligence scouts, though they often tell lies, and mistakes frequently occur through language misunderstandings. Natives being also easy prey to the slightest rumor and incapable of independent thought, you should keep their movements under constant supervision.

Chapter IX
The Battle

1. *The long voyage, the sweltering march—all has been* for *this*

When you encounter the enemy after landing, regard yourself as an avenger come at last face to face with his father's murderer. The discomforts of the long sea voyage and the rigors of the sweltering march have been but months of watching and waiting for the moment when you may slay this enemy. Here before you is the man whose death will lighten your heart of its burden of brooding anger. If you fail to destroy him utterly, you can never rest at peace. And the first blow is the vital blow.

2. *Squalls, mist, and night are our allies*

Westerners—being very superior people, very effeminate, and very cowardly—have an intense dislike of fighting in the rain or the mist, or at night. Night, in particular (though it is excellent for dancing), they cannot conceive to be a proper time for war. In this, if we seize upon it, lies our great opportunity.

3. *Battle movements in extreme heat*

(i) Sweat running into the eyes

Since this makes it difficult to take proper aim when shooting, it is necessary to bind a cloth about the temples beneath the steel helmet, that the sweat may be absorbed before reaching the eyes.

(ii) Keep the sun at your back

To fight facing the sun not only makes taking aim difficult, but means that the enemy can clearly see us, while we cannot discover them. From ancient times great generals have always fought with the sun behind them. Choose the time and direction of your attack carefully.

(iii) Bullets travel farther, targets appear nearer

Hot air offers less resistance than cold, and bullets travel farther through it. The sun's rays are strong and objects stand out clearly—hence it is easy to judge your target to be nearer than it actually is. You should bear these points in mind when shooting.

(iv) Be considerate to weapons

As a result of excessive external and internal heat, gun-barrels may expand and the efficiency of recoil and counter-recoil mechanisms may be impaired. Limit your rate and period of fire within reasonable bounds, check your weapon periodically, and do what repairs you can. And when you rest, treat your weapon kindly and give it protection from the direct rays of the sun.

4. *Hindering the flight of the enemy*
To check the withdrawal of enemy forces, one of your principal aims should be to outflank the enemy and gain control of catchment areas, wells, and springs to his rear.

5. Guarding strategic areas
When keeping guard over natural resources, railways, and harbors, small bodies of troops will be left to control large areas, and much ingenuity will be required of them. By constructing roadblocks, by winning the natives over to our side, or by utilizing natural obstacles such as cliffs, dense forest, and marshland, you must seek to tire out the enemy without exhausting yourselves.

Together with taking proper measures to ensure your own water supplies, you should contrive ways of denying water to the enemy. You should also exercise particular vigilance at night, and in times of rain or mist, you should ensure as far as possible that if the enemy launches an attack, it can be only from a very considerable distance away and during the heat of the day.

Chapter X
Anti-Gas Precautions

1. *Do not discard your respirators*
There is a possibility that the present enemy, unlike the Chinese Army, may use gas. If you discard your respirator as being a nuisance, it cannot help you in your time of need.

2. *Movement with respirators fitted*
In hot climates, when standing still it is easy enough to wear a respirator for an hour or more at a time, but to wear it for as much as an hour while on the march or fighting is more than can reasonably be expected.

Movement or operations in complete anti-gas equipment should be limited to fifteen minutes. If this time is exceeded, the soldier becomes markedly exhausted, and special care must be taken to allow him time for recovery. Movement of horses with respirators fitted should generally be restricted to fifteen minutes at a time.

3. *Putting on your respirator*
When fitting the respirator over your face it is apt to slip because of sweat and prove very troublesome to fix, so put your chin well inside the mask, and, using this as a steadier, pull the side straps strongly backward and upward with both hands, taking care that the mask fits firmly and correctly over the forehead.

4. *Care of the respirator*
After use it is essential to dry the respirator, removing all sweat with a cloth.

5 *Keep the canister dry*
Because damp is common in tropical regions you must keep the stopper fitted at the base of the respirator canister and the oiled paper firmly attached.

When landing or crossing rivers, grasp the flexible hose so that no water enters it, and again, do not forget the canister stopper.

6. *Do not wear anti-gas clothing next to your skin*
If you wear the rubber cape next to your naked skin, expecting it to be less hot that way, you will on the contrary expose yourself even more to the direct heat of the sun's rays, and, what is more, you will render yourself more liable to harm from gas. You must always wear some clothing beneath the rubber cape. To relieve the heat a little when in full anti-gas equipment, it is permissible at times to pour water over the anti-gas clothing.

Chapter XI
For Signal Troops

1. *Water for the radio earth*
In the dry season ground resistance to the radio earth is exceedingly strong, and in stony places or on sand by the coast you should pour plenty of water onto the ground around the earth. If water is not available you may bury in the ground a quantity of crushed melon, papaya,

or vegetables of high water content, and insert the radio earth into this. Or, should you select a place where there are trees and grass, you may sometimes find that two or three hundred meters of old insulated wire (the longer the better) stretched along the ground will serve as an effective substitute for the earth.

2. *Points to note on radio signals*
    (i) Special care must be taken to keep the radio free of damp. For this:
        (a) If the crystal becomes damp, its oscillation powers may be impaired or completely lost. When not in use, keep it wrapped in grease-proof paper.
        (b) In wet weather the "super" receiver in current use soon ceases local oscillation on shortwaves. Care must be taken of the tubes and dry battery.
        (c) Since both transmission sets for use by Army signal units and fixed transmission sets are of high voltage, special precautions must be taken in wet weather against damp or drops of rain. Before loading high voltage it is necessary to dry the set either with an electric fan or in the warmth generated by switching on the filaments alone.
    (ii) The pigment of "Empire Tube," used for connecting wire throughout the set, melts in the heat, and the wires become glued together, with an adverse effect on insulation.
    (iii) Keep the batteries as dry as possible, and store them in a cool place.
    (iv) Since air-cooled engines soon suffer in hot weather from insufficient cooling, it is necessary when running them to watch the temperature of the cylinder heads and avoid setting the engines on fire.
    (v) Because of static interference it is frequently difficult to use the medium-wave.
    (vi) Keys short-circuit through sweat from the hands, or reception is rendered difficult by short-circuits in the receivers resulting from sweat flowing from head, face, and ears.

3. *When you use semaphore*
    Since the strong rays of the sun have an over-stimulating effect on the eyes, it is essential for the signaler to wear protective glasses. For signaling by reflected rays in direct sunlight, red is the most effective color.

4. *Arrangement of watches for signal troops*
    Signal work is tiring, and watches for signal troops should, if possible, last no longer than two hours.

Chapter XII
For Motorized Troops

1. *Get through by determination*

If a man can pass, so can a motor vehicle.

If the road is too narrow, cut a way through; if there is a cliff in the way, let forty or fifty men in a bunch haul you up it.

Motor vehicles get through by determination. Force your way ahead, even if you have to carry the thing on your shoulders.

2. *Is the vehicle in good running order?*

It only requires a single bolt or nut to work loose and fall off, and the vehicle may not move. No matter how tired you are, check and grease thoroughly. Do not break down in your moment of peril! Oil, water, and air—are they all right? Is the battery charged?

3. *A drop of petrol is a drop of blood*

Petrol is the lifeblood of motor vehicles. Without it they cannot move. Since petrol evaporates quickly in hot climates, do not open the throttle too wide.

Starting is easy, so switch off the engine as soon as you come to a halt.

4. *Do not work the engine recklessly*

Do not shoot off at high speed as soon as you have started the engine.

The oil, being warm, has become thin. On asphalt roads especially, where the heat is intensified by reflection from the surface, if you suddenly increase the revolutions, the spread of oil will cause a fire. Drive gently and slowly for at least the first five minutes.

5. *When they get wet*

If saltwater has entered the crankcase, change the oil at once. If you leave things as they are, the water will be drawn up into the cylinders, where it will rust the pistons or cylinder walls, and result in fire.

If caught in a squall it does not matter if you yourself get wet, but see to it that no water gets to the various electrical fittings. If it does, wipe them dry immediately.

6. *Oil and water*

When oil heats up in hot weather, it becomes thin and loses its viscosity.

In this state it washes down into the crankcase the soot on the piston heads, which clean the cylinder walls. Consequently you cannot assume that all is well simply because the oil is sufficient in quantity. Test the oil for viscosity between the tips of your finger and thumb, and examine its color. If it is dark with soot it must be changed.

Examine the cooling water whenever you stop, and keep it constantly replenished. But do not use water with any salt content. Take a supply of good water with you when you start out.

Chapter XIII
Cherish Your Weapons

1. *Rust, mildew, misting*

Rifles, like soldiers, dislike the heat. When soldiers rest they should give their rifles a rest, too, offering them, in place of water, large drinks of oil.

Parts containing air or water (e.g., recoil buffers) expand, and precision weapons suffer a marked deterioration in accuracy.

Iron rusts, leather mildews, and glass mists. You must give constant attention to your equipment and weapons to prevent such deterioration.

2. *Keep the gas cylinder lock at its lowest marking*

Since the breech mechanism of automatic weapons moves very freely in high temperature, you should keep the gas cylinder lock at its lowest marking.

Furthermore, you should use a lubricant of high heat-resistant qualities and, if necessary, drain some off to reduce the quantity.

3. *See that binoculars and optical mechanisms do not moisten*

Since binoculars and all types of optical mechanisms are particularly sensitive to extreme heat, care must be taken to protect them. A sudden change in temperature, too, can considerably lower their degree of accuracy, perhaps causing moisture to form on the lenses. It is important to wrap them in cloth at night and prevent any great variation between their night and day temperatures.

Chapter XIV
Provisions

1. *Water supplies and disinfection*

You can get dirty water anywhere, but pure water is not so readily available. Since the natives defecate and urinate quite freely in all lakes and streams, and even the water which the natives use for drinking is full of germs, it is safest to drink only water which has been properly purified by filtering. Furthermore, do not neglect to take creosote pills regularly.

If you discover a source of good drinking water, see that no one defiles it, and if necessary set sentries to watch over it. When you are perspiring heavily, drink warm tea with about 0.8 percent of salt dissolved in it. To disinfect wells, place chloride of lime in an empty bottle, add water, shake until the mixture is clear, and pour the contents into the well. When the water you draw has a faint taste of chloride of lime, it is safely disinfected.

2. *How to keep cooked cereals from going stale*

(i) Pure boiled rice is better than rice and barley hash.

(ii) Wash the rice well before boiling.

(iii) After cooking until firm, allow some time for the moisture to evaporate before packing the rice into your container.

(iv) It is better to cook in a mess tin than in a large pot.

(v) Take two or three salted plums with each meal.

(vi) When cooking, it is best to add a little salt, a salted plum, or a small quantity of vinegar.

(vii) One preservative tablet should be added to each mess tin of rice during cooking.

(viii) Wash mess tins and rice baskets in boiling water and dry thoroughly before packing them with rice.

(ix) When carrying enough for two meals, pack each meal separately.

(x) In packing you should pack lightly and, if possible, place a piece of hemp cloth beneath the lid to absorb moisture.

(xi) Attach mess tins and rice baskets to the outside of your pack, protect them with leafy sprigs, etc., and when you rest do not expose them to the sun's rays.

(xii) As subsidiary foods, dried or tinned goods are recommended. But do not open tins until immediately before the meal.

(xiii) Store all between-meal rations for the march in a dry bag.

(xiv) Keeping the cooked rice in cellophane is extremely effective.

3. *What fruits can you eat?*

The use of fruits can have a great nutritive value. The following types of fruit are dangerous, but most others can be eaten:

(i) Those of excessively vivid coloring.

(ii) Those of excessively strong scent.

(iii) Those of excessively sweet and saccharine taste.

(iv) Those of excessive beauty in shape.

(v) Those growing on low bushes amid beautifully colored or mottled leaves.

(vi) When eating mangoes, do not drink milk (goat's milk) or spirits at the same time.

Chapter XV
Hygiene

As previously explained, a tropical campaign is a war waged against a whole army of diseases. Those which you should be particularly careful to avoid are malaria, sunstroke, beriberi, and snakebite. Besides this, there is a year-round danger, throughout the tropics, from such diseases as cholera, typhus, bubonic plague, smallpox, tuberculosis, and leprosy. Moreover, the enemy may, in desperation, resort to warfare by means of these terrible germs. You must be constantly on your guard, and refrain from incautious use of foodstuffs and wells abandoned by the enemy.

Perhaps because the heat drives even the dogs mad, there is a large incidence of rabies. If you are bitten by a dog, you must report at once for medical examination.

1. *How do you contract malaria?*

Malaria is to be avoided at all costs. The success or failure of tropical campaigns has depended, since ancient times, on how far this disease can be checked. One new malaria case in one's own army is a far more dangerous source of infection than any number of cases among the natives. Report for examination and treatment early, not for your own sake alone, but for the sake of the whole Army.

Malaria is carried by mosquitoes. The malarial mosquito is almost nonexistent in Japan, but breeds in large numbers all over the tropics. There are many varieties, but the easiest way to recognize them all is by their peculiarity of keeping their hindquarters raised when at rest. You might think that, since mosquito larvae are generally hatched in dirty, stagnant water, the malarial mosquito would have similar tastes, but the malarial mosquito's habits are cleaner and it dislikes stagnant water. It is most commonly found by clear mountain streams or at places near the coast where sea water and river water intermingle.

Since mosquitoes are common in Japan in thick woods, you might expect them to be equally plentiful in jungle regions; but the malarial mosquito is rarely found in the jungle away from the sea. In Java and Malaya, in fact, there are even places where the clearing of jungle areas has been restricted by law as a method of controlling malaria. The malarial mosquito is most active from dusk to midnight, but is less in evidence during the latter half of the night. There is a jungle mosquito too, but, unlike the malarial mosquito, it is active throughout the day. You should be on your guard by day too, since the bite of this mosquito can result in a fever. It is most important, of course, to hang your mosquito net at night, but precautions against being bitten by day are no less necessary. Take your anti-malarial medicine as directed, use your anti-mosquito kit, and apply the anti-mosquito ointment.

2. What is sunstroke?

Sunstroke is a sickness caused by the sun's rays. People who are in a weak state after an illness, whose appetite is poor, who are suffering from insufficient sleep, or who are chronic malarial cases should be particularly careful, since it is they who are the most likely victims of this sickness. The first symptoms of sunstroke are heavy sweating, a high temperature, and a flushed face; but gradually sweating ceases, the vitality weakens, breathing becomes labored, the pulse rate quickens, the face turns pallid, and the patient stumbles and seems ready to fall at any moment. If at this stage the patient rests immediately in some shady spot, he will revive, but if nothing is done he will lapse into unconsciousness and fall.

3. To avoid sunstroke

The best preventatives are ample stocks of drinking water, sufficient sleep, and a well-filled stomach.

4. If someone gets it, what do you do?

Unhitch his pack, remove his clothing, lay him down in a shady spot where there is a breeze, keep his head raised, fan him, give him water to drink, and splash cold water all over his body. If his breathing is weak, apply artificial respiration. Keep him quiet, and even when he has revived do not allow him to move for some time.

5. *Do not be bitten by snakes*

Tropical snakes are of many varieties and all are equipped with deadly poisons. If you do not take immediate counter-measures when bitten, the probability is that you will die.

Snakes are found in the greatest number in dense forest on high land or in the vicinity of freshwater, but they live also on the plains and on the branches of trees. Since they move away at the sight of man, soldiers in the vanguard may, without harm to themselves, clear a path for those following by walking along and beating the undergrowth with bamboo poles. People are only bitten when they tread on a snake or accidentally grasp one together with the branch of a tree. When bitten, apply tight bandages immediately on the affected limb between the wound and your heart, to prevent the poison from flowing in that direction, and then pierce the wound with some small knife and suck a fairly large quantity of the blood into your mouth. You must then receive treatment from a medical orderly. Since the treatment varies with the type of snake, it is vitally important that you should be able to describe the snake which bit you.

6. *Do not get beriberi*

Beriberi is chiefly a disease arising from vitamin deficiency, and is particularly easy to contract in the tropics. Do not exist on an unbalanced diet. Eat as much fresh vegetables and fruit as you can.

Chapter XVI
Hygiene for Horses

If you do not exercise great care with horses until they have become accustomed to the heat, they will quickly weaken. The first things to watch out for are sunstroke, heatstroke, and laminitis. Many horses are also afflicted by tripanosoma infection, caused by worms in the bloodstream. To prevent the occurrence of these diseases is the most important part of horse hygiene in the tropics.

1. *Value your horses*

Horses cannot speak. No matter how hot it is, nor how thirsty or tired they may be, they do as they are told and work on until they die. They deserve your sympathy and loving care.

Things to remember are: fill their stomachs full; give them plenty of green grass and hay; if there are no cereals available, rice stalks or straw will do. Anything which a horse will eat is fodder. Give the horses fresh water several times a day, and do not forget to give them salt to lick. On the move their heads should be protected from the sun's rays by sun hoods or by the use of grass and leafy branches. Whenever possible it is best for them to rest by day and move at night.

2. *Sunstroke and heatstroke*

The most dangerous disease for horses is very similar to the sunstroke from which human beings suffer. Their breathing becomes quick and they break out into a great sweat all over the body. Horses soon lose spirit, and even if you rest them they will continue to hang their heads dispiritedly and will refuse food.

The best preventatives are sun hoods (or grass and branches), plenty of water and fodder, and salt to improve their digestion.

3. *Laminitis, or founder*

This is a disease of the hoofs, inducing severe lameness, which occurs after strenuous activity in the heat, or after long train or boat journeys. At times it is brought on by the same causes responsible for sunstroke and heatstroke. A feature of the disease is that the lameness is not discernible while the horse is walking, but becomes clearly noticeable when it stands at rest. For on-the-spot treatment it is good to cool the hoofs in water, stop feeding cereals, and give more green grass and hay.

4. *What is tripanosoma infection?*

This is an infectious disease carried by flies and mosquitoes, and confined to hot-climate countries. It affects cattle and dogs besides horses. When animals contract this disease they are liable, like chronic malaria sufferers among human beings, to occasional bouts of high fever; their spirit flags, their blood gradually deteriorates, and in many cases they die.

The best way to prevent the disease is to devise means of protecting the horses, as far as possible, from horsefly and other insect bites.

5. *Use of water oxen and Chinese oxen*

Water oxen are massively built but comparatively gentle beasts. They are practiced in movement through marshy ground and have great strength. When loading things on them, place the load on the rump. Once every hour, throw water over them or rub their bodies with mud. For food, give them hay, green grass, and a small quantity of cereals;

but it is important to allow them about two hours to ruminate after the feed. Chinese oxen should be treated much as Japanese oxen. It is advisable not to wear or use anything red, as oxen generally dislike this color.

Chapter XVII
Movement in Special Terrain

In the tropics bamboo groves, jungles, and sugarcane plantations are common. Movement in these is much as was laid down for forest land. Apart from attention to the usual anti-gas and fire precautions, a cloth should be tied across the mouth and nose, and gloves should be worn to give protection from thorns and brambles.

Below are given certain points on which special care should be taken.

1. *Movement in bamboo groves*

The bamboo groves differ from those in Japan in that any number of bamboo canes grow in a cluster from one trunk, and are spiked with thorns, so that it is impossible to step into their midst. When traversing bamboo groves, move through the areas where the bamboos are less dense and lop off lower branches or make cuts in trunks so that the white sections will serve as route markers. Should you make a frontal attack on a bamboo grove, it is best to make a concerted rush from close quarters. When using bamboo groves in defense they are conveniently employed either as obstacles or for concealment; but there is the disadvantage, in this latter respect, that the terrible noise of enemy bullets crashing through the bamboos can have a demoralizing effect upon troops.

2. *Movement in jungle*

By jungle is meant dense forest in which a large variety of trees, grasses, and thorny plants are all closely entangled together. Such places are the haunts of dangerous animals, poisonous snakes, and harmful insects, and since this is extremely difficult terrain for the passage of troops, it will be necessary to form special operation units for the task. This type of terrain is regarded by the weak spirited Westerners as impenetrable, and for this reason—in order to out maneuver them—we must from time to time force our way through it. With proper preparation and determination it can be done. Maintenance of direction and good supplies of water are the supremely important factors.

3. *Movement in sugarcane plantations*

In movement through sugarcane plantations, which are very similar to the kaoliang fields of Manchuria, special care must be exercised to maintain correct direction. For this, scouts should be sent ahead to mark the trail, either carrying ladders or surveying the land from treetops. The use of compasses might also prove advantageous.

During an attack, such terrain provides opportunities for detours or outflanking movements of a local nature.

In defense a considerable obstacle can be constructed by breaking off lengths (40 to 80 centimeters) of sugarcane and binding them with rope, criss-crossed and higgledy-piggledy, to steel wires.

4. *Movement in marshy land and paddy fields*

French Indochina and Thailand come close to Japan in the intensive cultivation of rice; there are paddy fields everywhere. There are also large stretches of marshland. In traversing such terrain it is often best for each man to be equipped with snowshoes and poles, and for heavy armaments to be pulled along on sledges and covered with sugarcane, straw, or hurdles.

When advancing on snowshoes you should pause between movements as little as possible, to avoid sinking into the mud, and if the shoes should become deeply wedged you should take the full weight of your body on the poles and slowly extricate the shoes one at a time. Wherever possible you should pick your way along places where there is rice stubble to support you or where the mud has dried. Field and mountain artillery, when the ground to be traversed is only slightly damp, may be manhandled across if the wheels are fitted with tank tracks.

Chapter XVIII
Conclusion

At stake in the present war, without a doubt, is the future prosperity or decline of the Empire. Slowly, little by little, like a man strangling his victim with a soft cord of silken floss, America has been prohibiting the export to Japan of oil and steel. Why such cautious methods? The reason, perhaps, is a fear that to deny all supplies at one stroke might drive Japan, in desperation, to invade South Asia. And if the rubber and tin of the South were to be seized by Japan, it would create a situation far more intolerable to America than even the present lack of steel and oil is to Japan. America's policy so far has been one of weakening Japan without rousing her to violent indignation.

We have already, perhaps, left things too late. If we remain patient a moment longer, Japan's aircraft, warships, and road transport may be forced to a standstill. Five years have passed since the outbreak of the China Incident. More than a hundred thousand of your comrades have perished on the mainland; and the greater part of the armaments with which Chiang K'ai-shek killed those men was sold to him by England and America. England and America, whose desire it is to hold the Far East in a permanent state of subjugation and colonization, dread the thought of any solidarity between Asian peoples, and for some time all their policies have been directed towards the instigation of war between Japan and China. Our allies, Germany and Italy, are engaged in a life-and-death struggle with England, America, and the Soviet Union on the European continent; America, having given full support to England, is already virtually a participant in that war. For the sake of Japan's own existence, and because of our moral obligations as members of the Tripartite Alliance, it is impossible for us to endure the present situation a moment longer. We embark now upon that great mission which calls upon Japan, as the representative of all the peoples of the Far East, to deal a resolute and final blow to centuries of European aggression in these lands. Our peerless Navy is prepared, and ready to strike with its full strength. The formula indicating its numerical strength in relation to the fleets of England and America is 3:5:5, but if you include in the calculation its superiority in equipment and morale, that ratio becomes 7:5:5. Half the British fleet, moreover, has been destroyed by Germany. As far as our Navy is concerned, now is the great opportunity. The umbilical cord of the Chungking regime runs to England and America. If this is not speedily cut, the Sino-Japanese war will drag on endlessly. The final reckoning of our holy crusade will come on the battlefields ahead. Hundreds of thousands of the heroic dead will be watching over us. The supreme offering for which the souls of your departed comrades long is victory in this battle. To show our heartfelt gratitude to the Navy, which is dominating a thousand miles of ocean, sweeping the seas clear of enemy obstacles, and protecting us day and night with tireless devotion, we must requite such labors with comparable fruits of battle.

We Japanese, heirs to two thousand six hundred years of a glorious past, have now, in response to the trust placed in us by His Majesty the Commander-in-Chief, risen in the cause of the peoples of Asia, and embarked upon a noble and solemn undertaking which will change the course of world history. Officers and men, the eyes of the whole world will be upon you in this campaign, and, working together in community of spirit, you must demonstrate to the world the true worth of Japanese manhood. The implementation of the task of the Showa Restoration, which is to realize His Imperial Majesty's desire for peace in the Far East, and to set Asia free, rests squarely on our shoulders.

Corpses drifting swollen in the sea-depths,
Corpses rotting in the mountain grass—
We shall die, by the side of our lord we shall die
We shall not look back.

Appendix 2

The East Asia Federation Movement*

In 1931, while commanding a division in Manchuria, Major-General Kanji Ishihara promulgated the doctrines of the Toa Renmei Undo (East Asia Federation Movement), of which he remained the de facto leader until his death in 1949.

The basic principle of the movement was that "Asians should not fight Asians." It urged that in any future war the peoples of Asia should fight together—if they fought at all. It proposed the creation of Manchuria as an independent state as the first step towards an East Asia Federation of Japan, Manchuria, and China, and such other Asian nations as wished to join. The objectives of the Federation were to be promotion of mutual economic welfare, mutual support against aggression from any quarter, and joint action to prevent the spread of communism.

General Ishihara was insistent that Japan should avoid war with China, and urged that all Japanese troops should be withdrawn from the Asian mainland as soon as General Chang K'ai-shek's government recognized the independence of Manchuria.

In 1939 Colonel Masanobu Tsuji was appointed to the Headquarters Staff of the Japanese Expeditionary Forces in China, located in Nanking. He was a supporter of General Ishihara and strongly opposed to the extension of military operations in China, which he believed would eventually lead Japan to destruction.

---

* This appendix is by H. V. Howe.

On taking up his appointment, he quickly realized the intense hostility of the Chinese population to Japan—largely due to the indiscipline and misconduct of Japanese troops in China. He took drastic and unpopular steps to restore discipline—going so far as to issue, with the authority of General Itagaki, Chief of Staff of the forces in China, a proclamation that "Japanese troops operating in China were lowering the dignity of the Imperial Army." At the time, Japanese-sponsored pro-Japanese political movements, led by Japanese ex-Army officers and professional pro-Japanese Chinese—regarded as traitors by their fellow countrymen—were endeavoring to secure Chinese support for Japan against the Chinese Nationalist Government. The most important of these organizations was the Taimin-hui (Great People's Society).

Colonel Tsuji was sharply critical of such associations, saying, "The Chinese people will never be impressed by this sort of thing. A popular movement dominated by mercenary motives is as useless as writing on water. If the Japanese who carry out such movements are fools, then the Chinese who participate in them are servile. I pay my respects to the Chinese leaders in Chungking rather than to the Chinese professing a dubious pro-Japanese stand and staying behind in occupied territories."

Colonel Tsuji disbanded the Taimin-hui and ordered out of China all Japanese connected with the movement. In its place he created a branch of the Toa Renmei Undo, based on the free will of the Chinese people, and aided and abetted its growth in central and southern China.

General Tojo's government disapproved of the movement, placed General Ishihara on the retired list, relieved Colonel Tsuji of his post at Nanking, and recalled him to Tokyo.

Since the war, the influence of the Toa Renmei Undo movement has substantially increased in Japan, and Colonel Tsuji has risen to prominence in it. The movement no longer advocates any form of federation of Asian nations, but still urges their cooperation for mutual economic benefit. It adheres to the principle that "Asians must never again fight Asians," and rejects absolutely any suggestion that Japanese troops should ever be required to fight because of Japan's becoming involved in a quarrel between America and any other nation.

It urges that all Asian nations should maintain absolute neutrality in the event of conflict involving American and European powers.

Appendix 3

The British Garrison in Malaya*

The garrison in Malaya comprised: 9th Indian Division (2 brigades); 11th Indian Division (2brigades); 8th Australian Division (2 brigades); 18th British Division (3 brigades); and 12th, 28th, 44th, and 45th Indian brigades—a total of 13 brigades. In addition, Singapore fortress troops on the island consisted of two Malayan brigades.

The British official history of the campaign (*The War Against Japan*, vol. 1; H.M.S.O., 1957) states on p. 473 that the total British casualties in Malaya were 138,708 (of whom more than 130,000 were prisoners of war). With the exception of the relatively small number who escaped or were evacuated, this figure represents the strength of the British and Commonwealth forces in Malaya.

---

* This appendix is by H. V. Howe.

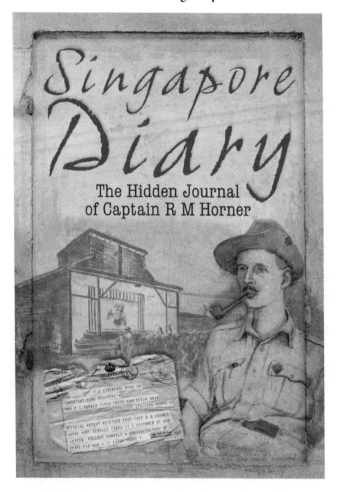

SINGAPORE DIARY 1942—1945
The Hidden Journal of Captain R M Horner

1-86227-339-1

This amazing account supported by anecdotes, cartoons and stories, provides a unique insight into Japanese POW life. It charts the war from the capitulation of Singapore through to its liberation, whilst candidly describing the emotional challenges faced by Horner and his fellow inmates through the loss of friends and separation from family. This incredible diary contains reproductions of images drawn by fellow POWs, including the famous cartoonist Ronald Searle.

OLIVER LINDSAY
with the
MEMORIES OF JOHN R HARRIS

The BATTLE FOR
HONG KONG
1941–1945

Hostage *to* Fortune

Foreword by
FIELD MARSHAL LORD BRAMALL

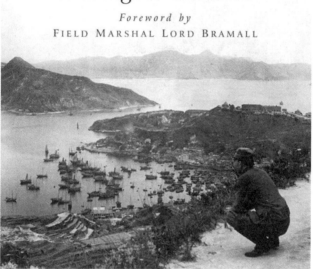

THE BATTLE FOR HONG KONG 1941—1945
Hostage to Fortune

1-86227-315-4

This is a remarkable new study on the liberation of Hong Kong from the Japanese, addressing many important questions regarding the Far Eastern war and occupation of the Colony which have never been fully explored. Including a mass of unpublished official material, part of which is drawn from original war diaries, this is the most thorough enquiry to date into the debacle which led to over 12,000 British, Canadian, Indian and Chinese defenders surrendering Hong Kong on Christmas Day 1941.

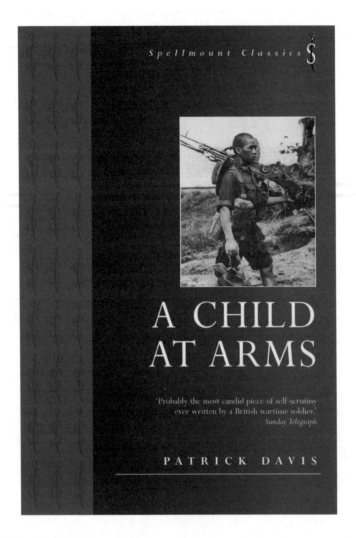

A CHILD AT ARMS

1-86227-337-5

Patrick Davis was posted as a novice 'hostilities only' officer to a veteran Gurkha battalion fighting during the desperate campaigns in Burma as Slim and his 'Forgotten Army' demonstrated to the world the myth of Japanese invincibility, driving the enemy before them in streaming defeat. This is the narrative of a young officer's fears and triumphs, of the discomforts and tragedies attendant on battle, the terrors and confusion in the midst of battle against a fanatically tenacious enemy. An excellent account of the relationship between British officer and Gurkha volunteer, it remains one of the finest pieces of writing to emerge from World War II.